Ups and Downs along the Black Sea in the reverse footsteps of Xenophon

Penny Young

Twopenny Press

2010

First published in the UK in 2010 by:

Twopenny Press
www.twopennypress.co.uk

Copyright © Penny Young 2010

ISBN 978-0-9561703-1-6

Front cover illustration by Owen Robertson
Back cover photograph by Ted Burt

Typeset in Adobe Garamond, designed and produced by Gilmour Print, www.gilmourprint.co.uk

To Alice, Andy and Ian

Contents

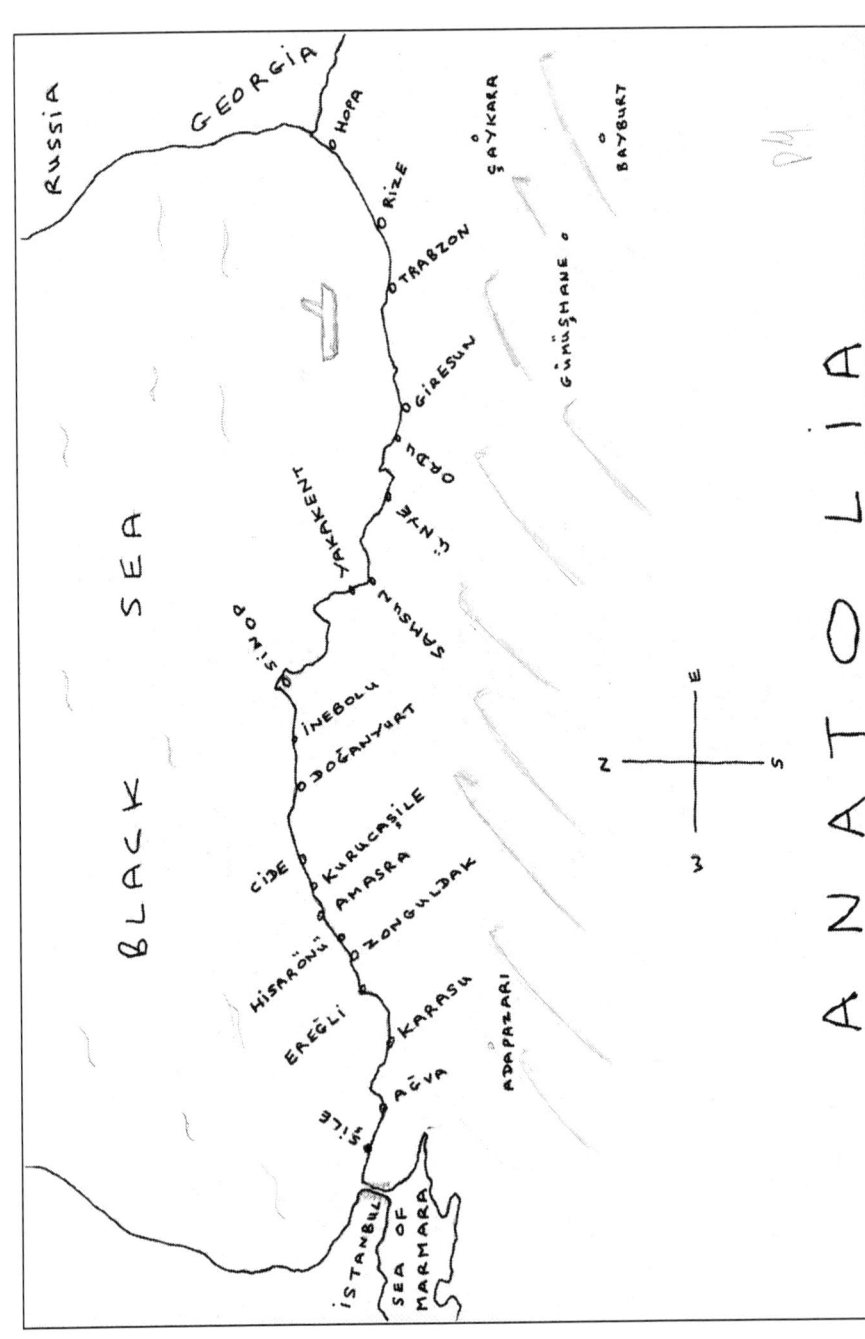

Prologue

On the spur of the moment, in the summer of 1997, I took a break from freelance reporting to make a bicycle journey along the eastern part of Turkey's Black Sea coastline. Not only was I having a mid-life crisis, but I also didn't feel very well and, as it turned out, I wasn't. The fling with my beloved bicycle therefore turned out to be my last to date. Although the journey was not a long one, both in terms of the number of miles/kilometres covered and the time span – about one month – it was an epic journey for me in many ways, extremely tough both physically and mentally. It was sheer will power that got me up those perpendicular slopes. It was also an historic journey. The roads along the coast have since been modernised. Huge motorways have been constructed and numerous, well-lit tunnels gouged out through the lovely cliffs. There are still some stretches where a cyclist can experience the twists and turns and the gruelling ups and downs that I had to tackle, but the route that I took has largely changed forever. The soaring Black Sea mountains are, of course, still there, vast, remote, breathtakingly beautiful and indifferent to man's trivial pursuits.

I was not alone during the journey. As well as the host of living Turks I met along the way, great peoples and figures from history and mythology jostled and haunted me as I passed by. As the writer Neal Ascherson marvellously describes in his panoramic book, *Black Sea*, the area has been the great divide between Europe and the steppes of Asia for thousands of years. The ancient Greeks sailed along the coast on legendary journeys, built their city-states and marvelled at the descendents of the 'barbaric' Scythian nomads who inhabited the countryside and the mountains. The Persians, the Romans, the Byzantines and the Russians came and went, and it was the Turks, themselves nomads from the steppes of Central Asia, who inherited the land.

There is not a vast amount of literature on the Anatolian Black Sea area. One of the most detailed descriptions comes from William J. Hamilton in his two-volume *Researches in Asia Minor, Pontus and Armenia*. This was published with his own excellent maps in 1842. Hamilton walked everywhere, minutely observing and recording what he saw and thought. He even timed parts of his journeys. There is John Freely's usefully detailed *The Black Sea Coast of Turkey*, published in 1996. Lilo Linke's *Allah Dethroned – a Journey through Modern Turkey*, published in 1937, is also well worth reading. Rose Macaulay's romantic novel, *The Towers of Trebizond*, is, deservedly, a classic. It begins with the famous line: '"Take my camel, dear," said my aunt Dot, as she climbed down from this animal on her return from High Mass.' And then, of course, there is Xenophon's *Persian Expedition*, the so-called *Anabasis*, which literally means 'the journey up'. It was Xenophon and his Ten Thousand rampaging Greek mercenaries who, in particular, kept me company on my journey along the Black Sea.

So who was Xenophon? Every schoolboy who ever had to study the classics would have known very well who Xenophon was – and probably hated him as he laboriously and painfully translated his *Anabasis* from Greek into English. Unlike the earlier legendary Greek heroes, the life of Xenophon is reasonably well documented. He was born in Athens during the first Peloponnesian War around 430 BCE and died some eighty years later, it is to be hoped at home, in his bed and attended by his beloved sons. His moment in history had come in the spring of 401 BCE when he volunteered to join an army of ten thousand Greek mercenaries, who had been unwittingly recruited by the wily and ambitious Persian prince, Cyrus the Younger, to help him overthrow his brother, King Artaxerxes II. Cyrus lost the battle of Cunaxa near Babylon, however, and was killed. Xenophon and the Ten Thousand found themselves in the middle of a foreign country, two thousand miles from home, and beset by very angry Persians, loyal to their triumphant King. It was decided democratically, Greek-style, that they should march northwards up the Tigris valley and make their way over the mountains to the shores of the Euxine (Black Sea) and what they hoped would be the welcoming arms of the Greek colonists who would help them get back to Greece. Xenophon was among the generals elected by the soldiers to lead them home. He appeared largely to take control and directed the retreat up the Tigris valley and into Anatolia during the snow-filled winter of 401-400 BCE.

Xenophon wrote his fascinating account of the journey in relative tranquillity between 379 and 371 BCE. The march home of Xenophon and the Ten Thousand was action-packed. They had to fight for their lives practically every day. Many men died, either in battle or through extreme hardship. During my journey, I saw no dead bodies nor did I have to fight too hard for my food supplies. Nevertheless, I felt that Xenophon would have understood and empathised with my ups and downs along the Black Sea in his reverse footsteps. In a very small way, some of my adventures echoed his.

All the quotations heading the chapters are from Xenophon's *Anabasis*. I used various translations, including one by Rex Warner that happened to be on my bookshelf. I also consulted J C Stobart's *The Glory that was Greece*. As Xenophon did, I am publishing an account of my journey several years after it took place. Unlike Xenophon, I was able to keep a detailed diary of my expedition. It is unlikely that Xenophon would have asked anybody to read through his account of his journey. In my own case, I would like to thank Nick Stanley for reading through mine with great care and attention. Any faults, errors or misplaced commas are entirely my own. I have used the Turkish spelling for words, phrases and proper names, including İstanbul. I realise that there have been many changes both in Turkey and along the Black Sea since my journey. I, too, have, of course, changed. What follows, however, is what I wrote and thought in that summer of 1997.

Penny Young, 2010

1
Polonezköy to Ağva

If we want to get across the mountain with the minimum of inconvenience, then, I think, what we must consider is how to ensure that our casualties in dead and wounded are as light as possible.

Tucked away behind a wall of mountains stretching from the east of İstanbul to the border with Georgia, Turkey's Asian Black Sea region is a world apart. It is a moody, brooding land of fierce storms, battered by north-westerly gales and torrential rains. Summer, when it comes, lasts just two months and the country people spend most of their time busily preparing for the long winter as if for a siege, gathering up every stick of firewood they can find and harvesting every wisp of hay for animal fodder. The land is richly green and fertile, famous for its cherry and hazel nut trees and the tea and tobacco plants that flourish in the sticky humidity on the central and eastern coastal plains and lower foothills. The mountains, which begin as swelling humps in the west, soar to nearly 4,000 metres, more than 13,000 feet, in the east near the border with the former Soviet Union, and pockets of snow can still be found up there in mid July.

It was a sudden inspiration to take my bicycle over to Turkey and explore part of this Black Sea coastline. I had visited the region once before in the early 1980s but had only survived there a couple of days before catching the bus back to İstanbul, exhausted by the overwhelming attention from the locals, who were obviously unaccustomed to single, female travellers. Since then, I had visited Turkey many times and lived for stretches in Ankara and İstanbul, building up a grasp of the language and a love for the country. I thought it would be fun to go back and have another go at the Black Sea, this time with my own transport. My friend, Andy Byfield, was also at this time living in a small village outside İstanbul close to the Black Sea. It would, I thought, make a good point to pedal off from.

I bought a return air ticket to İstanbul, a new pair of cycling gloves, an expensive pair of padded cycling underpants – a sore bottom for hundreds of miles is a terrible thing – and two reinforced bicycle tyres. Then, I packed up my beloved bicycle, graceful as a cygnet and strong as the proverbial ox, half filled a couple of bicycle bags and flew out on 28 June 1997. This was my birthday and I was even closer to heaven. I tried not to think about the exact number of years it represented. Andy met me at İstanbul's Atatürk airport, waving and smiling, head and shoulders over most of the Turks crowding excitedly round the international arrivals gateway. The bicycle was loaded into the back of his jeep and we drove off – no taxis, oh what a treat – into the hot, Turkish, June night, speeding in his chariot along the sea, past İstanbul's massive, fortified land walls, part of which were first built in 413 CE, and up the smelly Golden Horn, to swing around İstanbul and head back towards the Bosphorus, past the illuminated battlements of the fortress of Rumeli Hisarı, over the second suspension bridge and onto the other side of İstanbul which lies in Anatolia, ancient Asia Minor.

Andy was living in Polonezköy. The village was founded in the middle of the nineteenth century by Polish soldiers who had joined the Ottoman army to fight against Russia. Every weekend, the İstanbulus are quite prepared to sit in long, belching, traffic jams winding through the hills for the splendid eating and drinking to be done there. Andy was renting a shack attached to the summer house of a Turkish family. It was a romantic place, the gardens shady and sweet with pink, climbing roses. Andy is a plants and flowers man and knows where every orchid, bulb and endemic species of this and that is growing on the hills, building sites, valleys, rubbish dumps, mountains and coastlines of Turkey. His garden in Polonezköy was filled with plants, shrubs and flowers crammed into pots of every size, bulbous, leafy hostas spilling over dahlias, white bleeding hearts blooming cheek by jowl with lilies, orange trees and promising wisteria cuttings. Roses bloomed and aspens whispered. I wanted him to give me a clue about what I might see on my trip, especially if I made it up into the mountains.

I stayed a couple of days, swinging in a hammock in the shade of the weeping aspens, trying to relax and to think myself into a long cycle ride, wondering if my mind, back and leg muscles were going to withstand the vertical ups and downs, the peaks and troughs. I opened the maps a thousand times. My eye ran along the coastline taking in the mining city of Zonguldak, the towns of Sinop and Samsun, and moving eastwards towards Trabzon and Rize where the slopes would be planted with tea all the way to the border with Georgia. I struggled to make sense of the complicated history of the area with its wars and catastrophes.

The region is a narrow coastal strip of land, sweatily squeezed between what the Turks call Kara Deniz (the Black Sea) and the mountains. In classical times, the area east of Byzantium (Constantinople, İstanbul) in Asia Minor was divided up into Bithynia, Paphlagonia and Pontus and was colonised from around 800 BCE, by thrusting, young Greeks who established a series of city-states along the coast. The sea's original name was the 'Axeinos Pontos' or the 'inhospitable sea', no doubt because of the unpredictability of the weather and the terrible and terrifying storms that blew up without warning. 'Axeinos' could have been based on the Persian 'Axaina' meaning 'dark' or 'black'. The Greek colonists called the sea the 'Euxeinus Pontos', which meant the 'hospitable sea', in the hope that the name might placate the sea god so that he would grant seamen a safe journey across the dangerous waters. It is thought that the first Greek sailors ventured onto the Black Sea in the thirteenth century BCE, keeping close to the shore, following the sinuous curves of the land, fearful of deep water. They were recorded in mythology as Jason and the Argonauts, who braved the storms to retrieve the Golden Fleece from the land of Colchis (present day Georgia).

Nearly a thousand years later, Xenophon, a handsome, young Athenian (of course he was handsome) took control of an army of Greek mercenaries who had been fighting near Babylon. Xenophon led the Greeks north-westwards out of Persia, through the Armenian plateau, over the Black Sea mountains near Trabzon, and westwards along the Black Sea coast back to Greece. It is thought the path they took over the mountains led over today's Zigana Pass. We know all about his journey and the battles, plunderings and adventures of the Ten Thousand along the way because Xenophon obligingly left posterity a detailed account of the famous trip, although he modestly wrote about himself in the third person. He called his book the *Anabasis* or *The Journey Upwards*. This was a little disingenuous because there were lots of downs as well. Our paths would meet and cross as I followed, ghost-like, in the reverse footsteps of Xenophon.

One hundred years or so after Xenophon's famous journey, the region became known as the Kingdom of Pontus, whose kings were descended from Parthian warriors and who were nearly all named Mithridates. The most famous was Mithridates Eupator Dionysus of Pontus, who was called the Great. Born in Sinop, he inherited the kingdom from his father at the age of eleven and became very good at mixing poisons. He deluded himself into thinking that he could challenge the might of the Romans behind the Pontic mountains. He failed, and the Romans took over the coastal colonies, which became part of the Byzantine empire. The city of Trabzon (ancient Trebizond), perched on a hill overlooking the sea, achieved greatness in 1204 CE when the Emperor Alexius Comnenus moved the seat of his Byzantine establishment to the safety of the historic, Black Sea town, after the Crusaders sacked Constantinople. The Comneni kingdom was whittled away until Trabzon was taken by the Osmanlı Turks, eight years after the fall of Constantinople in 1453, when the Byzantine remnant was absorbed within the mighty Ottoman empire.

The wars through the nineteenth century between the Ottomans and Russia and the occupation by the Russians of Trabzon for two years between 1916 and 1918 hastened the departure of the Pontic Greeks from the Black Sea region. The area went into a decline, which was made worse by the closed borders into the Soviet Union and the loss of the traditional trading routes to the east. The final blow for the Greeks came when the Turkish Republic was established in 1923 and thousands more were sent 'home' to Greece in the exchange of populations. (Thousands of Turks, who spoke no Turkish and had lived in Greece for generations, were likewise forced to return to Turkey.) The Black Sea region became a backwater. Over the following decades, most of the population, fed up with the lack of opportunities, packed their bags, locked their front doors and wept as they headed off to find work in the country's more prosperous cities over the mountains or even further afield in Western Europe.

As I flicked through the travel books, it sounded as if the wars, troubles and harshness of the climate meant that most of the buildings that might have had major tourist-pulling power had crumbled into decay decades earlier. All the books warned about the difficulties of getting around with the lack of decent roads and the frequency of landslides. In fact, nothing seemed to have really changed on the transport front since the journey of Xenophon and his weary, frostbitten and footsore men in 400 BCE. They found the roads so bad, they took a break every so often by sailing along parts of the coast.

I wondered if I would even make it to Şile, the first seaside town along the coast from Polonezköy. Andy just laughed and watered his plants, cooked delicious Turkish dishes and fixed the shack's windows. In typical Turkish style, the electricity came and went while the water in the pipes spluttered to a stop and then suddenly gushed out a lurid, browny red. The coming on and off of the electricity and water did not coincide. I searched out bottles and a bucket, filled them up with water while there was some and positioned them strategically next to the toilet, just like old times.

In the evening, we sat in the cool of the garden, watching the fireflies flickering through the garden under the aspen trees. They glowed as they flew, on off, beep beep, hoping to attract a mate, sending a beam of light, a hopeful signal of love through the darkness. At night, the wood worm audibly chomped on the beams in the roof, their tiny, powerful jaws feasting, leaving piles of dust fresh on the floor in the morning. I slept stretched out luxuriously on the top of a high couch, feeling as if the sea were lapping around its legs but I was balanced in the middle, well away from the edge. I sailed over the ocean in the glimmering dark and there were no storms.

On the morning of the day of my departure, the alarm went off like a bomb. I peeled myself out of my couch and shook off any debris that might have fallen down from the busy ceiling during the night. It was late, half past five, and the morning was already coming in through the open window. It is always best to be on the road by then, hurrying to beat the sun and the lion heat. I slipped outside to check that the bicycle was still there and she was, leaning gracefully against the wall, snoozing. I hung the bicycle bags gently over the back wheel, trying not to wake her up. The air was fresh and the Black Sea so close. I ate standing up – bread, cheese and eggs, which had been hard-boiled the night before – unable to sit down, walking around in nervous impatience, wasting energy. Although the food was fresh, it tasted dry and dull and I had to force it down. It was almost impossible to swallow. It is essential to eat before, during and after a bicycle journey otherwise you lose energy. As Xenophon so thoughtfully wrote: 'It is better then to fight now that we have had a meal, than to fight tomorrow on an empty stomach.' Cycling is a snacker's charter. Whatever you eat gets burned up before you can say 'bicycle pump'. But, at that time in the morning, it is so difficult to put anything into a reluctant stomach.

A squeeze of the tyres to make sure they were still firm and hard, snapping on the new cycling gloves, bags balanced, glasses on, everything in place, a pilot checking her instruments were all working before a long haul flight, and the journey began. I wheeled the bicycle down the path, brushing past the climbing roses, and paused at the gate to look back at Andy standing outside the door, smiling and waving encouragingly.

The goal, as far as there was one, was to get onto the Black Sea coast and cycle along it until I arrived at Turkey's border with Georgia, or as near as I could get in the handful of weeks I was allowing for the journey. I turned left out of the gate, carefully got on the saddle and was off, swooping like a bird down the hill – oh the exhilaration – and out of Polonezköy, trying not to notice how bad the surface of the roads was.

It was going to be a fine day. The early morning was cool with floating pockets of mist in the dips of the hills. I was making my way over to the coast along the small, country lanes. There was just enough traffic to stop me feeling completely isolated. A young Turkish couple came by in a car heading in the opposite direction. They stopped and asked where İstanbul was. I wondered what they were doing so early in the morning and where they had come from. I vaguely pointed behind me and over the hills, amused that I, a foreigner, was being asked the way. I must have looked far more organised than I felt. To be honest, I felt a mix of emotions. I was glad to be back on the bicycle with the whole day stretching ahead, but I was apprehensive about dealing with the long journey, frightened as ever of the unknown and what might/could happen. A jumble of feelings. On all the journeys, there was always the worry about being raped and murdered by lunatics on lonely stretches of the road – although to be fair to the Turks, I had never heard of such an event in Turkey. Nevertheless, it is always in the back of one's mind. There was also the problem of being unfit. I never cycled far in England, much preferring to travel along unknown roads, to cover distances and arrive somewhere new. On this journey in 1997, there was not going to be much time to acclimatise, to ease the muscles in slowly. I was already into the lower foothills.

They were smoothly forested with plunging valleys, sweep, dip, the road swooping and curving. The bicycle and I stopped at every bend to gaze in awe at the view. It was as if a giant hand had taken a paint brush, dipped it in a pot of twiggy, dark green paint, smeared it over the countryside, and then with a sharp knife tidily levelled it off. If only something similar had been done with the road surfaces, which were impossible, almost impassable. They were constructed from a soup of glutinous tar mixed with stones and pebbles. The result was rough and bumpy and it was almost impossible for my tyres to get a grip, especially going uphill. I kept stopping to lean breathless and appalled over the handlebars, thinking I was going to die with the strain and wondering whether it was going to be like this all the way to Georgia. By car, I was still less than two hours away from İstanbul. It was fortunate the lovely views were there to distract me from the rising panic. I passed glorious, old, wooden houses, their balconies and verandahs draped with vines and red with geraniums planted in rusting olive oil tins. Bundles of onions hung from beams and washing lines were loaded with vests and knickers, gleaming white in descending order of size, from adults down to babies and through all the stages in between, an artistic visual representation of the seven ages of man. Lovely to look at. So glad they aren't mine. Don't let's get romantic here. Keep things in perspective. Gleaming fireflies winking in the dark, don't wink at me.

My first view of the Black Sea came unexpectedly as I was approaching Şile. I had toiled to the top of a height and was looking down over the hills and there it was in the distance, a piece of streaky, grey glass stretching to the horizon. No wonder it was thought in the old days that the world was flat and if you sailed too far out you would fall over the edge. If you took a ship and headed directly northwards over this small, largely landlocked sea, you would reach Ukraine and Russia after two or three days' sailing. I did not linger long admiring the view. The sun had cleared the mist away and now blazed down on my head. My arms and shoulders were covered up but my knees were beginning to go red. My energy began to fade and I needed to eat something more substantial than bread and olives. Head down, I pedalled on to Şile.

I first visited the little Turkish holiday village in 1983, also in the month of June, catching the bus from Üsküdar on the Asian side of İstanbul with a young man whom I had met in a restaurant in the Sultanahmet area of the city. He was a gentle man, quiet and withdrawn. His university studies had been interrupted by the violent, political unrest in Turkey in the late 1970s and he, like so many others, had lost his way. Many of his friends and the people he admired, writers and intellectuals, were in prison or had been in prison, persecuted for their left wing, liberal views. He was working in a bookshop in İstanbul until he could get a clearer picture of the future and was having an intense, long distance relationship with a foreign woman. I was a sympathetic and unexpected interlude. We stayed in a dumpy pension in Şile, run by a free-thinking manager. We were allowed to share a room, no questions asked. Our room had a balcony overlooking the sea and we drank Turkish red wine and ate strong, black olives. He told me longingly and lovingly all about his girl friend, the books they read, the thoughts they shared and the music they both liked. We baked, like two lobsters, side by side on the beach because the sea was far too cold for swimming.

More than fifteen years later, here I was cycling into Şile and it was a very different place. Development had arrived. Concrete, box-like, holiday houses had been unimaginatively laid out in dull, straight rows. They marched over the hills, which once had formed such a picturesque backdrop to what had been a small fishing village. There were dusty brick and cement works and busy factories selling the necessary building tools: iron, tiles, wood, stone and marble. The construction industry was booming in Turkey and the coastlines were filling up with holiday villages, second and third homes and apartment blocks. Great chunks of the Mediterranean and Aegean coastline had long been swept away under a tidal wave of concrete and the Black Sea coast was following fast. Many of the buildings were empty and unfinished, eyeless boxes, the builders waiting for money from the purchasers before they could be completed. It was sad to see how people were rushing to sell their spare plots of land, their gardens and their corn patches to get probably more money than they would ever manage to earn in a lifetime.

Şile's long main street with its little shops and tea houses overlooking the sea was still recognisable, however. The restaurant, where I had eaten lunch with the young man some fifteen years before, was still there, still decorated in Alpine Swiss style. I clambered off the saddle, aching in every limb, and leaned the bicycle up against the window where I could keep a careful eye on her. The ground rocked a little. I went in and ordered my favourite Turkish soup made with lentils, mercimek çorbası, always delicious. I spooned it down along with my memories.

The price of the soup was written up on a blackboard outside the restaurant – 70,000 TL. The man in charge, however, wanted me to give him a 100,000 TL note. I handed one over. 'No change,' he muttered. I waited. He gave me my change, slowly and reluctantly, six coins, each worth 5,000 TL. I took two and left four. Their value was so infinitesimal, I could not even count how much they were worth. The man grinned. Honour was satisfied on both sides. Outside, I filled up my water bottle from an ornate stone fountain opposite and set off on the back road to Ağva, the next seaside town.

Despite the new developments crowding outside Şile in the direction of İstanbul, the views on the eastern side were unspoiled and breathtaking. The roads, too, remained deliciously empty. The air roared with the sound of birds singing, the chirp of grasshoppers and the creaking rattle of the frogs hiding in the ditches. I met a tortoise slowly plodding across the road. Just in case, I stopped, picked him up and carried him over into the undergrowth, his little wrinkled head tucked anxiously inside his shell, legs rowing in the air.

I was hugging the sea route now with sea views all the time. The Black Sea is rarely black; its colour is difficult to pin down. It is a much less inviting sea than the blue, sparkling Mediterranean and certainly more inscrutable. That afternoon, it was an imperturbable, stony blue. The scenery was gorgeous with sweeping, densely wooded hills and there were blown butterflies like fragile bits of coloured paper, purple flax, red, rock roses and yellow daisies. But the road surface was so smashed and the hills so high, I kept getting off to walk. This brought its own problems. Pushing a loaded bicycle – however lightly loaded – up slippery, rutted hills is simply killing. You finish up too tired to do anything, walk or ride. I continued to feel as if I was going to die, but there was nothing to do except to struggle on.

I cycled through a tiny village and found a square tea house behind white-washed walls directly on the road just before it turned up yet another hill. The men sitting outside in the shade watched me arrive, their mouths open in astonishment, and continued to stare in silence as I painfully dismounted, leaned the bicycle up against a wall and limped into the compound. They pointed to a chair in the shade and called to the man to bring a glass of tea. They nodded approvingly as I heaped the lumps of sugar in for a quick fix of energy. Then the questions began. Where had I come from? What was I doing? Where was I going? They were interested and enthusiastic. It was a fairly standard reaction from the Turks I met on the journey. They loved the idea that a woman could feel comfortable enough in their country to cycle through it on her own, although they also always used the words 'brave' and 'courageous', well aware of the potential problems for females – especially the men. I did not pay for the tea. This was to become a feature of the trip. The tea drinkers waved me off with rapture. I couldn't let them down. I toiled up the hill. I had to keep cycling – well, at least until I was out of sight.

I struggled to stay on the saddle as long as I could but the hills, made worse by the horrible, uneven surfaces, kept beating me. I was even worried about the downward stretches, pulling on the brakes all the time, fearful of twisting a wheel in a particularly deep hole or killing myself by tumbling head first over the handlebars. In the end, desperation made me bold and I rode my lightweight, touring bicycle as if she were a heavyweight, mountain bike, rattling, crashing and juddering over the enormous holes and the bone-breaking ripples of tarmac like frozen, black waves. Even the final flat stretch into Ağva was a disaster in the shape of long stretches of slippery white chalk mixed with large, loose stones, almost impossible to cycle over. It had taken me ten hours to cover around fifty miles, eighty kilometres or so. At that rate it was going to take me a month of Sundays to get over to the east of the Black Sea region – and I had only just begun.

And, meanwhile, where was the sea? Painfully, but triumphantly, I cycled in search down the long, straight and empty road which led into town, either negotiating with extreme care a very regular line of bumps possibly put in to cut traffic speed (!?) or managing to wiggle around them at the edges. Every sharp movement now caused 'interesting' sensation from my backside downwards. I was so tired and relieved I had arrived, I paid no attention to the looks and stares of astonishment from the people in the street and the giggles from the kids. Ağva neither looked nor felt like a seaside town at all. I thought I would worry about where the sea was later and concentrate on finding a cheap place to stay. If I hurried, I could spend an hour on the beach, wherever it was, before the sun, still round and hot in the sky, disappeared for the day.

I spotted a motel up a side street. I could hardly swing my legs to get off the saddle. There were what seemed to be hundreds of school children milling around outside marshalled by a teacher. He came up to me, smiling purposefully. My heart sank. I told him I was looking for a cheap place to stay.

'Good,' he said, 'you can stay here and you will speak to my students in English. It will be such good practice for them.'

Not right now! But I couldn't be rude. He meant so well and was obviously thrilled at this completely unexpected opportunity.

'What shall I talk to them about?' I said weakly.

'Tell them who you are and where you've come from. Just chat to them. They'll appreciate it so much.'

The very last thing on earth I wanted to do was to engage in general conversation with a bunch of young, teenaged boys, who crowded eagerly round me, staring at the bicycle and me. I forced my face into a smile. Lucretia Borgia would have recognised such a smile and stepped backwards for her own safety. 'I'm really sorry,' I said, 'but I'm a bit tired at the moment. Maybe later. It would be wonderful.'

I fled into what looked like the motel's tea house to ask about a room for the night. The price sounded reasonable, a few pounds, but they asked me to wait ten minutes before seeing the room. I couldn't understand why they wanted me to wait and I didn't care. In Turkey ten minutes could mean anything. Making my excuses, I continued on down the street into what appeared to be the town square. I was struck by the number of boys – all boys – speeding round the streets on brand-new, gaily painted, mountain bikes. Times had changed in Turkey. Twenty years before, their fathers could not have dreamed of such riches. There was more progress taking up most of one side of the square in the shape of a large supermarket, another new phenomenon that would no doubt slowly kill off the millions of small Turkish stores, which would be unable to compete. I'm sorry to say I went in because at that point I had an overwhelming need for some very sweet, Black Sea chocolate. The man at the till was having an animated conversation with somebody via his mobile telephone. I asked him where the sea was and where a cheap place to stay was likely to be. He gestured vaguely behind the square and I went to investigate.

The sea was still out of sight, but I found Göksu Pansiyon. It was a smart, new, clean looking building with a well-established vine shading a seating area outside. I went in to find the owner, a young, good-looking, modern man, in a comfortable large office next to a bar. The establishment would not have looked out of place in an English seaside town. He was sitting busily working at a computer and was efficient and organised. He took me upstairs through a side entrance to a self-contained flatlet incorporating two double bedrooms, a kitchen and a bathroom with a shower attached to a natural gas cylinder. This meant there was hot water. I could have one of the rooms for the equivalent of £3.50. The room had a balcony with a washing line and was big enough to take my bicycle. Happy, happy days.

The clock was ticking. I rushed out to buy bread, cheese and biscuits for the next day and found a small store, the sort where boxes of washing powder, tins of tomato paste, candles and packets of cumin, pepper corns, rice and spaghetti reach from floor to ceiling. The owner was sitting comfortably tucked away behind an old-fashioned wooden desk. He was watching the news on television. The man being interviewed was the permanently scowling Mesut Yılmaz. He had just become prime minister after the forced collapse of the coalition government of Necmettin Erbakan, leader of the Refah party and the first Islamist prime minister since the establishment of the secular Turkish Republic. In contrast to Yilmaz, Erbakan looked like a genial Santa Claus.

'What do you think of the new government?' I asked.

'At least we've got rid of the fascists,' he replied.

'And how do you think they'll do?'

His answer was a shrug. I left the grocer watching the politicians on TV telling everybody how good things were going to be, and went to find the sea.

Ağva was a pleasant little town built alongside a river which ran into a creek that led into the sea. The creek was overshadowed by a massive outcrop of densely wooded rock, formed from layer upon layer of stone. It looked like a wedding cake that had been pushed by giant hands towards the sea. The hands had stopped pushing just before the cake would have tumbled in. The ancient Greeks thought the hands belonged to the mythical giants they called the Cyclopes. The huge, stone structure made a cool and shady backdrop for the town. Ottoman wooden houses with shutters and balconies lined the narrow streets leading down to the creek and the river. In İstanbul, many similar buildings had been done up and were selling for a fortune. You could have probably snapped one up in Ağva for the equivalent of a few thousand pounds.

I walked down to the creek to admire the fishing and pleasure boats, built in Noah's Ark style, tied up alongside. The sun was still hot although it was late afternoon and I was pleased I had arrived in time. The sea was away in the distance lapping against a long, sandy beach, the dunes stretching westwards back towards

Şile and the mouth of the Bosphorus. As well as being cold, the Black Sea is heavily polluted, so I lay on the sand and watched, from a safe distance, yet another school party. The teachers were using coloured flags to signal to different groups of children what they wanted them to do. In fact, I like Turkish children. They are articulate and enthusiastic, the girls and boys mixing and chatting in an apparently relaxed manner, maybe because they are so accustomed to the company of their numerous brothers and sisters. I fell asleep on my back and then on my front to the sound of the children's laughter.

Back in the flat, I washed away the sand and the journey under a hot and wonderful shower. The bicycle was leaning doe-like against the wall. I went over her feeling the tyres and checking screws. Although I was completely untechnical, only just about capable of changing inner tubes – and then it took me two hours to do so – it made me feel better to communicate in this way with the bicycle. I was sure she appreciated the attention. However, what I found threw me into a blind panic. One of the two gear lever wires was fraying and was only connected by a few strands. How could I have left England with the bicycle in such a condition! The first day's cycling had already taught me that I needed every single one of my gears. The strain on the gear levers and wires could only increase. A fraying wire would snap in no time. The only professional bike shop I could think of was far away in Ortaköy in İstanbul. I leaned against the wall wondering what the alternatives were.

The sound of bicycle bells floated in through the open balcony door. I went outside and looked more closely at the mountain bikes wheeling round the streets. The bikes were new and sophisticated. Somebody somewhere must be able to fix them. I went downstairs to find the boss. He had given me his business card so I knew that he was using his computer to run an import/export company, as well as his pension. This was an impressively organised, new age man. Even his name was reassuring. It was Gökhan Toprakcı, which literally meant Mr Sky-inn Earth-man. That covered practically everything.

I found Mr Toprakcı sitting at ease with his wife and two small children, drinking tea at a comfortable table under the vine. I wondered what 'gear wire' was in Turkish. All my good dictionaries were at home. Fortunately, Mr Toprakcı was an uncommonly clever man. He could have been the prototype for Inspector Bucket, Dickens' sharp detective in *Bleak House*, who always knew what everybody was going to think or say before they had thought or said it. Mr Toprakcı looked at my face and told me to sit down and drink a glass of tea. I did so. It was the way to behave in Turkey, even if it was past six o'clock in the evening and you were worrying that all the bicycle repair shops would be hanging up their tools for the day. I sipped my tea in a seething agony of impatience. I had a problem with my bicycle, I told him. Mr Toprakcı suggested that I brought her down so that he could take a look. This I did. I asked if there were any bicycle repair shops in town. With so many bikes on the streets, somebody must be repairing them. Of course there were, he said, and laughed, his wife joining in. Would they still be open? I asked nervously. Of course they would.

The Turks have very close family relations and there are different words to describe the maternal and paternal aunts and uncles. It turned out that Mr Toprakcı's 'Amca,' that's to say the brother of his father, ran a bicycle repair shop close by. After several more slim glasses of sugared tea and more laughter at my too apparent anxiety, he told his small daughter to take me over the road to Amca. I took her hand and tried not to hurry. I was frightened of pulling her over. Amca, who looked remarkably young, was to be found in a tumbledown shed in a side street about fifty yards away. The notice in the cracked and cobwebbed window said 'Genel Tamirci', 'General Repair Man'. I hurried in scarcely able to see through the gloom. As my eyes became accustomed to the lack of light, I was able to see wheels and bits of wire and things in corners and a work bench scattered with old screwdrivers and tools. 'I have a big problem,' I said and showed him the gear lever wire. And just in case he was unable to see for himself how badly it was fraying, I pointed out the good one.

'That's a small problem,' he said, and selecting a long piece of wire hanging on the wall, he matched it side by side with mine. Then he picked up a chair and carried it outside the shop underneath a shady plane tree growing in the middle of the road. 'Sit down,' he said. 'Relax.'

The Turks are ever clever and diplomatic. Amca did not want to hurt my feelings, but he did want to get rid of the person telling him how to do his business, whose anxiety filled his small workshop. I felt soothed and cared for and went to look at the elegant, Ottoman houses and gaze over the river which I knew I would be crossing at some point in the morning. I would not after all, have to return to İstanbul to get the bike fixed.

I went back to see how she was getting on. Oh joyful sight. She had a brand-new, gleaming, gear lever wire and Amca was just tightening up the tension. He charged me the equivalent of 75p. Overwhelmed with relief, I pedalled off and joined the young boys swooping and wheeling like evening swallows round the streets on their machines, I, on mine, testing out my gear levers and thinking about the route eastwards the next day. I had discussed it with Andy before I left. On my map, the stretch of road through to the next seaside town of Karasu (Black Water) was marked as incomplete. Andy remembered doing it once before in a four-wheel drive vehicle. The question was had the track been surfaced since then. I returned to the pension.

Mr Toprakcı was pleased at my pleasure and relief over my repaired bicycle. I sat down at the table and he asked me what I needed to know next. He could see on my face, he said, that there were other questions and problems. Good old

Inspector Bucket. We discussed the route to Karasu. I could probably get as far as a small village on the coast called Kerpe fairly easily but after that he thought the road stopped. If he were right, I would have to go back inland to the town of Kandıra, continue south to the town of Sakarya (formerly Adapazarı) and return to the coast from there.

'And now,' said this very intelligent man, 'what next?' I wanted a restaurant, did I? That was easy. His friend in the place on the beach would take care of me, and he hurried me up the street.

It was a cavernous restaurant overlooking the creek and I seemed to be the only customer. I asked for an İskender kebab. This is made with hot slices of meat cut from the layers of döner lamb on the spit, pitta bread, cold yoghurt and tomatoes. While I waited, I turned to the subtle and ambiguous world of Henry James – I had brought along *The Golden Bowl*, one of his many truly great novels. I always had several books with me. It is unbearable to have nothing to read. It also gave me something to do if I wanted to mind my own business. No sooner had I turned the first page than the manager of the restaurant had introduced himself and was sitting opposite me at my table. He was smoking a cigarette and blew the smoke in my face. He had brought with him the usual photographs of his 'friends', happy, European holiday makers who had been royally entertained by him at his small place down by the river. Look what a wonderful time they had all had together. After dinner, you must come and have a good time too. We can drink, have coffee, do anything you want. He looked at me hard. He was overweight but good-looking in a debauched sort of way. He reminded me of Victor Komarovsky in the film, Dr. Zhivago. He offered me a cigarette, which I pointedly declined. I was tired, I said. I had a headache. I needed to wash my hair. I had cycled eighty kilometres that day and would be getting up at the crack of dawn to cycle lots more. It made no difference. He sat there, solidly, looking at me. Fortunately, at that point, my dinner arrived and he moved off, rather like an oil tanker. He expected to see me later, he said.

I ate my dinner reflectively. Sex on a plate. That was how it usually was. If only I wanted all these men, instead of just one or two every so often, it would have made life much easier. What do you do if you want sex but happen to be selective about who you go to bed with? When you're hungry, you can eat. If you're tired, you can sleep; thirsty, well you can drink something. Sex is a nagging, irritating ache afflicting the animal kingdom. You can do some of it on your own but it isn't so nice. I ate my kebab, scraping up the tomato and yoghurt remains with my knife, which I licked regardless of cultures. Then I turned my back on the darkening creek and the shimmering sea and went back to the safety of the Göksu Pansiyon and out of the naughty night.

Back home, my room was well equipped. It had a working bedside lamp which I could unplug and use the socket to plug in my anti-mosquito device, a neat little affair into which you slipped a tablet which then gave off a smell all night, relatively odourless for us but pretty nasty for mosquitos. It worked, even in a large room with high ceilings. What with the river and the creek and the woods overhanging the town, I knew the mosquitoes would be more troublesome than Mr Komorovsky could ever have been. I had spent so many miserable nights on various trips over the years, being dive-bombed for hours, that sinister whine vibrating in the ears, then waking up to find face, arms and hands, sometimes even my feet, on fire. Occasionally, I burned anti-mosquito coils but the nights were always longer than the coils were.

I patted my dear bicycle, leaning up against the wall and dozing quietly. Was it unhealthy to love a machine? We had done so much together, been in so many adventures and ridiculous situations. When you travel alone, you have to talk to somebody as the hours tick past on the road. The Irish writer, Flann O'Brien, described the people who were turning into bicycles because they used them so much, including the postman who had cycled twenty-nine miles every single day for forty years. Food for thought.

I lay down to sleep, aching everywhere. It was only around 9 pm, but I was going to get up early. The alarm was set for five o'clock although the idea of getting back on the saddle after just eight hours was almost inconceivable. I slept, despite the lights shining through the windows from the shops opposite and the arrival of one of Mr Toprakcı's small daughters onto my balcony, curious to see who was there. I could hear him explaining to her that it was 'the foreigner'. He and his family were just next door in the adjoining flat which shared the balcony. It was reassuring to have them close by.

2
Ağva to Karasu

While we are marching, Timasion is to ride ahead with the cavalry, keeping his eye on us and also investigating what lies ahead, so that nothing can take us by surprise.

It was still quite dark at five o'clock and Ağva was blanketed in a heavy sea mist. It was cold outside and I felt terrible having to get up from a deliciously warm and comfortable bed. It took a huge effort of will to do so. My clothes hanging on the balcony were still wet. This was always a miserable state of affairs. However I arranged them, in or on the bicycle bags, they would smell later on. I forced down some bread and cheese, which was at least relatively fresh from the day before, filled my water bottle and started to carry my bicycle and bags downstairs, trying not to make too much noise and wake the family up. The key was in the door as Mr Bucket had told me it would be. Out I went into the street, slipping outside like a thief in the night, the air heavy and wet, strapping on the bags, snapping on my gloves, shivering in the cold, but suddenly catching the excitement of the coming day as the dark imperceptibly turned into a glimmering light. Quickly, quickly, not to miss a second, before the rest of the world got up; a new day all to myself, another beginning, another chance.

I got back gingerly on the saddle, admiring the mended gear wire, took a last look round and made my way back onto the long main street to head out of town. The day stretched gloriously ahead, although I was anxious about having to leave the coast and head inland. It meant that I was going to miss the tiny village of Kerpe and its beautiful, rock harbour, which was called Port Calpe in ancient times. After much burning, killing, plundering and taking of slaves around and about, Xenophon and the Ten Thousand, who had split up at Heraclea, modern-day Ereğli, some to sail along the coast and some to march inland, reconvened at Port Calpe. In the *Anabasis*, Xenophon described 'a promontory jutting out in the sea, and the part that faces the sea itself is a steep cliff of not less than twenty fathoms at its lowest point'. He obviously thought the site was perfect for a port city: there was a spring of plentiful spring water, quantities of timber for shipbuilding and the soil was earthy and free from stones. But no olive trees would grow there. So the Greek mercenaries continued their journey, marching westwards across country towards Byzantium, burying a great number of men who had died in the fighting as they went.

I too was going to have to cross country (no dead bodies hopefully) owing to the lack of a reasonable coastal road, although I was, of course, going in the opposite direction. It meant that the distance I had to go to get back onto the coast was doubled. It would be impossible for me to cycle down to Sakarya and then back to the Black Sea and Karasu – about 140 kilometres or eighty-six miles – all in one day. But I didn't want to stay overnight in Sakarya. I knew it would be a large town and too busy for my liking. The problem was how to get a correct assessment of the road. It is always difficult to get a bicycle-eye view of the road from people. Very few are able to imagine travelling anywhere by bicycle, particularly the Turks, who often have hazy notions about how far away somewhere is, generally estimating distance in terms of how long it will take by car. 'It's only five minutes away,' is meaningless when travelling on two wheels. Most motorists rarely have any idea about the road surfaces, or at least the impact it could have on cyclists. In Turkey, I was also discovering that a road might be covered in tarmac but it was still practically impossible to cycle on it.

The mist was still heavy and cycling along by the river creek felt rather like trying to pedal along the bottom of the sea. My hair and face were soon running with water, my shirt was soaked through and my bicycle bags were beaded with silver drops of dew. There was no point in wearing my cycle glasses, so necessary against sun, dust, stones and flies; they were misting up too badly. For once I wanted the sun to come quickly to dry everything off. Outside Ağva, I turned towards Kandira and began to climb up through the hills, up up, ever up, sometimes down but mostly up. I considered the position. I was travelling eastwards. The hills were getting steadily higher and would soon become full-blown mountains. I was still only playing around in the foothills. It might have been easier to catch the bus to Georgia and freewheel (well, almost) back to İstanbul. It was too late now. I resolved to stay on the saddle as much as I could. I had learned the hard way the day before that once you started walking, it was practically impossible to get back on.

There was much to occupy the eye and mind. The spiders had been busy working overnight; their webs were draped and laced over the bushes and trees like pearl necklaces. Folds of mist like sea foam filled the valleys, and bells tinkled round the necks of the cows grazing with their calves down the lanes. They were beautiful animals, clean and brown with soulful eyes and short horns on shapely heads. They turned to stare in astonishment at the unfamiliar creature looming up on wheels through the mist. They were all wearing necklaces of blue beads against the evil, blue eye (oh dear), which I later found out were on sale everywhere in hardware shops. There was very little traffic and this suited me fine. I didn't want any nosey drivers pulling over in the mist to find out what I was doing. Like the Ten Thousand, I didn't want any nasty surprises either. There was always that slight anxiety.

The hills, jagged and in shadow, kept the sun away for a long time. Sometimes there was a gleam over a peak but then it would disappear again. Just from that radiant gleam, I knew the coming sun was full and hot and burning and, despite my general dampness, I was relieved after all that I was being protected for so long. The countryside was glorious. Purple flax and yellow cistus roses filled the hedgerows and I was cycling through waves of yellow and black butterflies. A dog snoozed comfortably on the top of a haystack. He didn't see me. Fortunately. The women worked hard in this country, up at the crack of dawn, feeding the animals, forking hay. 'Only reapers reaping early' . . . Spinning up and wheeling down, I felt as if I were flying. The countryside spread out before me like the illustrations in a child's book of how it should be: cornfields, rivers, bridges, red-roofed houses and timbered villages, tucked away among the trees. I stopped off at a tea house in a village where the men were watching the news on television. The item was about the evacuation from Hong Kong by the British. What did I think about that, they asked. 'We've gone, at last,' I said. They liked that and laughed. There was more free tea.

It would have been almost perfect but for the roads. Once again, I was experiencing gluey, sticky surfaces to make even Xenophon's tough soldiers weep. The road was apparently in the throes of being repaired. I passed monster road diggers and mounds of round stones, which I was becoming familiar with slipping loosely under my wheels, but I rarely saw any workmen. They must have always been on a tea break whenever I passed by. The tarmac being laid seemed to lack a vital ingredient to make it hold together. It was melting all over the roads in waves and swirls and ridges. It gripped my tyres like glue and I felt as if I were rowing against the tide. At one point I got off the bicycle in despair before I fell off – and found my feet sinking into the road surface. I got back on hurriedly. Now my shoes were covered in sticky tar which made pedalling even more difficult. I tried to cycle right on the edge of the road on the old earthen surface. I battled on, swooping and sticking and bouncing, the wind roaring in my ears on the odd occasion I could go at a reasonable speed downhill. By the time I cycled in to Kandira, I was completely exhausted.

A shop was selling börek in the market place. This is one of the most popular and substantial snacks in Turkey. Made in layers from flaky pastry, börek is filled with minced meat or white cheese. When it is hot and fresh, it is simply delicious. Börek was just what I wanted. I asked for a big plateful and watched with pleasure as a large slice of the kind stuffed with meat was cut off for me. The horrors of the gluey road faded and I recovered sufficiently to be able to speak. The inevitable television was on in the corner and as usual it was news time. The Turks are quite happy to talk about politics or religion at the drop of a hat and I asked the börekçi what he thought about the ousting by the military of Necmettin Erbakan and his Islamist Welfare Party, Refah. He looked at me with clear, greeny-brown eyes – devout people always seem to have clear eyes that look at you directly without fear or favour.

'The Welfare Party will come back,' he said.

'But they are Muslims and want a non-secular Turkey.'

'We are all Muslims,' he replied. 'The Welfare Party, Refah, will come back. The other parties say they are democratic. They have no religion, but the problem is that they don't have any democracy either. We may as well stick with Welfare. They will definitely return.'

He charged me almost nothing for the börek. I went outside into the square to ask the taxi drivers about the state of the road along the coast. It was the usual story. They simply could not believe that anybody could be cycling anywhere and assumed I wanted a lift to Karasu. Patiently, I asked them which road they would take if they were going there. They would go via Sakarya, they said, there was no coast road.

So that confirmed it. I had to go further inland and back up again to the coast and Karasu. I bought an extravagant bottle of fresh water, drank half, put the rest into my water bottle and rode on. It was only another ten miles to the small town of Kaynarca and it was a relatively easy run. On arrival, I went into yet another restaurant and this time consumed a steaming hot bowl of lentil soup. The town was a pleasant place but the people in the restaurant were only able to deal with a foreign woman on a bicycle by pretending she wasn't there. They did this very successfully. I was served the soup and handed the bill as if I simply did not exist. But it was the cheapest bowl of soup I had ever had – 50,000 TL, the equivalent of 20p, half the price everywhere else. I never paid so little again. Honest people, even if they didn't like single, foreign women on bicycles.

The road inland to Sakarya was less extreme, with long gentle sweeps up and rushes down. The hills receded and the countryside opened up, a patchwork of colour, green, yellow and gold with mature trees pleasantly shady in the middle of the fields. The road surfaces were still not wonderful and I began to realise they never would be. The excitement on this leg of the journey was provided by a man on a motorcycle. He roared closely up behind me. My heart sank. Motorcyclists have often given me problems – the worst occasion was when I got pulled over by two members of Hezbollah on a Honda motorcycle in South Lebanon, who thought I was an Israeli spy on a bike and considered shooting me. This encounter wasn't nearly as dramatic but was a nuisance all the same. The man slowed down and rode alongside me, like a sticky, annoying, buzzing fly. He was smiling hopefully. Furious, I skidded to a halt and screamed at him to continue his journey AT ONCE. I bitterly resent being harassed by men. He pulled ahead and I cycled on slowly. The road was completely empty. What if . . . I saw him ahead of me. He had stopped and was talking to an elderly man by the side of the road. I decided I was going to get my own back.

I cycled up and stopped. Mr Motorcycle turned round and saw me. He flashed what he obviously hoped would be an irresistible smile, dazzlingly white-toothed underneath his black moustache. He obviously thought his luck was in after all. His smile faded as soon as he heard what I was saying, loudly, to the poor old man who looked as if he wanted to disappear. 'This man is following me,' I roared. 'I want you to go and report him to the police immediately. At once, do you hear? It is a disgrace. A disgrace for Turkey. If you don't report him, I will, as soon as I can.'

It was a truly magnificent performance and I enjoyed every second of it. The word for 'disgrace', 'ayıp', is much stronger in Turkish than in English and is similar to the Arabic. It is one of my favourite words. I continued to point accusingly (a very rude action in Turkey) at the old man who was shifting from foot to foot in consternation and embarrassment. I continued to ignore the motorcyclist who, I think, was squirming; certainly he had stopped smiling. The old man muttered that there was a village just a few minutes away and I should go there if I wanted to report anybody, but I interrupted. 'I am busy,' I shouted. 'You must go and tell them what has happened.' And I pointed at him again.

They stood side by side in silence. No woman, except their wives or mothers, had probably ever shouted at them before. I pedalled away, gleeful. As I toiled up a hill, struggling against the wind, I heard the sound of a motorcycle coming up behind me. I started to sweat slightly. Would he knock me off my bike and run me over to get his revenge? He passed me and, without a backward look, was gone.

The rest of the journey to Sakarya was relatively uneventful and without any further surprises. I could see from my map that there were short cuts through the hills, which would lead back towards the coast and avoid having to go into Sakarya itself. They were drawn as thin, purple lines, which the map glossary described as 'very bad roads'. I wondered how they could be worse than the ones I had already experienced. One of them even looked short enough to walk. It was only a few miles or so. Optimism and the capacity to forget how you felt five minutes beforehand are great weapons in the travel armoury. I stopped at a garage to fill up my water bottle and to ask about the route. A man with a weathered skin and a fresh, outdoors look told me how easy it would be. 'Go down the road a few kilometres,' he said, 'continue round the bend, not too fast or you'll miss the turning, and it's sharp right.' He was interrupted by the garage man, who reminded him that he was a forester. It was easy for him, but it wouldn't be so easy for me, he said. It was better to go to Sakarya and on from there.

I cycled on regretfully thinking what a coward I was and how pleasant it would have been to get right off the beaten track and onto a woodland trail. I looked out for the turning but it must have been so small I missed it. On the outskirts of the town, I stood on the road, which led back up to the coast and Karasu, and tried to wave down a bus. They all roared past, the drivers giving no sign of even having seen me. In the old days they would have screeched to a halt, loaded my bicycle onto the roof rack and continued on. The old Turkish buses were great. People used to transport their household goods, including their mattresses and kitchen sinks, across the country packed on to roof racks. It used to take hours to load up at the bus stations but was so much more interesting.

'They can't take you. They're full and there's no room for bicycles,' said a passer-by who had been observing me from a distance. 'You'll have to cycle.' He said it rather gloatingly.

It was another thirty miles or so to Karasu and I knew I had done enough that day. Maybe, I thought, there would be an old style bus in town that could accommodate the bicycle, and pedalled, painfully, on. It was only another five miles in to the centre of Sakarya but because I had mentally switched off by then, it seemed much further. In the central square there were scores of buses heading for the Black Sea, but none with a roof rack. I would have to wait for the big coach from İstanbul. This would have space in its luggage compartment. It would come within two hours, I was told. I went for a walk in Sakarya's new, pedestrianised shopping centre and checked the rate of exchange in the change money shops. As usual every other currency, including the pound, was gaining every day at the expense of the Turkish lira. There were always Turks queuing up to buy dollars which they kept to sell at a later date. When I first visited Turkey in 1979, there were 80 TL to the pound. Eighteen years later, the exchange rate that day in 1997 in Sakarya stood at 254,000 TL.

I was tired, my legs ached and the day was hot, burningly so outside in full sunlight. I went back to the cool gloom of the bus office and watched a young, rosy-cheeked barber in his shop opposite, his towels tidily hanging up to dry over a clothes-horse. He seemed to have no clients that afternoon and he sat and smoked cigarettes or chatted to the people brewing endless tea and coffee in a tiny cubby-hole next door. I would have liked to have gone in, sat in his comfortable chair and had him wash my hair. It felt so dirty from the road. I knew such an event would have brought the town to a halt. I dozed, leaning my head against the back of the chair, hoping I wasn't sleeping with my mouth open. After four hours, the bus from İstanbul still had not arrived. The office man was beginning to get irritated at being asked where it was so many times. 'I don't know. It's late,' he said. 'I don't know where it is.'

I went outside in despair. The next mini bus to the Black Sea was about to depart. By now it was late in the afternoon and there were fewer passengers. I even recognised the driver who had come and gone, probably several times, while I had been kicking my heels in the office. I asked him again whether the bike could somehow be squeezed in. It was impossible, he said. 'OK,' I said. 'What if I took a row of seats? How much would I have to pay?'

The three tickets cost the equivalent of £3. I suspect I may have paid an inflated price. Never mind. I rushed to squash the bags under the seats and managed to get the bicycle into the row. I squeezed in next to her, pretending to be comfortable. As usual, I was more concerned about the bicycle and whether any bit of her would be damaged. There was still no sign of the coach from İstanbul and I waved goodbye to the office man, feeling rather guilty that I had abandoned him. He looked relieved to be rid of the bicycle and me from his office. Maybe I had been sleeping with my mouth open! We roared off on the switchback road to Karasu. The journey took about an hour. I hung on to the bicycle, trying to stop her ripping my legs, looking out of the window and very gratified to see that the road surfaces were as bad as the ones I had ridden on earlier in the day. And I was safe and sound, high up in a bus.

My heart sank as we drove into Karasu, a nondescript, chaotic, down-at-heel town, with not a hotel, cheap or otherwise, in sight. We stopped to let some passengers off and I made a miserable move to get off too, thinking we had reached our destination. But the driver indicated we were continuing. We headed out of town and I suddenly realised that Karasu was very much a Turkish town, built well away from the beach. This was typical of the Turkish towns along the Black Sea. Unlike the sea-going Greeks, who had loved the sea and built beautiful cities with harbours, the Turks had built their residential areas well away from the coast, their backs turned firmly against the unpredictable sea, the mighty storms and the shifting sands. We were making for Karasu Plaj, a new, summer holiday development literally being built slap bang on the fine, white, Black Sea sand dunes.

It was a developer's dream and an environmentalist's nightmare. Rows and rows of identical villas and apartment blocks in lines faced the sea, while on the beach itself scores of tents had been put up in which entire families were camping with minimal facilities. They looked like refugee camps. I had heard Andy back in his office in İstanbul so often bemoaning the erosion of the dunes along the Black Sea and the loss of the sea plants and birds that grow and nest there. I was seeing this for myself at Karasu Plaj. This was Turkish sea-side development at its short-sighted worst, unplanned and unregulated. This was about making lots of quick bucks and to hell with the consequences.

I felt guilty about being so scathing when I saw the children having a wonderful time on the stretch of sand that was still free of building work. But soon there would be nothing left of the natural environment. It would be swallowed up under tons of concrete and breeze blocks. The only consolation was that the buildings were flimsy; they would never be able to withstand the Black Sea storms and the harsh weather. I was sure that one day Karasu Plaj would be a crumbling ghost town. I remembered travelling along the Mediterranean once with a member of Turkish Greenpeace. She stared in miserable silence at the monstrous, new developments along the coastline. 'One day all this concrete will have gone,' she said finally. 'That is the only way I can bear to look at it.'

I cycled up and down the streets, looking for a reasonably priced room, but everything was geared up for families and too expensive for a single person. So I took a dark and smelly but cheap room in a hotel along the front. It confirmed my theory. Although the building was recently built, it was already like a slum, damp and cracked – although it did have hot water in the shower room. It also had a large, open roof area, with washing lines. I could hang out my horrible, smelly clothes from Ağva, although by then it was so late the sun had virtually died, taking the heat with it. In early July along the Mediterranean, the nights would have been hot and breathless but along the Black Sea, the climate was similar to that of northern Europe. I went out to buy some food for the next day and a can of beer to drink in private on the roof that evening.

The street along the sea was crowded with parading teenagers, would-be lovers of both sexes, the boys in tight, sexy jeans and loose shirts strutting their stuff, the girls dressed likewise, some in short skirts. This, however, was Turkey. These teenagers could only look and long, at least in public. As night fell, the atmosphere was taught and strained. Over the way, the lights of the funfair twinkled out and the amusements spun, rocked and twirled, glittered and moaned. The most popular attraction appeared to be a giant chair boat which shot stomach-churningly high into the air and plunged back down again, eliciting long, drawn out, rhythmic, rocking groans from the girls packed inside, 'ooooooh' up, 'aaaaaah' down. It went on in the same rhythm for hours through the night, 'oooooooh, aaaaaah'. The ups and downs of love.

I decided to eat in the restaurant of the hotel, which was as dark and dank as the rest of the building but at least fairly busy, so the food in the display cabinets would be fresh. The best places to eat in Turkey are the cheap ordinary restaurants which proliferate in the towns where the men tend to eat out in the early evenings. But Karasu town was too far for me to go after a day's cycling and the only alternative to the hotel restaurant seemed to be take-away pizza huts. I ordered a plate of meze, a selection of Turkish hors d'oeuvres, made from vegetables, meats and fish which have been stuffed, pureed, mashed or oiled into delectable dishes, along with plates of olives, pickled cucumbers and cheese. Divine. I wanted a lot of water, a whole jug of it. The water that came out of Turkish taps was generally excellent, but the restaurants were beginning to sell tiny bottles of spring water to make more money. I asked the waiter for a jug of water. Unfortunately, I was using the word for 'tray', asking in effect for a tray of water. This caused a great deal of confusion until I solved the mystery by looking up the word for jug in my pocket dictionary. Confusing words can be dangerous. On this occasion it merely confirmed to the restaurant staff that I was indeed crazy.

My tiny room had a tiny balcony and, after the excitement of dinner, I went outside to see what was happening. The youths were still parading like young, sleek wolves up and down the street. The more practical ones were playing snooker in a games room just opposite the hotel. The lights were blazing and the noise from the funfair was terrible. How was I to sleep? But I did. It was a relief in the early morning though to slip outside into the fresh, sea air and cycle away from the crash box of Karasu Plaj, round the roundabout and along the coast towards my next stop, the iron and steel town of Ereğli.

3
Karasu to Ereğli

The soldiers held an assembly here and discussed the question of whether they should travel the rest of the way out of the area of the Euxine by land or by sea.

In retrospect, I laughed to think how stupid I had been to think that there could have been a chunk of motorway running eastwards from Karasu. The road was marked on the map in important, double red lines. These actually meant that the road was under construction. In fact, a surface had been laid but it was, like so many of the other newer surfaces along the Black Sea coast, stony, meltingly glutinous and slippery. It was a painful ride that morning, forcing the pedals round, gloomily thinking there were hundreds more miles to go, which were bound to be exactly the same. It was all made worse because the road was as flat as a board, at least to start with. Non-cyclists think that riding on the flat is preferable to cycling in hills or mountains but the truth is exactly the opposite. However painful cycling is up and down slopes, riding on the flat for any distance is excruciating. Muscles need variety. They need to be challenged.

The map indicated that the beaches from Karasu most of the way into Ereğli were fine and sandy and suitable for swimming. It also looked as if the road ran alongside the sea for a while. I had been looking forward to the ride, but the new developments were spreading like a disease, ugly and scarring, and there were no open views of the sea or the beaches. Some of the houses were built on stilts in traditional style to protect them from rising damp, but they were still unattractive cement blocks and, no doubt, still freezing cold.

The road finally turned inland and there was some hard cycling to be done up steep inclines. Challenging or not, I wasn't surprised at all that Xenophon and his men had chosen to sail or march inland along this stretch of the Black Sea country rather than exhaust themselves over endless, perpendicular hills. I tried to stay on the saddle as long as I could, only getting off when I was virtually immobile or about to go backwards. It was practically impossible to push the bicycle up some of the slopes because they were so sheer and slippery. It took all my strength and willpower to carry on, sweating and furious, hair sticking to head, body running with perspiration, glasses slipping down nose. It was a curious experience changing up through the gears and feeling one's legs dissolving into jelly which poured into a mould and then slowly reset again. I played mental games to get up the hills, trying not to look at the distance to go before the road headed downwards again, or fixing the mind in another time and place, anything to avoid contemplating the agonising haul ahead. Sometimes, when the road corkscrewed up and away into the distance, obscured by bends and trees, I watched the progress of any car or lorry that overtook me, watching like a cat in front of a mouse-hole to glimpse when the vehicle dipped down instead of pointing upwards. Other times, I closed my eyes or turned away refusing to look because I knew it would be too disheartening. I felt as if I were swimming against the tide, hanging on to the wheel of my boat, pushing on against the storm and the winds.

Travelling alone is indeed a lonely business, holding up a mirror to life. There is plenty of time, almost too much, for reflection and agonising analysis. As the hours ticked past, there was plenty of time to go through the boxes and drawers in the mind, peering in, blowing off the dust, trying to tidy up and accommodate the contents. There were some drawers which were quickly slammed shut even as they were opened, leaning against them to stop them sliding open again. I wrote scores of letters in my head to people I hadn't seen or spoken to for years. It must have been an unconscious way of trying to hang on to my own identity. Nobody knew me. I was to people only how I appeared to them, a crazy, foreign woman doing things most Turkish women could never have done, obviously unloved by my family or why should I have been there, alone and unprotected, no husband, brother, father to look after me.

'Are you married?'

'No.'

'Do you have children?'

'No.'

'Why not?'

I was asked that series of questions daily by men and women in shops and tea houses, even when I stopped in the street or the middle of a village to ask the way. Most people were unable to conceive of such a life and felt sorry for me for being in such an unfortunate position. Sometimes I felt so battered by the questions and overwhelmed by their obvious sympathy that I started to feel sorry for myself and wondered how on earth I had come to be in such a strange and unbelievable situation. There were, of course, those who smiled and understood, wonderful people, and then the world lit up and was real.

Away from the sea, the countryside was beautiful, the forests green and impenetrable. There were orchards of hazelnut trees and vegetable gardens – shove it in that rich soil and it grew. Red-roofed houses peeped through the trees, perched on the heights and nestled in the valleys. All the villages had names like 'the little village under the hill', 'the village on the hill', 'the village over the hill'. There were many picturesque, Ottoman houses, deserted and derelict, the worms feasting on the magnificent timbers. Their owners had long gone away to work in İstanbul or Europe. These houses were the stuff to weave romantic dreams around, flowers in pots, white vests on the line in descending order, a kettle boiling on the stove for tea, a man with clear eyes, who would come in at the end of the day, leaving his shoes outside the door.

Stick with the dreams and cycle on.

I reached Akçakoca, which was spread out over the cliffs and filled with hotels and restaurants, an unusually lively Black Sea town. I even saw some foreigners, a fairly rare sight, and stopped to ask them where they were from – exactly what I hated the Turks asking me. They were Danes, on a weekend break from Ankara. They were very impressed that I had cycled from Polonezköy. This made me feel a great deal better. I wanted a bowl of lovely soup, but I had arrived so early that nothing seemed to be open apart from a fruit and vegetable market in full swing near the bus station. There were buses leaving for Ereğli. This made me feel reassured. I had a safety net if anything went wrong. I bought a handful of peaches and two large tomatoes, feeling rather guilty. The Turks buy their food in kilos, whole bags of oranges and tomatoes, sacks of potatoes and trays of eggs. But the market stallholders were generally accommodating. They no doubt felt sorry for me too!

Cycling out of Akçakoca, I passed a soup house which was just opening its doors, and went in for a bowl of lentils. The atmosphere was unusually gloomy; nobody was speaking to anybody, neither the patron nor the customers. It made my soup taste lukewarm and insipid. Although I knew before the trip began that the Black Sea region was cut off from the rest of Anatolian Turkey by mountains, I was beginning to see for myself just how remote the area was and why over the decades many Black Sea people had gone to look for opportunities elsewhere. The soup man looked as if he were thinking of all the bowls of soup he would have to sell that day to break even. Either that or his favourite football team had lost the night before. I was glad to leave, shake off the shadows and get back on the road. It was a relatively straight run through Alaplı into Ereğli, hugging the coastline and along the sea. The major problem was the narrowness of the road. This made the journey a dice of death with the lorries, which were by then numerous, heralding the approach of Turkey's major coal mining and iron and steel producing towns.

At first sight, Ereğli looked rather daunting with its belching, flaring chimneys and conveyor belts and bridges of the iron and steel works, which sprawled spaghetti-like over the western approach into the city, like a giant, labyrinthine nightmare. It was difficult to think that Ereğli was founded by the Greeks around 560 BCE as Heraclea Pontica and that here their legendary hero, Heracles (Hercules) had plunged down to the underworld to fetch up Cerberus, the three-headed watchdog of Hades, as his twelfth and final labour – depending which account of the labours you read. Here, Xenophon and his plundering and battered band of mercenaries argued about the best way to continue their journey. I cycled in wishing a handsome hero would pay some attention to me, but I felt better when I found the road to the town centre over a green hill which effectively separated the foundries from the town of Ereğli itself.

Once I was safely up, over and down into the east end, only a chimney towering up from behind the hill and belching out thick white smoke indicated the industrial chaos spread out underneath it. The non-industrial part of Ereğli lay before me, with green parks and a wide boulevard running along the sea the length of the town. I cycled along it, almost out of town, wondering about places to stay, and spotted three smartly dressed ladies who looked as if they were off on a social visit to gossip and drink coffee. I drew up alongside and asked whether there were any pensions further along the coast or whether the only available accommodation would be in hotels back in the town centre. They were attractive, motherly women, amazed to see me and to be asked such questions. I could imagine their cool, shuttered houses with crisp, clean sheets on the beds, sweet Turkish coffee in the kitchen and hot water in the spotless bathroom, and almost asked them if they had a room to rent. Accommodation was limited, they told me. Few tourists visited Ereğli. So I turned back into the town and stopped to eat my two tomatoes and peaches together with my stale bread and melting cheese next to a water fountain under a tree in the gardens along the sea. Two boys on mountain bikes cycled up to have a drink. They stared with a professional eye at my bicycle leaning beside me and looked at me curiously, but they did not say anything and I was too tired to speak. I sat in a daze, letting my muscles relax. There was no question of continuing on that day. There had to be a hotel.

And so there was and it wasn't far away. Otel Eken was a new building on the sea front overlooking the parks. It appeared to be the only hotel in town, surprising for such an industrially important Turkish city. With seemingly no or little competition, I was prepared for the hotel to be expensive. A room with a shower, however, was around £5. The man behind the front desk was in a world of his own, engrossed in reading a newspaper. He invited me to go upstairs to look at the rooms. They were still unmade from the night before, the doors open, the bed sheets tumbled and the ashtrays full. There were no chambermaids to be seen and the hotel seemed empty. I found some clean sheets from an unused bed in one of the rooms and chose the least dirty room with a small balcony and a panoramic view directly over the sea. I carried the bicycle lovingly upstairs and moved us in, the amiable hotelier downstairs apparently completely happy with the arrangement. He had more important things to do, such as studying the day's racing tips and the horse-race programme.

Once again, I had arrived early enough to see the town and this was another reason why I started cycling at the crack of dawn. Half the fun of Turkey lies in seeing its busy, provincial life and poking around the markets and shops. Turkey is not only about fabulous, historical sites and, in any case, the Black Sea coast is not as rich in antiquities as the Mediterranean and Aegean coasts are. I could not expect to see the 'mosques, khans, castle and huge blocks of stones and architectural fragments of the ancient city', which, according to *Johnston's General Gazetteer*, were still in evidence in Ereğli in the 1870s when it was an important port in the Ottoman Empire, exporting timber, silk and wax and importing iron. I was impressed, however, by the extent of the ambitious parks and gardens, which were being laid out the length of the sea front, thus opening up the town to the sea.

Strolling down the glaring white promenade in the sizzling heat of the day, I admired the flower-beds that were being dug out and the brand-new park benches, elaborate fountains and intricate water channels being installed. There were children's amusement areas painted stickily in bright, garish colours. Admonishing notice boards were displayed everywhere: 'Protect the grass', and 'Without greenery, the world is in darkness', they declared. The local council, run by the centre-right Motherland Party, had obviously decided it was time to convince the citizens of Ereğli that their future was indeed safe in its hands. I had begun to notice on the trip that even the smallest villages along the Black Sea had offices belonging to the major and even minor political parties in Turkey, in many cases right next door to each other, all draped with signs and banners. The battle was on for the hearts and minds of Turkey's rapidly growing electorate. In Ereğli, the results were fairly impressive for the environment. However cynical the politics might or might not have been, the green development along the sea front gave the town a comfortable, positive atmosphere, despite the lack of tourists. There was an echo of the town's glorious past in the Greek and Roman remnants thoughtfully scattered through the park in the shape of marble baths, tombstones and pillars, a treasure trail of antiquities.

The Greek city of Heraclea was rich enough to send presents to Xenophon and his Greek soldiers, including 4,000 bushels of barley-meal, 2,000 jars of wine, twenty oxen and a hundred sheep. The good citizens no doubt hoped the mercenaries would have a wonderful party, get drunk and go away. (When the Greeks reached Port Calpe, the Heracleans shipped them barley, cattle and wine in case they thought about returning.) Some of Xenophon's men decided that Heraclea was wealthy enough to give them substantially more, if not willingly, then by force. The people of Ereğli rushed to gather up the provisions on sale outside the city and carry them back inside the walls. They shut and locked the gates and manned the towers. As a result, there was much arguing among the Ten Thousand left stewing outside, some blaming others for the situation and everybody arguing about the best way to get home. Xenophon had had enough. He considered boarding a boat and sailing away on his own into the sunset. But he didn't.

My heart, withered by the horrors of Karasu and its concrete tentacles spreading along the beaches, lifted. I felt euphoric and light-headed, which wasn't surprising given the hours I had spent on the road that day and the fact that the sun was now beating down overhead. No wonder the Motherland gardeners and painters were nowhere to be seen. They had all sensibly gone to drink tea in one of the shady kiosks. The parks and promenade were virtually deserted. Stupidly, I had put on a sleeveless dress and I began to feel so ill, I wondered if I would make it back to the hotel without collapsing. My mouth was already puffy and swollen from over exposure to the sun and my face was burned. Now my body seemed to be swelling too. I felt sun-dazzled, the glare of the light so bright I felt as if I were a tiny figure lost somewhere in an Impressionistic painting. I staggered back to the hotel. The lobby was deserted; the man had obviously gone to discuss the horse-racing with his friends. I took my key from behind the desk and tottered up the stairs to collapse on my bed and sink into a hot unconsciousness.

I came to a couple of hours later, the roaring in my ears fading as I dragged myself up from what felt like the bottom of the ocean. My room was bathed in a rich, shimmering light reflected off the wide expanse of water outside the window. The most beautiful light in the world is that which is reflected off the Bosphorus in İstanbul, a subtle ever-changing pattern of light and shade, a brimming, ethereal light which the Ottomans understood and loved, and so they built their summer houses along the water-front with long windows and balconies to catch as much of it as they could. I got up and went onto my balcony to look down into the square beneath and the triumphant statue of Turkey's founder, Kemal Atatürk, standing in the middle. I could see the factory chimney belching out smoke from behind the hill, which cut Eregli in two. The day was cooler and people were going outside again. Two boys balancing on one bike shot down the road racing the traffic, shrieking gleefully. There was even a handful of girls riding bicycles, something I had never seen before in Turkey. The women on the streets were a mixture, some dressed in traditional, dull-coloured, long skirts and headscarves, others wearing tight shorts and tee shirts. Often a traditionally dressed girl walked side by side with her fashion-conscious girl friend. I watched as two young women crossed the road and glittered off down the promenade. They were dressed to kill. One had blond hair and was wearing lime green shorts and shirt and high-heeled shoes. The other, who had black hair, was squeezed into tight, black trousers and a slinky, black top. I wondered if they were my first sighting of the girls from the former Soviet Empire, who had come to Turkey to do a variety of business including the oldest one in the book. The Turks called the women 'Natashas'. I had already noticed earlier in the day that one of the food stalls along the sea front had information written up in Russian. Nobody appeared to be paying the two girls much notice, but then the Turks are very discreet.

I decided it was time to go out and join the party. I was hungry too. I put on jeans and a loose shirt and lip salve instead of lipstick. I decided I didn't want any mistakes to be made along the Black Sea. I was regularly taken for a Russian, Bulgarian or Rumanian woman by shopkeepers in İstanbul and Ankara, probably because I had red henna'ed hair, wore denim jeans and had blue eyes.

'Russe, Bulgar, Romanya?' they would ask, hopefully, leaning forward, eyes gleaming with excitement, almost licking their lips.

'Brrritish,' I would say firmly, turning my back. Secretly I had always wanted to say that I was from Eastern Europe, to see what would happen next. But I had never dared.

Out of the hotel, I turned away from the sea and into the warren of back streets forming the commercial heart of Ereğli. This was Turkey, bustling, alive and vibrant, so different from the dull, sterile and identical shopping centres dominated by the chain stores back home. 'Buyurun,' called the shopkeepers and restaurant staff hovering in the doorways. It is a wonderful word, a concept rather. It means something like: 'I beg your pardon, we are at your service, please do us the honour of coming in.'

Labour is cheap in Turkey and families large. It meant that as soon as you stepped into a Turkish shop, scores of people appeared, willing and happy to serve you. This was unlike in England where shoppers queued to pay at one of two tills open, and where you could drop down dead and it would take some minutes for anybody to notice. Sometimes I wanted to be anonymous and just stare at the shelves in peace and then I missed the way one could browse in English shops. Sometimes, back in England though, I would close my eyes and hear 'buyurun' and weep that I was not in the bustle of Turkey, surrounded by that marvellous Turkish care, attention and excitement.

I stepped out into the streets of Ereğli feeling as if I were discovering it all anew for the first time. The magic never went. There were rows of gold shops with their bracelets, rings and necklaces glittering under bright, artificial lights. Quilt makers sat cross-legged on the floor of their small cabins, hand-stitching fluorescent purple and green eiderdowns. They were using mounds of soft goat and lambs' wool and white cotton, all of which could be found piled high in great sacks in nearby shops. Tailors sat in the gloom behind old-fashioned sewing machines busily turning out bespoke suits of clothes. There were countless grocery stores filled with sacks bursting with rice and lentils, and enormous tubs and jars – unscrew the tops and they were filled with black and green olives of different sizes and quality. A bewildering variety of feta cheeses coolly stewed in their own juice. In scores of hardware shops, shelves were crammed with red and blue plastic bowls, painted vases, plates and dishes, pepper grinders, Turkish teapots and many sizes of wooden spoons. Mops were propped up in the corners, their woolly heads like large, faceless dolls. Handicraft shops sold beads by the thousand, handmade lace, ribbons, bows, glittering sequins and skeins of autumn-coloured mohair wool.

In Turkey, the shops always open early in the morning and stay open late into the evening. The knack of walking down a street is to be able to look around and up and down and enjoy the tumbledown buildings and spot the ancient stone hans (originally places in which to stay and do business) without tripping into the gutter or over obstacles on the pavement. I stared at the buildings and the shopkeepers hanging around in their doorways stared back at me. Although I got irritated, how could I blame them? A funny-looking foreign woman. On her own.

If I had not been gazing upwards, I would have missed the Blue Hotel on the corner. I called it the Blue Hotel because it was still painted blue, although the paint was cracked and peeling. It was a large, square, substantial building, sadly empty and derelict inside. Through the open front door a gloomy staircase led upstairs, losing itself in the shadows at the top. The building looked as if it dated back to Ottoman times. The word 'otel' was traced over the facade but there was also Arabic writing engraved on a stone in the wall. It was exactly like the hotel in the classic, Turkish film, The Anatolian Hotel, made in the politically troubled times of the 1970s, a slow, searing story of a sexually hungry man in a down-at-heel provincial town. He committed suicide at the end of course, after murdering his decidedly unsexy lump of a wife. My Blue Hotel still had its telephone number on a sign hanging from a window on the first floor, Ereğli 362, the ghost of times past. It was rather like finding those yellowing advertisements at the back of books and in old magazines when you want to reply right away, call the phone number, hear a voice the other end and go back in time through a time warp.

While I walked around, I was sizing up the possibilities for dinner. I chose the biggest and poshest restaurant in town because the words 'İskender Kebab' were written over the door. Inside, everything was businesslike, the tables and chairs in strict rows, gleaming clean and the service immaculate. I wasn't asked any intrusive questions and could concentrate undisturbed on my food. It was a proper, old-fashioned İskender kebab house. The waiter automatically brought a bowl of salad and an extra dish of yoghurt to the table together with freshly baked, bouncy bread, like an Indian nan, and endless, sensible glasses of cold water. It was comfortable sitting in a corner watching the prosperous burghers of Ereğli coming in to eat, some of them bringing their large families as well. The Turks appear to have a great capacity to enjoy whatever they are doing. They never seem to get bored. I think it is because they have to work so hard for what they have and, of course, they love their families. After scrubbing my plate with the last bit of bread, I asked for the bill wondering if it would, like the restaurant, be big and posh. It was less than £2 and was one of the cheapest and best dinners I had on the entire trip.

Back in my room, I watched the evening from my balcony as if I were at the theatre. It was the cool time of the day. People were drifting along the parade, examining the cheap necklaces and trinkets and toys on sale in the kiosks along the front, eating a delicious assortment of nuts and rubbery 'dondurma', Turkish ice cream. A boat glided over the glass-like sea, decorated with flags, the children sitting right on the edge as children do, dangling their feet over the side. It was soothing just to sit and look. I was saving my energy. Three days into the trip and I had cycled around 150 miles over rough, precipitous terrain. I went to bed early, even before the sun had set, counting the hours before I had to get up and start pedalling. From my window I woke in the middle of the night to see the twinkling lights of the ships anchored off the coast.

4
Ereğli to Amasra through Hisarönü

I think that, in case all our efforts to secure sufficient boats are unsuccessful, we ought to request the cities on the coast to repair the roads, which, we gather are in a very bad condition.

My alarm clock woke me. I hadn't slept too badly despite the fact that I was unable to plug in my anti-mosquito device because the only socket available was in the shower room. It was pitch dark outside but with that tremble, that slight tremor in the air, which says the dawn is coming. I hate being woken up by the alarm. It jangles the nerves so and there are just a few seconds when I think that life is simply not worth living, an extreme, black hole of despair and misery, shaken off as soon as I get up but deep enough to make those moments fearful. It helped to have a routine, to force down food of some kind – on this Black Sea journey it was generally stale lumps of bread smeared with white feta cheese. I went on to the balcony to bring in my clothes and take down my precious piece of ancient string that acted as a washing line. The day was definitely on its way. Ereğli's fire brigade was up and busy, using their powerful jets to give an early morning, rather fierce bath to the multi-coloured petunias, marigolds and shrubs down in the square. The plants and flowers, dragged from sleep by the shock of cold water, probably felt like I did.

On my travels, I often feel that I am a spectator or occasional actor at a play, walking on stage, doing my bit and walking off again. There is a plot, I'm sure, but the number of characters involved is so large, it is difficult to follow the thread. As I watched from my balcony box in Ereğli, a young man followed by a young woman, his sister or his wife, walked out of the shadows and into the lights of the square. They were both dragging heavy suitcases and occasionally sitting down to rest. They were dressed as if they had come from an Anatolian village somewhere over the Black Sea mountains in eastern Turkey. They came from the direction of the bus station and were walking gloomily and separately. There was no holiday excitement. I wondered what their business was in Ereğli. I was watching them. Who was watching me?

I wheeled the bicycle, who kept her thoughts to herself, out into the fresh morning. I was heading that day for Zonguldak and beyond. I guessed my road was back over the hill and then out of Ereğli, winding away from the sea and heading inland. There was a track marked in purple on the map, running directly eastwards from Ereğli, but this meant that it was an earth road and only to be used in dry periods. It kept close to the sea, but I knew I would need a four-wheel drive to be able to negotiate it. At that stage of the trip, I had not yet promoted my bicycle to such exalted heights. That was to come. Two elderly men were sitting outside in a street on a hill just above the car park next to the square. I heard their voices echoing round the square before I saw them. It was Vladamir and Estragon as large as life, waiting for Godot in the centre of Ereğli. They certainly were not waiting for me. I shouted and shouted from down below, wanting to check the route out of town, but they totally ignored me. I simply did not exist in their play. The pair were having a loud animated discussion, although I couldn't catch enough of it to find out what the subject or subjects were. Was it the meaning of life, the identity of Godot or the results of the horse racing the day before? I left them to it.

I pelted up the hill and over to the western side of town – so easy when the road surface was good –and swooped down the other side. There, I found a road sign to Zonguldak and headed out of Ereğli, past the new, sprawling, concrete apartment blocks eating up the lovely countryside. I knew it was going to rain. So much for summer. There was a heavy, slightly sinister wetness in the air. Veils of mist and cloud obscured the views. I could only glimpse the plunging valleys, hills and forests. It felt as if I were cycling on the edge of the world, one slip and I would tumble into the precipice. It was a spectacular road, although the map didn't mark it out as a particularly picturesque one. The sky was thick with black clouds. The rain was coming. I could smell it. My legs felt flabby and pathetic and I couldn't go any faster; I couldn't run before the storm. I was climbing upwards as usual, trying to stay on the bicycle rather than beside it. I was cycling through Kurt Dağ, which means Wolf Mountain. That day it was living up to its name. If you look up the word 'kurt' in a good Turkish dictionary, you will find a Turkish saying: 'kurt dumanlı havayı sever', translated into English, means, 'The wolf likes foggy weather', but which figuratively means 'a rogue works in the dark'. I was certainly in the dark.

The Turks at least made sure drivers knew what was ahead of them and there were signs all along the route warning of the conditions to come. The most common sign, the one which was going to become an all too familiar understatement, read 'Bozuk Satıh', 'Uneven Surface'. One sign showed an open umbrella on which rain drops were gently pattering down to warn drivers that their cars might slip in wet conditions. Another showed a car balanced precariously above or below two parallel lines and looking as if it were about to topple off. This meant there were steep slopes ahead. Sometimes there were notices counting the number of kilometres to reach the top or bottom of the climb – mostly the top if you were travelling eastwards along the Black Sea. It was one of those signs that morning which told me I was going to have to climb up a ten-kilometre stretch, about six miles, to get to the 'top'. It would not have been too much of a challenge, except that I had already taken what felt like hours to climb up from the coast on a road surface that looked like a jigsaw puzzle with most pieces missing. It was also about to rain.

It was a killing, non-run upwards, pedalling away, trying to ignore the shouts and roars from the lorry drivers as they thundered past in their noisy, smelly lorries, belching out poisonous fumes from enormous exhaust pipes which usually pointed towards the kerb and therefore in my direction. I sometimes tried not to breathe. This was difficult given that I was struggling uphill on a bicycle. I could never make out what the drivers were shouting. It sounded just like the noise a large, fat animal might make before it was about to do something particularly disgusting. Oh for a machine gun to blast their tyres and watch their vehicles crash down the mountain side, preferably in flames as in all the films. Or maybe I needed a battle-axe to smash them over their stupid heads. (According to Xenophon, the Amazon ladies, who lived along the Black Sea, not only used bows and arrows but also battle-axes, which gives the phrase 'she's a battle-axe' a whole new meaning.) At least no lorry driver stopped that day to proposition me (this was becoming a fairly regular occurrence), probably because the weather was so bad, they wanted to get off the slippery slopes as quickly as they could and they thought that in any case a cold rain might dampen their hot ardour.

It began to rain on the downward run through the valley back towards the coast. The gods had held off until then. This was serious rain, blinding, soaking, sheeting down. There were few trees at this point to shelter under. The thick forests had given way to large outcrops of rocks through which the road had been blasted, although there were no bits wide enough to shelter under and even if there had been, I would have been far too frightened to creep underneath, given the frequent road signs warning motorists about the possibility of rock falls. This, I decided, was just the sort of weather when the land could start to move. There was nothing to be done except to keep going. I was too cold to stand still. At least everything in my bicycle bags was wrapped in plastic. I was mainly concerned about the strain on my brakes.

As it turned out, the surface on this stretch of the road was excellent, but it was so precipitous, it would have been suicide to have ridden without using any brakes. I pulled them hard and felt the bicycle skidding away from me. I could scarcely see. I had taken my glasses off, but the rain was driving with such force against my face I could hardly keep my eyes open. I roared down through the valley, past a group of young women who had got caught out by the weather. They were laughing with excitement and their clothes, long skirts and blouses, were sticking to them, their headscarves soaked. They were enjoying themselves. I wasn't. This was not funny. Early July along the Black Sea and it felt like winter. I shot past a bus shelter, slithered slowly to a stop and pushed the bicycle back up the hill to take refuge inside. There were four men waiting for a bus. They stared in amazement as I took off one of my rubber slip-on shoes and poured the water out slowly. Even I was impressed. I was cold and my shirt was sticking to me. One asked whether I had a coat. My Turkish wasn't adequate to explain that I had a jacket right at the bottom of one of the bags but it wasn't worth getting it out to have that soaked as well. It wouldn't have made me any warmer. (I badly needed a waterproof on the trip but had omitted to take one. A mistake.) They asked where I had come from and where I was going. They were young and good-looking and they appeared reluctant to have to go when their bus arrived. I felt like going with them, but the rain eased off and I continued.

It was a typical summer Black Sea storm. The rain clouds soon disappeared and the mists cleared. I had dropped back below the tree line and there were shafts of sunlight filtering through clearings in the dense, green forests. The air smelled good, the birds resumed their singing and everything looked clean and freshly washed. As the day warmed up, I quickly dried out as I cycled along. The mood changed so fast, one minute wet and depressed, the next excited, uplifted and triumphant. A heady cocktail of emotions. I was sad to leave that very beautiful valley, turn along the coast and cycle in under the cliffs towards the grey town of Zonguldak.

One guide-book to Turkey described Zonguldak as a 'large and ugly city, bang in the heart of Turkey's main coal district.' The guide book did not mention the exquisite Black Sea mountains and valleys within striking distance. I didn't see Zonguldak properly, although I wrote subsequently in my diary that it 'felt rather nice, tucked up against the hills.' I cycled straight through and out, over the railway line, passing the sprawling, grimy works beside the sea, which looked like a bleak, industrial scene from Dickens. The climb winding upwards and skirting the town was almost perpendicular. It was impossible I should ever get anywhere. I found that if I leaned forward, right over the handlebars, I got on better, but it was all rather daunting.

My water bottle was almost empty and I stopped at a bakery up one of the hills. A hot, new bread smell wafted out of the open door. Everything inside was white and covered with flour. There were tubs overflowing with creamy dough and machinery throbbing and shaking; everything was floury, warm and comfortable. It filled me with an incredible feeling of well-being, as if I were being enveloped in an eiderdown. A man came forward to take my bottle to fill it from a hose and I followed him further into the bakery to find a group of young workers sitting bare-chested on dusty sacks of flour, taking a rest. I tried not to stare as they smiled shyly but I was struck by their white skin, just like the creamy dough in the tubs, and their soft, round arms like new loaves of bread. They looked wholesome and fresh. It all fitted in to that concept of Flann O'Brien about turning into a bicycle, except these guys were turning into delicious loaves of bread. The machinery was too noisy and my Turkish too limited to explain that one. But I had a momentary desire to eat them.

I pushed on, worried about my capacity to keep going on such slopes. I was climbing into the rich suburbs outside Zonguldak, pretty village-like areas sprinkled over the cliffs, with well-kept villas and gardens, roses and grapevines climbing everywhere. I needed to use a toilet and stopped on a bend outside an immaculate villa where two men were outside washing a car. They showed me into the house to use their spotless downstairs toilet. I was worried about inadvertently making something dirty and tried not to splash the gleaming basin or the floor as I washed my hands.

Back outside, out the gate, and the road onwards looked like Jacob's ladder. I felt as if I were losing my balance. This needed thinking time. A little way ahead was a shuttered garage door with a level piece of ground in front. I wheeled the bicycle onto it, balanced her against the door and went to open my bags to get at some bread and cheese. The luggage rack, with the three bags attached to it, one either side, one on top, fell backwards off the back wheel. I looked around for a bolt which I presumed must have worked loose, but there was nothing to be found. It remained a mystery how the rack and the bags had stayed on the back wheel without anything holding them in place. I thought of the ride earlier through the pouring rain and remembered how the bags had seemed to slip forward as I was descending through the valley. I began to feel almost lucky. They could have fallen off a million times since.

I mentally ran though my options and decided the best one was to dump the bags and cycle down into Zonguldak, find a workshop and get the luggage rack fixed back on. My heart sank at the time I would lose and the idea of having to negotiate that steep climb up all over again, even minus the luggage. I wheeled the bicycle back down to the friendly house on the bend. Maybe I could leave my things there.

The two men looked rather surprised to see me return so soon. I explained what had happened as best I could, pointing to the problem. 'It's a big problem,' I mourned. The younger of the two men laughed. 'It's a small problem,' he said. 'You're lucky, you've come to the right house.' And he took me into the garage, which turned out to be, in effect, a workshop. I was indeed lucky. The man – his name was Okur – had brought his family home from Germany to stay with his father for a few months. Both men were engineers. In the garage workshop was every kind of screw and tool necessary to fix my luggage rack back on. Okur began to explain everything to me in German but I stopped him, telling him I could speak some Turkish but no German.

'I don't speak Turkish,' he said in Turkish, 'I can only speak German now.'

In fact, he could speak Turkish but he did so with a German accent, pausing slightly and thinking of the words first. He had been living with his family near Stuttgart for thirty-five years, returning to Turkey for the summer holidays. He called his wife and daughter downstairs. They came to collect me and, while he worked to repair my luggage rack, they showed me over the lovely house with its ceilings of wood and large, graceful rooms. It was richly furnished and comfortable with a large colour television in the sitting room. There was a magnificent view over the cliffs and the sea from a long balcony running the full length of the house. It was one of the new-style villas I had already admired in the green, hill suburbs outside Zonguldak, built with the help of hard-earned money from Germany in a style of architecture heavily influenced by Western Europe. Okur's wife, Şükran, who spoke Turkish as if she had never left her native country, was immaculately dressed in German clothes, her shining black hair – Turkish women have such enviable hair – left long and shaped down her neck, as a German woman would have it. They had obviously done well in Germany, where around two million Turks lived and worked, undeterred by ugly outbreaks of racism. I asked Şükran about the problems faced by the Turks in Germany, but she preferred not to go into the subject. She merely shrugged and smiled and said life was good there – but it was good to be home. Her husband came to join us as we sat on the balcony drinking coffee. I asked him whether he missed Turkey, living out of the country for so many years.

'When I come home,' he said simply, 'I always leave my window open at night so the sound of the sea can come in.'

As I left, Şükran wrapped up some of her homemade börek for me to eat on the journey and we exchanged addresses. When I got back to England, I sent the family a picture of Norwich cathedral to their German address. A few weeks later, I received a postcard from Şükran from their home town of Winterbach, a world away from Zonguldak.

As I went out of their gate – for the second time that morning – I admired the new screws holding the luggage rack in place. I felt so grateful I could hardly speak. I continued upwards on the road to Hisarönü. I was obviously getting fitter because my legs felt stronger as I toiled ever up, clutching the handlebars as if they were a ship's tiller in a force nine gale. Up and down, round and round over the hills. The houses had been built so recently you could still see where the woods had been cut down to make room for them. Most people I stopped to speak to automatically addressed me in fluent German, continuing to do so even when I replied in Turkish. I filled up my water bottle in one village and watched a beautiful, well-groomed young girl strolling along with her less well-dressed friends. She spoke to me, adjusting from German to Turkish when I told her I couldn't speak German. She was home from Germany on holiday to see her family and was going for a walk with her cousins. She stood out in the street, a foreigner, bringing with her an air of other places. Just as I did.

I continued on through sleepy villages, so close to Zonguldak but feeling remote and undisturbed. There were neat vegetable patches in the gardens and wild hollyhocks in the hedgerows. One of the bigger villages, Çatalağzı, stood in the shadow of a massive series of conveyor belts and railway lines, which ran down from the hills through the valley, taking coal to an electricity power station. It looked like something Heath Robinson would have created. I noticed an office for the Islamist Welfare Party. I couldn't see any other political party represented. I also noticed a bicycle repair shop and in fact there was one in every high street I passed that day, their doors open onto the road, bits of wheels spilling out, rubber tyres hanging up. It wasn't only the new mountain bikes for children that were providing business; bicycles were a cheap way to get around. Despite the influx of foreign money, the Black Sea remained cut off from the rest of Turkey, its people drained away by the prospect of a better living elsewhere. Zonguldak might have had rich suburbs but the shabby villages, numerous tea houses and bad roads told a story of the battle to survive and make a living.

The people had not lost their sense of humour though. I stopped outside a grocer's shop at the top of a particularly steep hill to recover and was approached by an old man. He asked me where I was from. I told him I was from England. He muttered something, smiling, and I just managed to catch the words: 'Sarah and Musa'. That was all he said, and laughed. He was referring to a thirteen-year-old English girl who had become a world story after getting pregnant by a Turkish waiter and marrying him in a religious service in Turkey with the consent of her parents. The English newspapers, I felt, had been far more critical of Turkey and its customs than of the English family. I began to try to apologise, ridiculously feeling responsible. But he just laughed again, obviously delighted with the conversation and our chance encounter.

There was magic in the air that day. The achievement of continuing along such a difficult route was immense, the pain of the cycling softened by the beauty of the countryside. There was nothing to indicate on my map that the road was a switchback up and down the cliffs nor that the scenery would be so stunningly beautiful. Other roads marked as 'routes with a view' could not begin to match the way from Zonguldak to Hisarönü, through leafy lanes delicious in the shade, the hills squeezing in and then drifting away, voices and laughter floating through a hedge in a garden filled with beehives. Green smells. I stopped and ate Şükran's neatly sliced börek. It was stuffed with minced meat, vegetables and herbs, twice as rich as it would have been in the shops. From the cliff tops, there were vast, sun-dazzled views over the Black Sea. It was an indeterminate colour that day, inscrutable and locked in to itself. The Black Sea is, in effect, an enormous pond surrounded by land. The only outlet is through the Bosphorus straits, twenty miles or thirty-two kilometres long, passing through İstanbul and into the Sea of Marmara.

I was able to look down from my eagle's eyrie into secluded sandy bays. I wanted to frame the pictures I saw and hang them on my wall. A woman sat all alone in the middle of a wide beach under a parasol. Her children paddled in the sea, silhouetted against the sun, small figures in a huge world. In another bay, a man bobbed around in the water in a large, black, rubber tyre – I had forgotten the pleasure. There were children swimming and playing, girls in pretty swim suits and shorts, little boys diving into the surf, spread-eagled in the green, transparent waves, looking like frogs frozen into the ice on the garden pond in the cold of winter. If these children lived here, they would have the roar of the Black Sea waves in their ears forever.

The distance I had travelled from Zonguldak was by then only about twenty miles, but I had lost count of the times I had struggled up to the top to whizz down to the bottom to climb up again. If I had been wearing seven-league boots, I could have stepped across from hill to hill, so intimate were the distances. I arrived in a one-street village, parked the bicycle carefully in the shade and went in to the small shop. The young man and his sister stared with horror at my sweating, sun-burned, red face and evident exhaustion. They rushed to get me a chair. I asked how much further I had to go. The man showed with his hands, up and down, that the switchback continued, but, he said, there was just one more village before I arrived in Hisarönü. I bought a bar of chocolate and a fizzy drink, something I never normally drink but I badly needed a quick energy fix. His sister opened the fridge, got out a bottle of ice-cold water and poured me a glass. Fancy, they said, fancy cycling from İstanbul. Drink it all.

The road to Hisarönü passed high along the cliffs, winding back away from the sea. The road was, of course, under construction. Things obviously had not changed along the Black Sea coast for thousands of years. Xenophon was so worried about the bad roads in 400 BCE that he managed to 'persuade the cities voluntarily' to repair them to facilitate the march of his men back home to Greece. He did this by pointing out to them 'that they would get rid of the Greeks all the sooner if the roads were in good repair.'

The old Turkey was sometimes not so far away. It is fine to be nostalgic about the good old days, but the oldness of the days was precisely why thousands of Black Sea people had abandoned and were continuing to abandon their homes in search of better prospects elsewhere. The small town of Hisarönü proved the point. I cycled in along the railway line, making a mental note about a cheap restaurant I spotted almost opposite the tiny railway station, and stopped at a tea house to ask about hotels. A group of middle-aged men sitting outside drinking glasses of tea greeted me with enthusiasm. There were two hotels, they said, and the cheaper one was right opposite, behind me. I turned and saw on a hill a long, low, wooden building with verandas and vines. Its windows were broken and it was derelict and decaying. I looked at it in silence, imagining how it must have been once upon a time. It stood next to an extraordinary old building, also of wood, and decorated with what looked like carved cattle horns. I had never seen such architecture before and thought, extravagantly, about the archaeological site at Çatalhöyük near Konya in southern Anatolia where the mysterious remains of the first known urban society in the world were being uncovered. The people of Çatalhöyük decorated their houses with real horns 9,500 years ago. I turned back to the tea house men.

'Antik,' they said, enjoying my pleasure.

I asked how old the horned house was. They shrugged.

'Antik, Antik,' they repeated.

'And the hotel,' I asked. 'Is it OK?'

'You had better stay in the one round the corner on the beach,' they replied. 'It would be better for you.'

I continued along the dusty road, turned left at the corner and headed down to the beach and the hotel. I patted the bicycle encouragingly, tied her to the railings underneath a rather posh awning covering the back entrance and went into the old-fashioned reception area. It was dark and desolate and I had to shout for someone to come. Two boys appeared. They looked astonished to see me. I was taken upstairs and shown an enormous room with a vast double bed, power points, a small shower room and a balcony with an interestingly obscured view of the sea (a crane and a mountain of giant rocks). The place was run down and dilapidated but cheap and perfectly acceptable. I went down to collect my bicycle and bags. The boys politely helped me, although I asked them not to. One asked me how long I would be staying. I told him I would be leaving the following day.

'What a shame,' he said. 'The Hisarönü Festival starts at the weekend. You should stay longer not to miss it. You'll have to come back next year for it.'

The woman of the hotel came up to the room to check up on me. She was plump and motherly, probably a lot younger than I was. Her hair was swept back into a dark bun. She spoke beautiful Turkish, clear and precise, every word of which I could understand. She was anxious and concerned, as if I had had an accident and she had to look after me. This was disconcerting. If I wanted a hot shower, I could ask her for the key, she said. Did I want a call at five o'clock in the morning? Thanks but no thanks, I said, I had my own clock. Would I want to eat in the restaurant later? There was fish and kebabs. 'Thanks,' I said thinking of the bill and mentally comparing it to the one I would get for dinner from the cheap restaurant I had seen coming in to town. (I was probably wrong about that. This was an honest woman.)

'You are a journalist,' she said. 'You must write and tell people how wonderful Hisarönü is so they come and stay. We have everything they would want, fine views, fine beaches and good swimming. I don't understand why they don't come.'

I assured her I would indeed be writing about Hisarönü and asked her the best way to negotiate to the beach. It was just outside, she said, and I should put cream on my face. Look how the sun was damaging it.

Outside, it was stiflingly hot. The hotel was next to a couple of restaurants, which looked equally sad and empty, draped in the dark green foliage of a eucalyptus tree. They were in a potentially prime spot on the edge of the beach but the great rock construction was going on directly in front, blocking out the sun and sea and everything else. I went to have a look. A sign announced helpfully that Hisarönü was building a fish barrage. I was to find similar barrages being built centre-stage in nearly every town and village along the Black Sea coast. It was doubtless a good idea for the fishermen who had to battle against the storms, but disastrous for the tourism industry. I stumbled westwards trying to find a break in the rocks to see where the beach was. It was a long walk away and the sun was so hot I took refuge in a small café in a dusty, newly planted rose garden along the front. I ordered yet another fizzy drink, wrote my diary and waited until it was a little cooler before going on to the beach.

It was fairly busy and I chose to sit near a woman, her four daughters and young son. They all stared at me, eyes round and mouths open, as I slipped off my dress and lay down in my bikini. I was so tired, I just wanted to lie still and float off. Unfortunately, the son came and sat as close to me as he could possibly get and talked and talked in disjointed sentences. I hoped the woman would rescue me but she was obviously delighted that somebody else was occupying her dear child. I lay down and tried to blot out the sound of the kid who continued to chatter on at what seemed like two inches from my ear. I opened my eyes and sat up. Mother and daughters had not moved. They were sitting in exactly the same position on the sand under their sun umbrella, eyes round and mouths open, staring at me. I didn't want to be rude but it was too much. I moved away and, left to myself, fell briefly and comfortably asleep.

The railway line and little station, with a range of busy timetables posted up on a wall, were behind the beach. This was a rare sight along the Black Sea. The people of Hisarönü enjoyed regular services along the coast to Zonguldak and the local towns and villages. There was also a service every morning to Ankara to the south over the mountains. This, I thought, must be a beautiful journey to make, chugging from village to village through the Black Sea forests and mountains, climbing at the journey's highest point to 1,250 metres, more than 4,000 feet. A train went through while I stood and watched, a proper train, with big, heavy, red carriages and windows you could open and lean out from, a guards van and several drivers. The train stopped on the lines and hundreds of people clambered down the high steps onto the tracks. They were coming home from work at the end of the day, hurrying home to their families.

The restaurant I had noticed earlier was close by. There was nobody inside and the vats for the food on the cooker at the back were, as far as I could see, empty. But I was lucky. The man scraped together a plate of rice and one of baked beans, Turkish-style, and I mixed them together and ate them with bread, thinking meanly but happily of the expensive (relatively speaking) fish dinner I was avoiding back 'home'.

I went off to explore Hisarönü. The town began as an important Greek colony in the seventh century BCE, called Tieum. Later on, as its Turkish name suggests, a castle was built there. Hisarönü was a dusty, rather sad, little place. There were lots of tea houses, a couple of hardware and grocery stores, a shoe mender's and various work-shops in the main street. But more shops were standing empty than were occupied, their old-fashioned shutters rolled down, dust and cobwebs begriming the windows and the heavy brass locks in the wooden doors rusted up. The owners had gone off to İstanbul or to Germany years before to make their fortune, although it looked as if some people were returning. There were a few concrete apartments being built further up the street over what were going to be rows of new shops. Or maybe these were being built optimistically for the tourist trade that was expected and hoped for.

I went up to a grocer store to ask about my route the following day. The young man was sitting outside. He was remote and unsmiling, unusually distant. Nevertheless, he gave me clear instructions, straight up the street and out of town, turn left, over the railway line and then over the river, turn right through the next village and join up with the main road to Bartın and Amasra.

I turned back towards the sea, feeling reassured, and two girls came up to me. They were smiling nervously. Both were wearing jeans. Modern girls. One spoke to me in English, delighted to find a foreigner – and a woman – whom she could speak to. She was thirteen, although she looked much older. She wanted to practise the English she was learning at her high school, she said. Her father was an engineer in Çaycuma, a town close by. He wanted his daughter to have a good education. She hoped to leave town as soon as she grew up, maybe go to England to carry on studying. I asked her whether she could see a future for herself in Hisarönü.

'Why should I want to stay here?' she said. 'There's no cinema, nothing for young people to do. The sea is filthy. We can't even swim. There is nothing for us here.'

The girls left me near the hotel. They said they felt uncomfortable because so many people were staring at us. I went back towards the barrage and turned right to see what the beach looked like east of the dam. The sight reinforced what the girl had just been telling me. A stinking sewage channel ran from the town straight through the beach and into the sea.

I returned to the hotel, creeping in to avoid being seen, past a couple of expensive Mercedes with German number plates parked close by. Later that night, the homely tinkle of teaspoons stirring cubes of sugar into Turkish glasses of black tea floated up underneath the balcony and into my room through the open door, the sound mingled with laughter, conversation and the lament of Turkish love songs. Some ex-Hisarönüs, who were obviously doing well in Germany, had driven back in time for the town's festival, and were catching up on the gossip and the state of play back home. I wondered if they too would leave their windows open to let the sea slip in at night.

I was eating my second hunk of Hisarönü bread by a quarter to five the next morning when there was a knock at my door. It was – I should have guessed – the anxious lady. My heart sank. Turkish conversation at such an hour.

'I was so worried about you last night. I thought maybe you hadn't eaten and I nearly came up to see how you were,' she said.

I made some excuse about having eaten a lot earlier in the day and began to make moves to go. She carried my bags down the stairs and stood and watched as I strapped everything on and got ready to leave. I tried not to feel irritated and ungrateful – kind woman, getting up to see me off, wanting me to remember the good people of Hisarönü. I preferred to leave without trailing clouds of glory, unobserved at that hour, unfussed, unhurried, mentally gearing up for the day ahead. She waved me off, anxiously kind, kindly anxious, reminding me to tell my friends to come and stay in Hisarönü. I cycled away feeling mean and guilty about missing the town's festival weekend. However, I have kept my word about remembering the good people of Hisarönü – and its castle, an added bonus. I spotted it as I took the eastern route out of the town. The old fortress – or what looked like the remains of one – stood marooned in a field. It looked rather like the ruins of one of the old family mansions to be seen in County Clare in Eire, the gable ends still standing and covered with ivy.

On I went, up the hill and briefly along the railway line, which went to Çaycuma and onwards to Ankara. I passed close by the river sparkling tirra lirra in the early morning sun. There were the remains of a fine hump-backed bridge of stone sadly crumbling away, another remnant of the town's glorious past. I crossed the river over a large, new structure to find that the road had disappeared and had been replaced with tracks and ruts. Marco Polo turned back here and made the rest up. I continued.

It was another hard ride, but a visually lovely one, passing through richly green cultivations, fields of maize like self-important soldiers standing heads up and backs straight in rows. The corn on the cob would be taken off to the towns and cities, heaped on the back of street barrows and sold freshly boiled to eat with a pinch of salt. The farmers in these parts made their own sturdy fences out of spare pieces of wood and planks to enclose their land. There was plenty of wood to use. There were endless forests of mature trees, the Black Sea light turning the leaves to a liquid, shining green, a sparkling emerald or a dark, glossy olive. It was a secret, noisy, silent, damp, sweet-smelling world apart, dotted with conical-shaped haycocks, plastic sheets or rubber tyres tied down on top, each pierced through with a long stake to hold the stack together. They looked like so many chess pieces waiting for their next move.

There were long climbs upwards, the views soaring and plunging, as did my spirits. I tried eating sweet biscuits, bread, cheese, nuts, but lost energy as soon as I gained it. I stopped at a gloomy soup shop in the outskirts of Bartın for something to eat and was infuriated by a toothless, mumbling, old fool with his sniggering boy assistants, amazed at a woman and a bicycle. The price of his soup was inflated <u>and</u> I had to pay for a miserable glass of bitter, stale tea to follow, which was usually complimentary. It put me in a bad mood and made me mentally strike Bartın off my list of towns to be revisited.

Onwards and upwards, fighting to stay on the saddle, even up the most slippery, rough slopes, with people staring in amazement at this lunatic that had appeared from the middle of nowhere. Some of the slopes were so steep that when the bicycle ground to a halt, there were false starts before I could move forward again. It was like being on a rocking horse, rocking madly to go anywhere, three rocks forward, two back. The reward came on the approach to Amasra as I swooped along like a fighter pilot, on the switchback edge of the cliff, the views stunning over the cool-coloured sea down below where the mountains plunged with a splash right into it. And I followed them, spiralling around the sides, headlong down into Amasra, jewel of the Black Sea coast.

5
Amasra to Kurucaşile

As they sailed along they saw Jason's Beach, where the Argo is said to have been moored . . .

The walled city of Amasra sits on a fortified promontory jutting out into the sea and connected to the mainland by a narrow isthmus. There are gently curving harbours on either side. Xenophon and his Ten Thousand sailed happily past in 400 BCE with a fair, following wind and recalled the exciting adventures of their heroes, Jason and his Argonauts, who had sailed by nearly a thousand years before them. Amasra (Sesamos, Amastris) is one of the oldest cities along the Black Sea coast. Everybody who was anybody throughout history stayed awhile and added to the fortifications. The picturesque ruins of the citadel and the defensive walls with their towers are largely Byzantine, built on Hellenistic foundations. Amasra is a gem, but as I hurtled down the hill, I could see that twentieth century vandals were busy. The beautiful, forested hills around Amasra were scarred by eyesores in the shape of incredibly ugly apartment blocks, some of them six storeys high. The unsympathetic, white slabs squatted precariously on the slopes, looking as if they could fall flat on their faces down the hills at any minute. They were a world away from the little, red-tiled houses down below nestling inside the old walls and spilling out around the bays.

I cycled in over the isthmus feeling exhausted and emotional. The tourist office was right at the entrance to the town. I practically fell inside its doors and burst into tears. The girls rushed to get a glass of water. I tried but failed to explain the mix of emotions: the overwhelming beauty of the countryside through which I had travelled, the ridiculousness of perpendicular cycling, spider-like, up and down slippery slopes and the triumph that I had done it. It was obvious they thought I should have caught the bus. This made me cry even harder. One of the girls took charge and led me off to what she said would be a cheap pension, the cheapest in town, she assured me, with a sea view along the eastern shore.

I guessed that the pension probably belonged to her father's sister's cousin, or something like that, and the price went up as we got closer, starting out at 750,000 Turkish lira in the office and had reached one million TL, around £4, by the time we arrived, she smiling so sweetly and innocently. The lady of the house was having breakfast with her children and a neighbour; olives, cheese, eggs and hot glasses of tea were all comfortably laid out on a table outside the front door. The Turks were generally so hospitable that I felt quite upset she didn't offer me a glass of tea and the chance to join them. I could have done with it at that moment.

We went upstairs to a room with a balcony overlooking the sea. There were three beds crammed inside. I could scarcely understand the woman's Turkish. She started sentences but never seemed to finish them. It was only when we had confirmed the higher price for the night that she told me the water was off because of a burst pipe. She was about twenty five years old, dressed traditionally in a long skirt and a headscarf loosely tied over her hair. Unusually for a Turkish woman, she smelled of sweat. I thought it must have been because of the stress of the burst water pipe and running her household, and felt better that I had been too tired to bargain over the price of the room. She seemed extremely grateful that I had turned up that day and made buckets of water available in the bathroom from an unknown source and took away my smelly, cycling clothes to wash them herself. The house was immaculately clean.

It was still quite early in the day. Despite the hard road, I had covered the forty miles, sixty-four kilometres or so, from Hisarönü in reasonable time. It was, however, already blisteringly hot in the full glare of the sun, far too hot to head for the inviting sandy beach, even though it was practically outside the door. I felt completely exhausted, but I had to go and explore.

It was Friday, market day, and the streets were filled with stalls lined up under awnings shaded by tall plane trees. The stalls were piled high with linen, clothes, pots and pans, kitchenware of all sorts and fruit and vegetables. Although it was the height of the holiday season, the town had a sleepy air about it. The fish restaurants, small hotels and pensions didn't appear to be rushed off their feet. The souvenir shops in a winding, narrow, back street, selling cheap, wooden ashtrays, statuettes and spoons, were not going to make their retirement fortune that day.

I managed to force my legs to carry me up to the citadel, slipping in like a lost shadow underneath the magnificent stone entrances. The steep, cobbled streets were picturesque, hung with trailing flowers, and the views of the green hills enclosing Amasra were splendid – despite the best attempts by the vandals. I had no energy to wander far. I felt dazed, bruised by the sun and battered by the journey. I staggered back down to the waterfront underneath the great walls of the castle where the sun was even hotter as it bounced off the blindingly white promenade and the sea. An ancient flight of stone steps led down from the walls, partially shaded by some trees. I sat down on a step to eat my lunch of bread, tomatoes, cheese and peaches. Afterwards, I walked back to the pension keeping in the shade as much as I could, stopping to telephone Andy far away in İstanbul from a call box on the way – a connection, somebody who knew me. He was off on a field trip to Uzbekistan the following week. 'Take me,' I thought.

Amasra was drowsing through the afternoon, its cottage gardens filled with hollyhocks. I stopped to admire a Greek Ottoman mansion, shuttered and empty, dreaming of its glorious past. A cat came past carrying a fat dead rat in its mouth. A second cat with three legs, furiously hopping to keep up, followed behind. Back at my pension, I hid from the sun on my balcony. Despite the heat, a hard core of holiday makers were out on the beach. A black-haired beauty, aged about fifteen, strolled down the street wearing only her one-piece swimming costume. A daring young lady. She climbed down the steps onto the sands and posed like a model, her long hair streaming down her back. The illusion burst, literally, when she turned round and a shimmering bubble of gum blew from her mouth. I went down from my Lady of Shalott seclusion to risk a quick swim in the sea, although I was careful to keep my head as far out of the water as possible. The beach was a riot of colour, a holiday wave of parasols, blue, white and yellow swirls spinning dizzily into the blue and I lay with my eyes shut and listened to the splash of waves on the shore, children spitting, screaming and laughing, pleasure boats spluttering, the rattle of a tractor in the distance, a confused cock crowing, all blending into a cacophony of sound, like the roar when you put your head under water. A smiling toddler floated in the water face downwards and bobbed up giggling. It was pleasant to sit surrounded by Turkish families on holiday. Unlike the family units in northern Europe, Turkish families spread out, only too pleased to take you in rather than to shut you out. This has its advantages and disadvantages. That afternoon it was pleasant to smile in sympathy at the jokes of the groups close to me, although I could hardly understand a word. I wondered if they were descended from the ancient Greeks, some of whom eventually converted to Islam and stayed behind. The Greeks and the Turks are fine-eyed, dark-haired and handsome people. There must have been some intermingling over the centuries.

I went back to my room to get dressed and go into town. I had decided to eat dinner on my balcony that evening. I bought bread, smooth white feta cheese, luscious black olives, a greasy tin of sardines, a melon and a bottle of red Turkish wine – Buzbağ, of course, cheap and excellent. Later, sitting on my balcony, glass of wine in hand, lots more still to go in the bottle hidden out of sight underneath the window sill, I munched on the cheese and olives, reflecting happily that there would be enough for the next day.

I was finishing my dinner when I got company. More people had moved in to the pension. It was a family from the town of Karabuk over the mountains inland. A young couple, who were expecting their first child, had taken the room next door together with the girl's parents. They were all going to have dinner on their balcony. I offered them a glass of wine and they invited me to share their dinner of green beans cooked in oil, plain macaroni with mayonnaise and water melon. They had hired somebody in to prepare the meal for them and wash up afterwards. The food was simple but delicious, They were upset when they found I couldn't eat much because, as I explained regretfully, I had already eaten. Fortunately, the family's Turkish was clear and smooth. The girl and her father were both teachers. She had spent a couple of years teaching in Dıyarbakır in the east of Turkey. The city was Kurdish and overwhelmed with refugees from the hundreds of villages that had been destroyed in the unresolved battles between the Turkish government and the Kurds over their human rights and need for an acknowledgement of their culture and identity. It was a vicious war which had cost thousands of lives, damaged Turkey's international standing, put writers, politicians and intellectuals in prison and made the chasm between the Kurds, who were generally referred to as 'Mountain Turks', and the Turks deeper and even more bitter. (Interestingly, in his *Anabasis*, Xenophon referred to the tribes, who lived in the mountains of Thrace, as 'Mountain Thracians', and described the fierce battles against them.) Most western Turks, however liberal, found it difficult to discuss the subject rationally, so strong was the prejudice against the Kurds and the grief over the numbers of soldiers who had been killed in the fighting. I asked the girl whether she had enjoyed her time in Dıyarbakır. It was an interesting experience, she said simply. It was obvious that she was glad to be back in the west of the country. Her father, however, went further than any Turk I had spoken to before who was not a human rights activist or involved politically. 'It is quite simple,' he said, 'they should get their human rights, the economy in the east should be improved and they should be able to live the way they want to.'

After that the conversation zipped along. Even if I didn't fully understand the meaning, I got the sense of it. It was wonderful sharing wine and thoughts with like-minded people. We talked about a hundred different subjects, life styles, politics, Turkey's secular history, the threat from fundamentalist Islam, education, the horrible buildings scarring the hills around Amasra, anything and everything. The girl's father did most of the talking, the others laughing at his enthusiasm and vehement way of speaking. At one point in the conversation, he reminded me about Margaret Thatcher. The Turks, he confided, had called her 'the Iron Lady'. ('Demir Bayan' in Turkish.)

'So did we,' I said.

I left them to watch television and went to check that the bicycle was happy parked far away from me for the night, outside in a small, enclosed courtyard at the back of the house. Her tyres were fine and everything was in place. I had locked her up as usual. The passage from the yard back through the house led directly out into the street and it looked as if the front door was always open. There was no point in taking chances. She was a very special bicycle. I went back upstairs to my room to study the map, trying to imagine what the next part of the journey would be like. The road from Amasra as far as the town of İnebolu, more than a hundred miles away to the east, 182 kilometres, was coloured yellow and green, much of it twisting in serpent-like coils, apparently running along the sea. I knew what it all *should* have meant, although by then I didn't have much faith in the map's symbols. I had been tried and tested on tortuous roads that were marked innocently as straight lines and fooled by roads that turned out to be reasonable, although they looked like snakes on the map. I stared and stared at the route, trying to decide how tough the cycling would be and how ambitious I should be about the distance I could cover. There was no point in trying to ask anybody. Xenophon and the Greek mercenaries had chosen to sail along this stretch of the coast rather than walk and ford the many deep rivers. The next town of any size was Kurucaşile just under thirty miles away. Not far, but somewhere to aim for.

I slept uneasily, hot in the night, my dreams shadowy and mountainous, the future threatening and the present meaningless. I was glad to get up, stuff a selection from last night's leftovers down my reluctant throat, fill up my water bottle from the tap – the water was back on – and go and wake up the bicycle from what I hoped had been more pleasant and restful dreams. The day was promising. It was that magic time when the dawn hovers just below the horizon and the darkness slowly changes into a glimmering half light filled with promise. The air was breathless and waiting, the shadows and nightmares melting away in front of the sun. No wonder people worshipped the sun as a god, the life giver, the fiery power who must be placated and obeyed. I wanted to get as far as I could before the god emerged in his full Apollonian glory and the real heat of the day began.

A tough road lay ahead, beginning with the steep climb out of Amasra. I had been mentally preparing for the climb back out of the bay as soon as I had begun the corkscrew descent into it the previous day. In fact, it wasn't as bad as I feared, possibly because I had set my mind on doing it, locking it in place with a dull clunk. There is, of course, a huge physical effort involved in mountain cycling but also a mental one. I often felt as if I were trying to haul up a heavy chain and connect it to a large hook, fighting to lift the iron links up and into place, sweating not to miss, staggering under the weight. When I managed to make the connection and heard it lock together, the triumph was sweet and the cycling went smoothly.

I was so busy hauling on the chain while trying to keep the bicycle's wheels on the road and moving that I hardly had time to look back at the view of Amasra, beautiful in the dawn, tucked away within her fortified walls washed by the enigmatic Black Sea, as they had been for millenia. I did, however, get a closer look at the monstrous apartment blocks. I would not have liked to have been inside them. There was already an air of dereliction about the buildings. Already the cement walls were cracked and crumbling. They looked like the inner city blocks which were built in Britain in the 1960s, soulless and dead, too high up and too exposed to the environment. The relentless, Black Sea weather would make sure those buildings crumbled long before time had licked Amasra's

Byzantine remains. I pedalled thoughtfully on, upwards and onwards, more ups than downs, no traffic. We were on our own, my dear bicycle and I, in a damp, misty world of forests and hills, closed in and remote.

I found out where my journey was going that morning unexpectedly, climbing up, on a bend and rounding a corner. The view was overwhelming. Awed, I stopped and stared. By comparison with the hills I had so far passed through, the view that stretched out before me looked to my inexperienced eyes like how I imagined the Himalayas. A panorama of bare mountain tops towered up as far as the eye could see, misty peaks folding into each other, secretive, fearsome. I felt overwhelmed, small and very insignificant. The ground felt as if it were slipping away from underneath me. This was definitely one of the views of the mountains of the Black Sea from the coast. A tea house was strategically balanced there on the edge of the road and, amazingly, a group of people were sitting under the awning just as if it was the most normal thing in the world to be up there at the crack of dawn. It was my turn to wonder. I got off my bicycle and wheeled it over. I needed a flat surface in order to regain my balance, get a grip on things. I greeted the group. They looked at me as if foreign tourists on a bicycle were always appearing from nowhere at that time in the morning. The tables were turned. From the number of beer bottles, I had a suspicion they had started the weekend early. Very early. Again, I couldn't understand a word they were saying to me. It didn't matter. I got back on the saddle and, feeling rather like a circus clown riding a wobbly bicycle over a high wire, plunged head first into the mist and the mountains.

The view had made me feel drunk with excitement and nervous anticipation. Aren't there those special moments when one feels as if one is seeing a different dimension, when one's personal problems and preoccupations are cut down to size, trivialized? The world is bigger and more wonderful than can be imagined and time is vast and endless, a couple of thousand years or so, a mere blip, a wink of an eye. Our little lives are so important to us, so unimportant in the great scheme of things.

My little life seemed rather precious as I sweated on, a dribble of perspiration, over precipitous, rough roads, pulling on the brakes or crouched over the handlebars, snailing up perpendicular slopes, kangarooing down the other side. Sometimes it felt like I was hanging on for dear life as the world rocked around me, whirling and spinning out of control. According to the map – huh – the road, which had swung inland, would turn back to run along the coast. But the glorious hills, dotted with houses in apparently inaccessible places obscured any views there might have been of the Black Sea. After that heady glimpse of a spacious world, I was back in more familiar intimate countryside, passing through villages, peering into cottage gardens to see stooping old ladies, who had come out at first light to check up on their cabbages and roses. I passed through one village in a forest and stopped for tea. As usual, I was spoken to in German. I asked them to change back to Turkish. As usual, I didn't have to pay for the tea. The young, fine-eyed, tea house owner came out with me to wave me off and have a look at my bicycle. His car was parked outside, with the multi-lingual word 'Fanatic' painted on it. I laughed and pointed to my bicycle. 'Me too,' I said. It was his turn to laugh.

Although there was rarely an alternative road on the journey, I always asked villagers whether I was going the right way, how far it was to where I was going and what the road was like. I felt reassured when the answers were roughly the same. That day I was having difficulty in making anybody understand where I was going. 'Kurucaşile', I kept saying, 'Kuru-ja-sheilé'. One old boy shrugged and I heard him say 'Kurrjasheile'. Just that slight alteration in the pronunciation made all the difference.

My heart sank as I cycled from the beauty of the countryside in to a down-at-heel, forgotten, little town lost somewhere on the Black Sea, Kurucaşile, ancient Kromna. Jason and his Argonauts and Xenophon and his Ten Thousand sailed past without stopping. It was still relatively early, around mid morning, but I didn't feel I could cope with any more slopes that day, even though the next town of Cide was a mere fifteen miles away, practically within walking distance. The first 'hotel' I found was a dump just off the main road that continued out of town. This looked like a seriously 'men only' kind of place. I leaned my weary bicycle against a ricketty table outside and went in to find the owner sitting chatting to a customer in a cavernous tea house underneath the hotel, a wood-burning stove like a pimple in the middle of the floor. Neither of the men looked in the least surprised to see me. I put on my best smile and asked how much the rooms were. About £3. Could I see one? Of course. And we went out of the tea house and in at a side entrance, up a flight of dirty, stone steps into a big hall, almost a long room in itself. The rooms led off the hall. I was shown a largish room, with two single beds and a broken down chair. The plaster on the walls was cracked and dirty. I asked to see the bathroom, which was at the other end of the hall. It was tiled and there was a shower and a Western-style toilet. This was broken and stinking. It was like going back in time to the Turkey I had first seen in 1979. All the cheap hotels used to be like this. The problem was I had got older and (slightly) fussier. I asked the man politely whether there were any other hotels in town. There was one other on the front near the sea. I would go and have a look, I said, and maybe come back if he didn't mind.

I hoped desperately I wouldn't have to.

I cycled into the town centre and down to the sea. It took me less than two minutes. The hotel was a new, concrete affair which looked like a palace compared to what I had just seen. I found the owner in the dining room restocking the small bar. He was young, slightly portly with his hair scraped back in a pony tail. He had a party coming from Trabzon for the weekend and all his rooms were taken. He was sympathetic, knowing what the other hotel was like. His mother was in the reception area and overheard. They conferred and she led me upstairs and showed me a small bedroom with three beds in it.

'You can sleep here with me and the child,' she said. 'You will be as my daughter.'

'A child?' I asked.

'A boy,' she said.

A BOY!

'He's only young,' she said, and smiled.

How to get out of that one! I just didn't fancy the idea. So I waffled on about having to get up very early the next morning. I told them I would go back for a beer later on.

I scurried back to the first hotel in case an unexpected coach load might arrive there at any moment. The man did not seem at all surprised to see me. The room was still free. He let me get on with things. I carried the bicycle carefully up the narrow, dark stairs, negotiated her through the door of my room and leaned her against one of the filthy walls. There was another door from the room leading out onto a balcony. This was filled with builder's rubble and the door refused to open. The window overlooking the balcony was a wide one, running the entire length of the room, letting in the glare of the sun and any curious eyes from the houses opposite. I pulled the filthy, old curtain across. I found a broom, swept the floor and went to explore upstairs. The building was unfinished. The stone steps continued to the roof. The owner's plan was obviously to wait until he had enough money and then add on another storey and create more bedrooms. Standing on the dusty landing among discarded bricks and lumps of metal was what looked remarkably like an old-fashioned clothes stand, roughly nailed together. I picked it up and rushed down to my room. At least I now had somewhere to hang up my clothes after I had washed them out in the bathroom. I fixed the smell in the toilet by throwing several buckets of water down it – shutting my eyes as I did so. It smelled so bad because the toilet chain didn't work. I then used the bucket to wash the tiled floor down. I brought a chair in from outside to put my things on, washed my clothes in the bucket and took a shower. I decided it was better to do everything then while the hotel was empty. There would be more people around in the evening. I tried not to think about getting up at five o'clock and having to use the bathroom the morning after the night before. I left it probably cleaner than it had ever been before. The 'clothes horse' was perfect to hang my wet towel and clothes on. It was time to brave the stares of the inhabitants and explore Kurucasile, although my heart sank a little. There was a long day to get through and it didn't look as if Kurucaşile was going to provide a great deal of opportunity for sight seeing.

It must have been a prosperous little town once upon a time. But now the once fine houses in the tiny square were skeletons of their former selves. The roofs had collapsed long ago and the inner timbers, like giant rib cages, were exposed to the sky. There were the usual tea houses and cafes, although even these had a feeling of emptiness and despair about them. How many glasses of tea costing less than six pence each did you have to sell to make a living? I took refuge in a courtyard restaurant with a pretty garden off the street leading down to the sea. The glass display case was groaning with meze and meat to be grilled and the soup vats were steaming. I ordered a bowl of lentil soup. It came with fresh bread and I ate it trying not to notice the excitement outside about the foreigner who was in town and the number of people who passed and re-passed the door, mouths open, to peer inside. I had got much better at 'not noticing' on my travels but it was hard work constantly feeling as if I were an exhibit at a freak show. Sometimes I thought the restaurants ought to have been paying me rather than me paying them. I felt quite excited at the prospect of a party from Trabzon arriving in town and went down to the harbour to explore, hoping I might see their coach arrive – excitement for me as well as the locals.

I often chose not to travel with a guide-book when I was cycling. It was extra weight to carry. Hotels and restaurants could always be found and it was tedious to read about all the sightseeing one could do if one had the energy for it – or not as the case might be. It was always preferable to stumble across things unexpectedly. So I was completely unprepared for the sight that greeted me down at the harbour, which rang with the sound of tapping, drilling and hammering from scores of boat building sheds. Despite its unprepossessing appearance, Kurucaşile was a major centre on the Black Sea for boat building and had been for centuries, the town's craftsmen turning out sturdy, oak-timbered, fishing and cargo boats. The Ottoman sultans looked no further than Kurucaşile to have their boats built for them. Maybe Xenophon's Ten Thousand, who were constantly looking for ships to escape the trudge along the coast, should have called in after all. With the changing times, the shipwrights were making pleasure boats as well, many of which were being sold to middle men in İstanbul, who then made a fortune selling them on across northern Europe. If Kurucaşile had been in Western Europe, it would have been a major tourist trap, stuffed with bed and breakfasts, ice cream parlours and souvenir shops selling wooden boats with 'Made in Kurucaşile' written on the sides. As it was, I was on my own as I wandered round the harbour admiring dozens of wooden boats in various stages of construction, from the initial timber frames to newly painted, gleaming beauties, many in what looked like a traditional blue and green livery. They were of a simple design, a square tower in the middle of the deck, like Noah's Ark. I had seen similar boats at Ağva. The whole trees and great logs of wood used in the construction were piled high outside the sheds. It was an impressive sight.

I carried on walking round the harbour, unable not to notice that the young trees the town had tried to plant around the port in hopeful, wooden cages had mostly died and had turned into dry twigs. The gloom of the place descended again. Beyond the harbour, some boys were swimming in the sea. The water looked green and cool and clean. Looking closely at the sea within the harbour, there were suspicious, brown lumps floating on the surface, horribly like what I had bucketed away earlier from the toilet in my hotel bathroom. I wondered what the party from Trabzon would make of it all. It was time to go and sit in the shade, drink a cold beer and wait for them to arrive.

The beer wasn't cold and the hotel was still empty. I was assiduously attended to by a teenaged boy who told me that he worked at the hotel during his holidays to make some money. The only activity was happening down on the small quay where a group of men were trying to move a new, bright orange boat closer to the edge. They were laying wooden planks in front of the boat and using a tractor to pull it along, inching it over the wood closer towards the side of the quay overhanging the beach. It seemed a laborious way to get a boat into the sea. A dog panted up to watch, got bored and ran off again.

The next bit of excitement came in the shape of three cars covered in decorations and balloons, which hooted their way down to the sea front. Nobody paid much attention. There was nobody to pay much attention. A young boy sat in the front seat of the first car, looking out of the open window. He was feebly fiddling with the tinsel and decorations on the bonnet of the car, waving occasionally and trying to smile. He was wearing a white, satin suit trimmed with fur and a spangled hat. He was off to be circumcised so he must have been about eight or nine years old. His little face was as white as his suit. I always felt sorry for the children to be chopped around at such an age. However, they all seemed to survive it and, hopefully, enjoyed the sweets and gifts showered upon them by their families on the big day. I caught a glimpse of the woman driving the car as it raced by. She was young with long, dark hair. It must have been his mother. She looked proud of her little prince and excited. I wondered where Dad was. Maybe working in Germany.

The boat was closer to the side of the quay; the men were working hard. The hotel owner dropped by for a chat. He came from Izmir on the Aegean coast, he told me. He had been running the hotel for just under six months and was happy living along the Black Sea in Kurucaşile, the peace, the countryside, the beauty. I asked him how he thought he could compete with the tourist resorts along the Mediterranean with its fine beaches and vast historical sites. He went away to the bar inside, rummaged around and returned armed with proof in the shape of books and pictures of Kurucaşile – in the old days – wonderful pictures of the town's graceful houses clustered around the harbour. It seemed too churlish to mention that the houses were in ruins, the new buildings, sadly like his hotel, were soulless and horrible and that the sea was filthy with the town's sewage running straight into it. I asked him where the guests generally came from. The hotel was full of holidaymakers at weekends, mainly from the Black Sea region, he said. He was expecting the party from Trabzon any time, although they had telephoned to say they would be arriving later than expected. The group would be worth a lot of money to him that weekend. I was sure, I said, that they would enjoy seeing all the boat building going on.

'The boats are sold for anything from £4,000 to £140,000,' he informed me proudly. 'They are sold to buyers in İstanbul and then sold on for a lot more money to buyers in Germany.'

'Why don't they sell them directly to Germany themselves?' I asked. He shrugged and smiled and went off to make more arrangements for the expected influx of guests.

By then the boat had been inched to the edge of the quay. I sat and watched, puzzled as to what would happen next. Why hadn't they rolled the boat onto the beach further round the harbour where there was direct access to the sea? At that moment, all was revealed when a lorry drove up on the beach and stopped underneath the quay. The sides of the lorry's trailer were unbolted. The boat was to be manoeuvred off the quay and onto the back of the lorry and then driven to İstanbul, no doubt to be shipped to Germany. It seemed an unnecessarily complicated operation.

The afternoon wore on and so did I, reading my book and writing my diary, wondering what I was doing with my life. I was sure the beaches and bays outside the town would be clean and lovely but I knew I didn't have the energy to try to get to them. It was hot walking in the full sun. The tea houses were filled with men sipping their endless glasses of tea. No doubt the women were sitting comfortably at home, also drinking tea and chatting to their friends. I could have gone out in a boat, but I didn't want to have to negotiate a reasonable fee and then to find that I was landed with a hopeful, would-be amorous boatman who would watch my every move. Sunbathing on the grubby beach in full view of the boat-wrights was out of the question and I didn't want to get too close to the brown, lumpy water. You had to laugh. Laugh, didn't I just. One thing kept me cheerful, however, it was the thought of having dinner in a convivial atmosphere later on, with the party from Trabzon. I wandered back to my hotel and this time noticed that somebody was building an enormous boat in the rubble and weeds of the next door garden.

The place was still empty and quiet. I slept for an hour or so and woke up ready for dinner. I wandered back to the front, peering in through a window into the dim interior of a fine, white mosque along the way. By now, the shopkeepers hardly bothered to stare at me, I had become such a familiar figure in town. A couple of people were sitting in the hotel's small garden and there were even some children splashing around, incredibly, in the slimy harbour. But the atmosphere wasn't nearly as busy as I had anticipated it would be. In fact, it felt a bit like a morgue. I wandered in to the dining room. It was deserted. A young boy appeared, the one who had brought me my beer earlier in the day. Where was the party from Trabzon, I asked. They hadn't come. Why? He didn't know, he said miserably. It was a disaster. He asked if I wanted to eat dinner and took me into the kitchen where he opened the top of an enormous freezer and pulled out large slabs of frozen trout. If I wanted meat, he said, he could get it from outside. My heart sank for the nineteenth time that day. I couldn't cope with the prospect of sitting in an empty, dusty dining room on my own, eating cooked lumps of frozen trout or greasy meat-balls brought in from god knows where. I stammered my excuses, trying not to look at the boy's anxious face, and left. I didn't see the hotel owner. Poor man. He was probably booking his passage to Hamburg.

I hurried up the street looking for dinner. My previous soup restaurant was ruled out on the grounds that it too was deserted. I was worried about salmonella poisoning from stale food, although the meze had probably been freshly made for the weekend rush – or maybe it dated back to the previous weekend. Terrible thought. I continued on and found a pizza house. It was deserted and shut up. It obviously had not seen a cooked piece of dough for years. 'Why is it closed?' I asked some men who were sitting close by outside a tea house. They shrugged.

There was no alternative. I bought some tomatoes, peaches and a melon at a fruit and vegetable stall on the corner near the mosque. The old gentleman was packing up for the day but he was so pleased to help me, scrupulously charging exactly the right amount of money. I bought some bread and went backwards and forwards across the street from shop to shop looking for a tin of sardines, which I finally managed to find. Yuk. For a treat, I bought a large packet of crisps 'chipz' which cost as much in Turkey as they did in England but there were more of them in the packet and the quality was much better. Then, loaded with my spoils, I went home.

There was great activity in my hotel. The owner was having around twenty brand-new mattresses delivered. They were being loaded up in the hall outside the bedrooms. It was very exciting. Hope springs eternal. Safe in my bedroom, I laid out my supper on one of the broken-down chairs and ate it, staring at the lurid pattern of red tulips on the grimy curtains. What was I achieving by all of this? What was I doing there, washed up on the coast of the Black Sea in towns long past their prime, as I was mine? They were questions that were not going to be answered just at that moment. I went to bed early, trying not to think of possible bugs in the crumbling walls. The half of melon I was saving for breakfast in the morning simmered sweetly all night on the chair beside me.

6
Kurucaşile to Doğanyurt

The Paphlagonians, too, were extremely clever at making away with stragglers, and during the night tried to do damage among those who were camping in advanced positions. As a result there was very bitter feeling on both sides.

The hotel owner was up before the dawn, at four o'clock as he had told me he would be, first spitting noisily and at length in the smelly bathroom and then sweeping up outside the tea house. I ate the rest of the melon and carried the bicycle gently down the stairs. I strapped on the bags and said goodbye to the owner. I felt grateful to him for letting me stay and for the fact that nobody had bothered me in the hotel. Off I cycled out of Kurucaşile upwards and eastwards in the cool of the morning, the sea splashed with pools of warm red with the sky matching. Despite the manic, yellow squiggles on the map, the road to Cide was surprisingly good. Once I was safely up into the mountains, I stayed there, balancing along the edge of the cliffs with the sea like a wrinkled, slate mirror beneath. I dipped, like the sea, up and down and relatively gently, rather than experiencing the terrible plunges to the bottom and scrambles back to the heights of previous days. There were no thundering, snorting, male lorries passing that day, just a couple of baby donkeys nuzzling poor old mummy who looked no older herself. The air smelled of wild mint and green ferns. I stopped in one village as an ass clattered out of control from a side turning to shoot in front of me, dragging a heavy, wooden plough on her way to the fields. The farmer, furious, pelted behind her, casting an evil look in my direction as if it were all my fault – a stranger with blue eyes from lands far away bringing bad luck.

I covered the fifteen or so miles to Cide quickly. The road in was straight and flat and passed along one of the best beaches I had seen so far – no sand, just clean, smooth stones. It was still early, only about seven o'clock in the morning. The beach was empty of people, even though the sun was up and it was easily hot enough to swim. It looked very tempting, but I had to get organised. I found a new but pleasant, tree-shaded pension by the tiny harbour. Two young sisters were preparing breakfast. They wanted two million TL, nearly £10, for a clean, white room, a double bed with crisp, cotton sheets, a new shower room in which all the plumbing seemed to work and, they assured me, constant hot water. The view from the Swiss chalet-style window looked inland over emerald, wooded hills folding into the distance. Sadly, the grim skeletons of new apartment blocks scarred the scene. The price for the night was high and I was sure there were cheaper places back the way I had come, but I liked the idea of the restaurant outside under a vine, and so accepted. One snag was where to put the bicycle. Their father, the girls said primly, would never let her into the bedroom. I tied her up to the railings outside under a tree in view of the front door, where I hoped she would be safe, and walked back along the road towards the beach.

It was a glorious day. I felt rich with time. Cide was a small seaside resort, built away from the town centre, which was tucked away further inland. There had probably been nothing there a few years before, apart from a handful of fishing boats and the small harbour. Now, low-rise, concrete holiday apartments and hotels were being built along the sea, although the building work didn't appear to be as frenzied as it was in Şile and Karasu which were closer to İstanbul. A map had been thoughtfully provided by the town council on a notice board showing the whereabouts of the mosques, hotels and hotels-to-be. On the wall of a café overlooking the sea was a sign proudly announcing the next meeting of members of the Society for Atatürk's Thoughts. It all felt a bit like Bournemouth.

The beach was still empty. I chose a place and sat down, spreading out a towel which I had smuggled out from the pension. What luxury it was, first to swim in the gently, rippling sea, so clean here that every stone lying on the bottom could be counted. It was shallow at the edge, plunging suddenly deep. Oh the sensual pleasure of that silky water on my aching, sweaty body, floating away the creaks and groans. The Black Sea is not as salty as the Mediterranean so one feels less buoyant in the water. It is also a colder sea. Walking into the Mediterranean in summer can be like stepping into a warm bath, but the Black Sea is cold and fresh, an altogether different experience. Looking back inland, the thickly forested hills sprang forward like lions, their great paws sliding to a stop just before the beach. Mosque minarets, like fireworks about to go off, pointed skywards.

I sunbathed for about two hours, watching a group of horses walking on their own down the street and listening to the sound of the sea swooshing over the stones. They looked like cakes, brown and white, flat, smooth and round, veined and patterned, good enough to eat. An old man sat motionless with his bicycle under a tree watching the sea. A girl came and settled on the beach. She was joined by her father – or maybe her husband. By ten o'clock, it was too hot to stay in the sun and I went off to explore the town.

It was Sunday so the gold shops, hardware stores and shoe shops were shut and the town quiet. Cide was a small, dusty place of about 6,000 people, but I think I spotted an office for every political party in Turkey. They would probably have won more votes if they had turned their offices into cinemas or snooker halls to give the bored youngsters in town something to do and somewhere to go. I stopped off to eat some more breakfast in a restaurant and watched as the man expertly rolled out a round piece of dough to make me a lahmacun, an ubiquitous, Turkish, fast food snack. He sprinkled it with minced meat, tomatoes and fresh parsley and served it up piping hot and bursting with freshly-chopped salad. The inevitable questions followed: what was I doing in Cide, why was I alone, why wasn't I married? He was obviously thrilled to see a tourist. 'We don't see tourists here in town,' he said. 'Do come back, won't you, any time.' He was dusty with flour and wholesome, like his lahmacuns.

I wandered through the streets drinking in the rich displays of purple wisteria that grows like a weed in Turkey, tumbling over gardens, houses, sheds and rubbish dumps. There were many Ottoman houses, redolent of richer times past. Most of them were derelict and falling down, the sky coming in through the roof, once magnificent gardens gone to seed. Some of the wrecks were up for sale, hopeful signs stuck up on wooden planks in the gardens. Often the telephone number for enquiries had the code for İstanbul, hundreds of miles away. My favourite house was a picturesque mansion, splendid in its own sunny acres of grassland. Two haycocks stood at the front. No doubt the large, square rooms inside had high, inlaid, wooden ceilings and double opening doors. There would be deep window seats and an enormous chimney in the kitchen over an iron range.

These lovely little towns were shadows of their former selves. Brick villas were being built on the outskirts of the town, pushing the countryside further and further back. Beyond, earth track roads wound up and into the as yet unspoiled hills and shady countryside temptingly beyond. The only way to travel through the Black Sea area, I decided, was by bicycle or on foot to get any feel for the way life had been, was – and the way it looked set to become. People stared at me as I walked slowly by staring at their town. I was able to ignore much of the attention I got, but I still didn't like the feeling of walking on stage and becoming the centre of attention, a character who wasn't simply carrying a spear, but inadvertently playing the lead role – like Maggie in *The Golden Bowl*, caught willy nilly in the glare of the circus spotlight.

I walked back down the long, straight, dusty road to the sea, trying to stay in the shade of the trees, passing the tiny bus station, which didn't look as if it had seen any activity for weeks. It was the weekend and the high season. By now, the Aegean and Mediterranean resorts would have been packed to bursting point. The Black Sea resorts simply could not compete. They seemed half asleep, drowsing through the brief summer. My pension certainly was not busy. I chatted with the owner, the father of the two girls. He told me he had been to London for a heart operation and asked why I was travelling alone. We joked about the 'joys' of marriage – and the advantages of being single. 'But you do need somebody to talk to,' he said.

I needed to change some money and he offered to buy my pounds, checking the rate of exchange on teletext from a colour television in the lounge. He gave me the exact amount. He would no doubt have kept any foreign money, which gained in value every day in Turkey. He was obviously an enterprising businessman. How else could he have invested in the pension and afforded expensive heart operations at a private London clinic. Not only did he have a pension in a prime position in front of the harbour, there was also a camping area in the garden with tents and chalets and a restaurant outside, the tables laid out enticingly. He was no doubt aware of the competition to come from the development further along the coast, situated right on the beach. It was obvious that at present business was tough. Around the bay, there were more restaurants, but they all seemed to be empty, not a customer in sight. Maybe it was too early in the day. I wondered how the people here made a living. Behind Cide, the new buildings ravaging the hillsides offered an answer. Either the Black Sea remained off the beaten track slowly dying or the region had to be developed. If only they could do it more sympathetically with the environment. If only they learned from Western Europe's mistakes.

I went off to explore the harbour. This was heavily polluted. Cide's sewage floated straight into it. The ducks swimming around on the edge seemed unconcerned by the nastiness surrounding them. I climbed onto the harbour wall to look over and into cleaner waters. The girls at the pension had told me that they always took a boat out beyond the harbour to swim and had done so since they were small. Somebody had written on a rock in Turkish: 'Loving is sweet but parting is very bitter.'

Up from the pension and across a bridge over the river running down the west side of the bay, there was a small corner shop. I bought a bottle of red wine and bread and cheese for the following day. Back at the pension, I opened the bottle and had a crafty glass – what bliss – and lay down to sleep for a couple of hours.

At four o'clock in the afternoon, the sun was still high in the sky. I forced myself up from what felt like the depths of the sea and off my bed and went outside with the bottle of wine concealed under my arm. One of the tables on the beach was partly in the shade of a willow tree next to a rowing boat. It reminded me of my father's small boat many years ago when I was a child. I sat down and hid the bottle under the table, filling my glass surreptitiously every so often, watching the ants run over the boat and the light and shadow moving as the sea breeze blew through the trees. An old woman, her sleeves rolled up revealing two strong arms, came down to the sea shore. She was carrying a large knife and a big fish. At the water's edge, she bent over and cut up and cleaned the fish in the smelly water. I made a mental note not to eat fish that evening. An extended Turkish family was sitting close behind me, fathers, mothers, cousins, uncles, aunts, all drinking coca cola and Turkish tea and having a jolly time. The girls were dressed up like chocolate boxes, very pleased with themselves, with frilly white dresses and pink bows in various decorative places. A small, fat brother threw stones at the ducks, which sailed gracefully away out of reach. I hoped he might fall in but he didn't. Unusually, the family ignored me. Maybe they spotted the bottle under the table and thought I was a very loose 'Natasha'. Anyway, I was glad to be left alone in my sunny wine haze.

Later that evening, while walking around the other side of the harbour, I came across the old woman who had been cleaning the fish. She was in a most unfortunate situation, sitting on the ground bowed under an enormous pile of sticks and kindling balanced on her back. She was unable to get up and a friend – maybe her sister – was holding on to her hands, tugging and pulling to get her up and onto her feet. Horrified at the plight of these two ladies, I offered to help, but they declined.

'We're used to it,' said the fish lady.

'I saw you earlier,' I said. 'You've been working all day.'

'What else can we do,' said the other. 'You have to work to live. Life's tough.'

I passed by guiltily, feeling immensely rich and privileged. Then, suddenly, I had a vision of myself at their age. If I didn't do something about my life, that's how I would end up – maybe without the friend! I ate a thoughtful dinner of rather sad meat balls and a limp salad sitting outside at the pension restaurant. There were a few other people eating there. They seemed absolutely unconcerned when an enormous lorry roared and shook its way past, blasting diesel fumes in all directions, hardly able to negotiate the bend. It was loaded down with building materials of one kind or another. I moved tables to get closer to the house and further away from the road. Two young men came up from the harbour. I guessed they were sailing round the coast. They came in for dinner, passing business for the owner, who was lying on a sofa inside, his health obviously not great despite his operation. After the meal, I went to pay him for my room and inquire about the bicycle over night. He assured me he would fetch her in – personally – at close of play. I could get out the next morning through a side door. The key would be in the lock inside.

I went upstairs and tried to sleep. It was always so hot in these concrete buildings in the summer (and freezing cold in the winter). I left the window wide open but there was no air. I was glad of my anti-mosquito plug. What with the river close by and the filthy state of the harbour, the mosquitoes at Cide were big and unpleasant.

I felt as if I hadn't slept at all before it was time to get up, the stars still shining outside in the sky over the darkness of the hills. I felt irritable and uneasy all day. Maybe it was because of the warm wind, almost like a desert wind, that blew relentlessly against me throughout the day. It dried me out and virtually blew the bicycle backwards. I drank even more water than usual, sucking it out of my bottle in desperation, very glad of the numerous water fountains the Turks construct everywhere, especially the ones that pipe water, delicious and cold, directly from the mountains. The road was marked on the map as picturesque and precipitous, hugging the coastline, but I was hardly aware of my surroundings, more intent on staying on the saddle and trying to lock my mind into place to keep going. I was heading for Doğanyurt, the biggest town on the map before İnebolu, which I knew I could never reach in one day cycling over such roads. It was still a sixty-six kilometre-ride to Doğanyurt, however, just over forty miles. I had asked in Cide what Doğanyurt was like and whether there would be a place to stay. The answer had been vague. The Turks don't like to tell you bad news. It makes them feel uncomfortable. So I was trying to prepare myself for the worst. What would be the worst? A derelict, seaside place with nowhere to stay? Well then, I would knock on the door of a house with a little old lady among the nodding hollyhocks in her garden and ask if she had a spare corner. Proper travellers did that all the time, didn't they? Proper travellers carried tents so they were self sufficient or rolled themselves up and slept in the hedges along with the tortoises. (I passed one that day on the roadside, safe in his house on his back, going nowhere in a hurry but getting there all the same.)

I cycled on, wondering what the hell I was doing and why I hadn't got married, had some kids and stayed at home washing up and weeding the garden. It was a day for opening those drawers in the mind, stirring through the dusty contents and slamming them shut again. There was very little traffic on the road, the odd early morning bus between villages, scores of wondering pairs of eyes inside turning to stare at me as it passed and then turning to look out from the back window as the bus lurched and jolted out of sight. That day I seemed to be passing lots of men, walking singly or in pairs down the road or waiting by the roadside. They were probably waiting for the bus or hoping to get a lift from the occasional taxi or van going by. It was uncomfortable having to cycle slowly towards them, usually uphill with no room for manoeuvre and aware of being intensely observed. Although Turkey had become a top tourist destination, the rural places were still very traditional. Women were protected by the men of the family and they certainly didn't ride bicycles. A Turkish girl I met in İstanbul had cycled all over south America and was planning a trip to Africa. She said she seldom cycled in her own country because of the attitude of the men. She could understand too well the insults and suggestions they muttered as she went past.

Earlier in the year, I had reported on a United Nations programme to train teachers to achieve better results in the small village schools. The Turkish co-ordinator told me that a pupil from one of the schools had performed so well, she had won a coveted place in one of Turkey's grammar schools. The villagers had presented the child with a bicycle as a reward.

'The extraordinary thing was,' he said, 'she was a *girl*, an 11-year-old *girl!*'

'Why shouldn't a girl get a bicycle?' I asked, wondering how he would phrase the answer.

'A *girl*!' he repeated, and lowered his voice to a conspiratorial whisper. 'It's the *sexual* thing, you know, in Turkey. Girls don't ride bikes. It is wonderful what that village did, truly wonderful.'

As I battled on through the mountains that day, I tried not to think of what was flitting through the minds of the men I passed. It made me more furious and anxious, almost unable to make my legs, turning into jelly, turn the wheels, my glasses slipping down my nose with sweat. Yet that day, nothing happened. Nobody did anything. Nobody even said anything, as far as I could tell. I came upon a lorry driver coming in the opposite direction round a bend in the road. He was thoughtfully clearing away the rocks that had tumbled down from the hillsides over the road. He didn't even see me as I scooted past, so intent was he on clearing the road. The mind is its own place, wrote Milton. It makes a hell of heaven and a heaven of hell. I stopped for some tea and yet more water in a tea house and asked once again about Doğanyurt and whether there were places to stay there. The hotel in the centre of the town was a 'poor place' and not fit for a woman to stay in, was the un-reassuring answer.

Doğanyurt means the home of the falcon. A picturesque name. It turned out to be another run-down place, beside a river running into the sea and tucked away underneath a cliff towering up on the eastern side. By the time I cycled in, I could hardly move my legs after the forty miles or so from Cide, whose clean, stony beaches (outside the harbour) seemed like a distant dream. Doğanyurt felt like the end of the world. Most of the shops were empty, the tea houses were all full, the roads were smashed and strewn with rubbish and nearly every building looked as if it was about to fall down. The atmosphere was one of washed-up despair. Just before the bridge into town, a sign had pointed in the direction of the beach and a pension. The 'hotel' in town would definitely be a no-hoper, so I went back and turned down the sandy track towards the beach. Around the corner loomed a concrete block. A young man was sweeping the patio area outside, tables and chairs piled up in a corner. He raised his eyebrows thoughtfully when he saw me and stopped sweeping. It was a new pension, not really ready for business yet, he said, but I could have one of the rooms upstairs for a small charge.

He took me up an outside staircase leading to the first floor. The walls and floors were of bare concrete, which was already starting to crumble. The shower room looked derelict rather than in the throes of being finished off. The toilet seat was smashed and the doors were broken. I was shown a room containing a double bed and a bedside cabinet. The curtains at the long picture window overlooking the tumbledown harbour were filthy and torn. There was just room for me and the bicycle. I made my decision. It was only for one night and it was very cheap. The man was being kind in letting me stay. I thanked him and accepted.

It was a blisteringly hot day and I felt filthy after the ride. I decided to tackle the shower and managed to coax a trickle of water out of the overhead pipe. By fiddling with the box of tricks on the wall, pulling this lever and pushing that button, I even persuaded the water to run warm. After the shower, there were my cycling clothes to be washed out, but there was a hole in the sink and no useful bucket as a standby. I went downstairs into the restaurant on the ground floor and asked the caretaker in the kitchen for one. After much rummaging around, he produced something suitable. I found a balcony in one of the larger dormitory rooms and hung my clothes up to dry over some old chairs. Having got organised, I went to take a closer look round the town and buy some food for the next day.

It was a short walk back up the track over the bridge and into town. The countryside round about was richly green and exquisite. With a bit of effort and a lot of money, Doğanyurt could be a dear little holiday town. But unlike in Cide, there seemed to be no will, opportunity or incentive to try. The men sat in the shade outside the tea houses playing dominoes, chatting or just watching the world – and me – go by. I found a bread shop in the centre where the baker was loading his shelves with warm, crusty, brown loaves. The smell of fresh baking wafted down the street. He smiled with pleasure when I complimented him on his bread. The other shops open in the town were miserable affairs, dark and empty of customers. I was sick of eating bread and cheese all the time and felt like a change. Close to the sea front, I saw a sign saying 'pide', the simple but delicious Turkish version of pizza. It was hanging up in what seemed to be a tea house. I hurried inside to see if it were true and whether they were still baking that day. The boy seemed surprised that I was surprised and asked for my order. I explained that I wanted a couple of pide to eat the next day. 'Will they still be OK to eat tomorrow?' I asked. 'Of course,' he said, 'I'll put them in a packet for you.' I sat and waited, conscious of the stares from the tea drinkers on the packed terrace outside. I asked the boy why there were so many people sitting around in the town. 'This is Turkey,' he said shortly. 'There aren't any jobs here. People can only work in the fields. Now it's summer and the hottest time of the day. What else can they do, apart from go to the tea house?'

It appeared to be only a short walk from the pide house to the sea and I tried to make my way down to the front to look at the view. I gave up, confounded by the smashed roads and the piles of stone lying around. I felt depressed and turned back out of town heading for the beach. On a path under the trees, a small, harmless-looking man coming in the other direction passed by. I – oh so stupidly – automatically wished him good day. After that, I was conscious of being followed, over the bridge and back onto the track down to the harbour. It was the same man. He stopped me, gabbling incoherently and making lewd suggestive moments with his hands. He scuttled off when I shouted at him and

I continued on, furious with myself for having been so stupid. Women on their own in such places do not speak at random to men. It was quite simple. I felt that the day was disintegrating and I needed a beer.

Back at the pension, the owner was sitting drinking beer with a friend who had dropped by. The friend was fair-haired, in his twenties, tall and lean. He looked more Western European than Turkish. I couldn't help thinking that his eyes were narrow and mean. We fell into conversation. He could speak English. He had worked in Western Europe, including England, driving lorries, he said. He had resented the poor wages the Turks were paid and hated the way they were treated, like second, even third class citizens. So, he had returned to his home in Doğanyurt. Although it was more difficult to earn any money, at least it was home. I asked him what he did to make a living in such a town, but he avoided answering the question. He told me he didn't like the Welfare Party because, he said, it was too close to Iran. He himself supported the Grey Wolf Party. He was watching me closely as he said this and saw that I blinked rather hard. The Grey Wolf Party did not have the best reputation in Turkey. It was an extreme, fiercely nationalistic party, with a history of militancy. The party's use of the picture of a wolf recalled the legend that a grey wolf led the original Turkish tribes out of Central Asia. It was a very macho, moustachioed organisation. Women's rights were not at the top of their agenda.

'What's wrong with the Grey Wolf Party?' he asked, challengingly.

'Eh, they don't like women very much,' I stammered.

He laughed, and his eyes looked warmer and less wolfish. I began to think that his treatment abroad had scarred him for life and made him into ripe material for the Grey Wolves' propaganda, although deep down he was a warm and wonderful human being. But all my suspicions came flooding back when the pension owner leaned over and had a long, whispered conversation with him during which they both laughed at length. This was not turning out to be the most relaxing of days. My imagination raced. What if the Grey Wolf, what if the pension owner (whose eyes had also started to appear sly and calculating) . . . later on . . .? But no, it was impossible. Any trouble and the business would be ruined, before it had even apparently begun. Everybody in town would by then know about the foreign woman staying near the harbour. I drank my beer and read my book, trying to suppress the rising hysteria. The Grey Wolf stood up to go. He said goodbye very politely and loped off. I continued to wonder what his business was in such an out-of-the-way place.

It was not the kind of town to go wandering off on one's own. The harbour was filled with boats but it was not a picturesque sight. It looked as if the boats might have last taken to the waves during the time of Xenophon. Several appeared to serve as poor, temporary homes, the decks covered over with make-shift roofs of corrugated iron. One boat even seemed to have a permanent roof of red tiles. I read my book and wrote my diary through the rest of the afternoon. The pension owner hosed down outside and watered the poor, tired shrubs planted hopefully at the front. I wondered why he didn't go and do some work on the pension itself. A few young men wandered up to drink a beer or two. I guessed it was probably the only place in town that served alcohol. I shifted indoors out of the sun and away from the prying eyes and had another beer at a table in the restaurant. I was served by the caretaker who I decided to get on my side.

'Will I be on my own tonight in the pension?' I asked.

'Yes, if nobody else comes,' he said.

This was something that must have been rather obvious but I hadn't got round to worrying about it until now. 'I think I might feel a bit frightened on my own,' I said. At that moment, the owner walked in. 'She says she might feel frightened on her own in the pension by herself,' the caretaker told him.

I asked the owner where he would be.

'In town,' he said. 'But you'll be fine. The caretaker is on the premises twenty-four hours a day.'

'Where does he sleep?' I asked.

'Down here.'

I thought this was rather unhelpful. The entrance to the pension was up the steps at the side of the building. Nobody would ever hear me screaming up there.

'Do you think anybody else will come to stay?' I asked hopefully.

'You never know. A foreigner, a tourist walked through last week. He stayed here on his own too.'

I thought wistfully of the foreigner, walking miles away in the shade of the forested hills. I wished he would come walking back down the track right then. It occurred to me that I had scarcely seen a foreigner since I had left Andy waving goodbye back in Polonezköy. I thought I might feel better if I ate something. I asked the caretaker to make me some köfte with a salad. He seemed a pleasant, harmless man. I decided to labour the earlier point.

'If I am frightened and scream in the night, will you hear me and come and help?' I asked as carelessly as I could, as if it were a joke.

'Of course I will. Don't worry. You'll be perfectly safe.'

I ate my dinner thoughtfully. The weather had become violent and uncomfortable, the wind hot and fierce. It whipped up clouds of dust, whirling them along over the harbour. Nature itself was distressed and I could hear the cows in the fields behind the pension mooing and the frogs gulping and bubbling frantically in the ditches. The sea was disturbed and angry. It moved like a bowl of water which was being slopped from side to side by a giant hand. Back upstairs, I looked around. I could shut the front door and lock it from the inside, which I did. It seemed that every door and every window inside the pension had been left open and was banging and rattling in the wind gusting through. I struggled to close them all. It was difficult because closing one created a current that blew open another. Some of the windows were broken and others had swelled and didn't fit in the frames properly. This created unexpected draughts. As I ran backwards and forwards, I noticed that the front door was open again. Somebody had opened it. Who? How? I went into my room and locked the door. It was dusk by then so I turned the light on, a bare, low-wattage bulb hanging from a cord in the middle of the ceiling. The bulb dimmed and flickered on and off as the wind blew even more strongly. Part of the picture window in the room refused to shut despite all my pushings and pullings and the wind made the filthy curtains flap over the bed. I began to feel as if I were unwillingly starring in a Hammer Horror movie. I sat on the bed and thought. Whoever had the key to open the front door probably had keys to open all the bedroom doors including mine. Even if I left the key in the lock inside, somebody could smash through the glass in the top half of the door or even break the flimsy door itself down. The wind was roaring so loudly outside, nobody would hear anything. I decided to barricade the door.

My hand shaking, I unlocked my bedroom door and scuttled to the front hall where I had seen a large bed board propped up against the wall. I carried that back to my room. There was a heavy bedside cabinet already in my room. I decided I needed at least another to put on top. I lugged one in from the dormitory room. Tipping the bed board on its side, I leaned it against my bedroom door, pinning it in place with one of the cabinets and putting the other cabinet on top. Whoever tried to get in would have to smash through an awful lot of wood first and by then I would be smashing all the windows and making enough noise to wake the dead. Exhausted, I finally went to bed.

The alarm roared at half past four. I was still alive. The barricade was still intact. I squeezed out of the room and went to use the bathroom. My face reflected back in the mirror stared monstrously red, sunburnt and distorted – or maybe that last bit was because of the glass. I felt a little silly about my fears the previous evening and decided to hide the traces. I took the bed board back to the hallway and manhandled the bedside cabinet back to the dormitory.

I crashed through the door – and stopped horrified. A man was lying on the bed nearest the door. He was looking at me in complete amazement. It was the good old caretaker who, because of my fears, must have decided to sleep near my room to guard it during the night. Now I felt incredibly and absolutely stupid. I couldn't possibly begin to explain why I was standing in his doorway with a bedside cabinet, having just crashed past with a bed board. If only he had told me the night before! I muttered a thank you and goodbye and turned and fled, rushing to get my bags and bicycle outside and down the stairs into a new dawn, where the fresh sea air was soft on my burning face and sweet on my soul.

7
Doğanyurt to İnebolu

When they had poured the libations and sung the paean, first of all two Thracians stood up and performed a dance to the flute, wearing full armour. They leapt high into the air with great agility and brandished their swords.

I cycled back up the track and over the bridge and headed eastwards through the town, the cliffs looming steeply above. I began to climb almost immediately, passing an army post on the bend. A soldier came out to stare. I wondered what there was to guard in Doğanyurt. I must have been the most exciting thing that had happened to him that year.

'Dinlen,' he said, 'Take it easy.' He went on urgently, 'Çok yokuş var.' 'There are a lot of hills.'

He was a very intelligent soldier. It was the first time anybody had been so clear about what lay ahead of me. İnebolu was a mere thirty kilometres away, around nineteen miles, but there were indeed a lot of hills along the way and I thought I would just give up and die several times along that road. The surface was horrible: tracks, ruts, and potholes, the stones glued together into a rough, lumpy mat. There were more signs of road works but little actual activity. I had to haul the bicycle up steep stretches of the road countless times, stopping and starting, drops of sweat rolling down my face, plopping over my nose and stinging in my eyes. I was also stopping to tug furiously and uncomfortably at my clothes; there were three sweaty layers: cotton underpants, padded cycling pants and my cycling shorts, all of which were soaked through all the time around the stomach. (If the lorry drivers had but known the horrid truth.)

It was stunningly beautiful countryside, the road zig zagging out of sight, down through heavily forested valleys and then lazily climbing up again through rocks and grassland. Perched on the edge, the world rocked and spun around me, a breathing, chirping, singing, croaking world, heavily scented by the green smell of the pine trees and the wild herbs. Bushes of yellow cistus rose grew like a weed everywhere. By the time I cycled into İnebolu, the clouds had dropped way below the mountain tops and the day had become dull and overcast.

İnebolu is built around the mouth of a river. The town was founded in the sixth century BCE by Greek colonists who named their settlement Abonuteichus. The Romans called it Ionopolis, a name the Turks adapted. I stopped on the bridge in the town centre to observe the wide streets on either side of the even wider riverbed. The river is called İnebolu Çayı, which means the İnebolu Stream. Although the water level was at a summer low, it was plain that the 'stream' would turn into a roaring torrent in the winter. Xenophon and his men sailed along this part of the coast, thus avoiding having to cross the many rivers, like İnebolu Çayı, pounding down from the mountains.

There were several handsome houses on the western side and a food market in full swing in front of the shops and workshops on the eastern side. The town looked grubby and grey under the overcast sky, which threatened rain. Ignoring the curious stares of the crowds, I got off my bicycle and guided it through the edge of the market and into the maze of narrow, back streets where, I judged, I would find the hotels. I asked a shopkeeper for directions and he led me to a street in which there were at least two. They were both dingy, cheap and much of a muchness, but I liked the relaxed hotel owner in the first one I went in to. He let me wheel the bicycle right inside the gloomy, old-fashioned lobby and park it among the chairs at the back. A room was available, he said, and gave me the key. I went upstairs to take a look. On the spacious landing was a government tourist poster of the sun setting over the Blue Mosque in İstanbul. The poster was dated 1979, coincidentally the year I first visited Turkey. The room was tucked away down a corridor and was small with a shower. This was all fine.

Back downstairs, the hotelier said that the woman would come to clean the room 'soon'. I collapsed into a chair to wait. The hotel clock struck the hour and then the half hour. On the reception desk, which was manned by a young boy, an antique telephone rang like a voice from the past. 'Hullo,' said the voice in my imagination. 'It's Ali here. Has he gone yet and can I put my fez back on?'

Kemal Atatürk, the man who forged the Turkish Republic from the ashes of the Ottoman Empire after the First World War, began his campaign against the occupying Allied forces along the Black Sea. After his victory, he chose to visit the conservative towns there to introduce his radical ideas about the kind of Turkey he wanted to create. He selected the important port of İnebolu in which to make a radical fashion statement. On 2 September 1925, he walked openly, albeit nervously, around the streets wearing a Panama hat as opposed to the traditional fez, which, he said, represented Ottoman backwardness. He then made an historic speech in the clubroom of İnebolu's branch of the Turkish Hearth organisation. Gentlemen, he said, the Turkish people, who had founded the Turkish Republic, had civilised ideas, but they also had to be civilised outwardly. He continued:

'A civilised, international dress is worthy and appropriate for our nation, and we will wear it. Boots or shoes on our feet, trousers on our legs, shirt and tie, jacket and waistcoat – and of course, to complete these, a cover with a brim on our head. I want to make this clear. This head-covering is called a "hat".'

It was a momentous occasion, and in İnebolu and the other provincial Black Sea towns, you could still get a feel of the enormity of what Atatürk did to turn the Turkish people towards the west away from the east and their old traditions.

He not only got rid of the fez, he also replaced the Ottoman Arabic alphabet with a modified Latin one, introduced women's rights, abolished Islam as a state religion, and laid down a secular constitution. Atatürk's driving goal was to create a unified Turkey in which belief and ethnic origin were subordinated to the concept of being a Turk in his or her own country, Turkey. He has been much criticised for his nationalistic ideas but, at the time, Atatürk was struggling to unite a country which was trying to emerge from the collapse of an antiquated empire and fight off the threat to its independence from Britain, Greece, France and Italy, all of which had their own various agendas for the territory and all of which invaded. As Patrick Kinross wrote in his biography, Atatürk 'transformed a crumbling, straggling empire, beset by enemies, into a compact homogeneous state, recognized by potential friends.' Atatürk believed that everybody was a Turk first and last and coined the saying: 'How happy is he who can call himself a Turk.' In doing so, he unwittingly sewed the seeds of bitterness and violence among the country's Kurdish minority.

İnebolu, the hotel owner informed me as I waited for my room to be prepared, was a town of the centre right True Path Party, the party of Tansu Çiller. He didn't like Refah, the Islamist Welfare Party, he said, they were too religious. As he spoke about the present, standing in the hotel lobby redolent of the past, I noticed what was being shown on the television. Nobody else seemed to notice except for me. The TV channel was playing a popular Turkish video. It featured two women, one dressed as a man in a black top hat and a black suit, the other with long blond hair and wearing a very revealing dress. The two women were rubbing suggestively up against each other, making as if to kiss each other passionately – and it was only about nine o'clock in the morning. This was followed by a keep fit lesson conducted by a nubile woman in the skimpiest and tightest of tunics. I was ever surprised at what Turkish television showed and at the apparent indifference of the people, the vast majority of whom are Muslim and, despite Atatürk's radical reforms, largely traditional in outlook and temperament. It was the eternal conflict between the values of the past and the present.

As if to reinforce the point, a man passed through the lobby and scowled with distaste and disapproval when he saw a lone woman in cycling gear, sprawled in a chair. His distaste hit me with force and I felt extremely uncomfortable. I decided that waiting for the cleaning lady was a futile exercise and headed upstairs, armed with a broom and a dustpan I found on the way. I dumped the dirty sheets outside, swept the floor, washed the dust off the surfaces with my own precious cloth, took a shower – the water was cold and spluttered out at random from a rusting shower head – put on my jeans and all my heavy clothes including a sweat shirt and a sleeveless jacket and ventured out to explore.

As I passed a tea house on the corner of my street, I waved at the group of men sitting outside smoking hubble bubbles, sucking on the long pipe and drawing up the tobacco smoke cooled by the water in the glass bowl. I felt as if they were old friends. As I had ventured up the street earlier, checking out the hotels, the men had greeted me with great respect, graciously welcoming me to İnebolu. One of them now got up again, bowed and repeated exactly what he had said before, his friends nodding in sympathy as he spoke.

'May I, on behalf of the people here in İnebolu, welcome you to our town. You are most welcome and if there is anything we can do to make your stay pleasant, you must let us know.'

Atatürk would have been a proud and vindicated man had he heard those courteous words.

I was glad of my sweater and jacket. The weather had definitely taken a turn for the worse. It was time for breakfast and I chose at random one of the many soup restaurants in the busy street. I sat facing the window so I could watch the comings and goings outside and began to make some notes in my diary. One of the waiters came up to take a look.

'What are you writing?' he asked and smiled with pleasure when I told him that I was a journalist and was describing the town.

'Today's market day in İnebolu,' he informed me. 'There's a market here on Tuesdays and Saturdays.'

A young boy came to listen. 'What language are you writing in?' he asked, staring in amazement at my notebook. 'English,' I replied.

I asked the waiter whether there was a museum to Atatürk in town. He shook his head. 'Maybe in Samsun.'

'Atatürk was a great man,' I said. 'It's a shame İnebolu doesn't have a museum. It is an important town.'

He nodded, beaming proudly.

Few Turks ever criticise or even consider criticising the founder of their Republic, especially in public. It could land them in prison. The words and deeds of Atatürk are instilled into them at an early age. In every school, there is an Atatürk corner displaying maps and charts detailing his progress in the battle for Turkey's independence, as well as photographs of him throughout his life and copies of his most famous sayings. His portraits and statues can be found in most shops, work places and town centres. His sayings are even cut into hillsides, particularly next to military installations. Turkey's army prides itself on upholding Turkey's secular constitution, even if it has to interfere, sometimes dramatically, with the political establishment.

I enjoyed my hot, lentil soup that I made even hotter by sprinkling on top a generous helping of the chopped up and dried, red chilli flakes which Turkish restaurants routinely provide next to the salt and pepper. Suddenly, there was an awful crash. The young lad hurrying upstairs carrying a tray packed with glasses had slipped and dropped the lot. There was a glorious smashing and tinkling as broken glass cascaded down the stairs. I watched, holding my breath, wondering what would happen. The boy stood frozen to the spot with horror at what he had done. Without a word, a waiter took a broom and began to sweep the glass away. The customers laughed quietly. I got up to pay my bill and made a joke to the man at the till, obviously the restaurant owner, about it being an expensive day. He shrugged philosophically and smiled. The Turkish concept of fate – God wills it – which they share with their Muslim brothers, is sometimes very attractive.

Although İnebolu did not have a museum dedicated to Atatürk, he dominated the small square, which I found up the street and around the corner from the restaurant. It was a grand display. The centrepiece was a large bust of the great man, that familiar, handsome face with its famously penetrating gaze. The bust was covered in gold leaf and therefore could not show the fairness of his hair and the colour of his fascinating eyes, which were piercing and an enigmatic, grey blue, rather like the colour of the Black Sea. Atatürk did not look Turkish at all. He was an Ottoman Moslem, a Macedonian, born plain Mustafa in the port of Salonika, then still in the Ottoman Empire, afterwards in Greece. (The date of his birth is uncertain. Andrew Mango said in his biography, *Atatürk*, which was published in 1999, that the most likely date was the winter of 1880/1881.) He acquired the nickname, Kemal, meaning 'perfection' when he was a boy at military school. In 1935, Turks were required to adopt family names. Mustafa Kemal dropped his Arab name of Mustafa and adopted the name Atatürk or 'Father Turk' – metaphorically 'Father of the Turks'. From then on he was Kemal Atatürk. On either side of the bust in İnebolu were two pictures, also covered with gold leaf. One depicted him with his famous hat in his hand, the second was of a boat on the Black Sea, marking the fact that the boatmen of İnebolu helped to transport munitions during the War of Independence and organised a regatta to welcome Atatürk with songs and dances in traditional style on his historic visit in 1925.

Wandering around İnebolu, one could see how wealthy the sea trade had made the town, enabling the Greek merchants to build their rich, timbered mansions on the hills above the port. Many of them were ruined; others had been restored to their former glory. I walked slowly up the winding, cobbled streets behind the port with my head, like a windmill, swivelling around from side to side and thrown backwards trying to take it all in. The streets were so narrow and the houses so high and on so many different levels that I had to keep crossing from one side of the street to the other to try to get a good view. Black cats crossed my path in all directions. An elderly gentleman leaned out of a wooden casement and asked me what on earth I was doing. 'Looking at your lovely houses,' I replied. He smiled with pleasure. 'Our houses are very old,' he said proudly. An elderly woman found me gazing with rapture at her neighbour's garden, which was down a flight of stone steps and tucked in to a narrow dell at the side of the house; every square inch was crammed with plants, flowers, shrubs and vegetables. I began to move away feeling rather rude to be invading somebody's privacy. 'Look, look,' she said. 'Do stay and look.' There were geraniums red on the stairway, cabbages, fig and pomegranate trees, the luscious orange fruit apparently turning into exquisite, orange flowers. Yellow iris bloomed (the sort in my garden back home) and white morning glory, so delicate, so rampant, wound its way insidiously through the undergrowth.

I met an old man as I was climbing up a particularly steep bit of the road. I was trying not to slip. He was inching his way downhill, using a stick as a support. As we passed, he stopped and announced: 'You know, I worked in Holland for ten years.' I tried to ask him more, whether he was happier now he was back home in Turkey and what it had been like in Holland for him, but he continued on his way, tap tapping down the hill.

The sky was very overcast and it looked like rain was on its way. The sea was flat and an indeterminate slate blue. I stopped for a cup of Turkish coffee at an unexpected tea house overlooking the sea and sat in the garden under a vine. Hens clucked and pecked in a corner. A handsome young man was sitting there too, surrounded by books and papers. He had a dazzling smile that revealed a charming gap in his front teeth. I wished I were a lot younger. He had blond hair and I was reminded of Atatürk's looks. I asked him where he was from. He was the son of the house and an electrical engineer, he said. His family had been born and bred in İnebolu. How lucky his family was to have such a beautiful house in such a spot, I observed. 'Yes,' he said, 'But the winters here are simply terrible. They are very long and it rains all the time.'

Even as he spoke, it began to rain and the drops sploshed through the leaves of the vine. We moved underneath the verandah and the rain pattered with a pleasant noise onto the tin roof. We sat in companionable silence. I was half asleep and trying to read. Mr Electrically Handsome was trying to work but kept stopping to look at the view below us. There were some people, dark blobs in the water, swimming in the sea. The fishing boats were heading for the harbour out of the rain, which was by then falling heavily. The boats looked like toys floating in a bath manned by little plastic men. I could have picked them up, poured the water out and propped the men against the taps to dry.

The rain stopped and as I left the café (there was no bill for the coffee), the muezzins began their calls to prayer. It was an unearthly sound bouncing up from the several mosques in the town beneath and from a handful scattered in the hills, their minarets pointing upwards like so many rocket launchers. I continued on and further upwards. Woodland tracks criss-crossed the hills, new houses at the top, old, wooden houses with gardens tucked away down below in the valley. They were well spaced out among the trees and practically invisible. There were flowers and vegetables, corn, cabbages and onions, wild feverfew, bay trees, rhubarb and haycocks, yellow iris, tumbling miniature roses and hibiscus climbing up fir trees, their red trumpets silently triumphant. Daisies and cows grew in the long grass. Stone steps, swept clean, led invitingly up to the front doors of houses. At the top were many pairs of shoes – in descending order of size – Turks always take their shoes off before entering the house. Doors and windows were open to let the air in and everything was neat and clean, even if the fences had been mended with beaten-out oil tins and some window panes were missing. Voices could be heard but, as if in a fairy tale, there was nobody to be seen. It was as if they had all disappeared or time was standing still. The very flies slept on the walls. I slipped past, feeling like a intruder, whispering nice things to the curious dogs, who were very much alive, to try to stop them barking. Most of the houses had their own satellite dishes on the side and at least one house had a generator ready to roar into action during a power cut. Above the valley were cool, pine forests. The mists were closing down low in a white curtain below the hill tops and the shapes of the trees, silhouetted high up on the edge, loomed through the milky whiteness.

On the way back down was a cemetery overgrown with grass and brambles. Some of the memorials on the older graves had been carved out using the Arabic script, possibly commemorating the ancestors of some of the people still living there. Some of the gravestones were topped with Ottoman-style turbans fashioned from stone. Newer gravestones were decorated with painted images of tulips and flowers. Nearly all of them, old and new, had the words, 'Ruhuna Fatiha' inscribed on them. Al-Fatiha is the first Sura or chapter in the Koran and the phrase loosely translated means 'A blessing on the soul'.

I passed underneath some cherry trees growing over a garden wall. The clusters of fruit were hanging temptingly down from the top branches; the lower ones had obviously been stripped of their fruit. Just as I was thinking what a waste it was, a lorry drove up and stopped. The men inside jumped out, climbed on to the roof of the cab and helped themselves, laughing like naughty boys, to the ripe, red fruit. It wasn't going to be wasted after all.

Back at the hotel, the chambermaid had been and gone. The filthy blanket on the bed had been carefully wrapped in a clean, white, cotton sheet which was held in place with large safety pins. During the night, there were incredible storms. The ground shook from the thunder as if it were going to split open and the lightening came and went as if an effects person were flicking a light switch on and off backstage. I snuggled down in my bed, trying not to breathe in the smell of the blanket. The rain poured down hard enough to drown in. It was difficult to sleep and I kept looking out of the window to watch the pools of water flooding the street outside. It was electrically exciting, but I wondered whether I was going to be able to start as usual at half past four in the morning. Would I need a boat rather than a bicycle? A Noah's Ark? I fell asleep and dreamed of my own clean blankets at home. In my dream, I went to get them.

8
İnebolu to Yakakent through Sinop

The generals of the Greeks entertained the ambassadors from Sinope. There was much friendly conversation and, among other things, each asked the other party what they wanted to know about the remainder of the journey.

The alarm clock exploded. I jumped out of my pit, rushed to the window and leaned out. The ground looked soaked. A man happened to be walking past. It didn't matter what time it was, day or night in Turkey, there was always somebody doing something nearby. I asked him if it was still raining. 'No, it's not,' he said, smiling. I forced myself to swallow some bread and cheese and carried the bicycle down the stairs. She had slept underneath the old poster of İstanbul to make her feel at home. I had to wake a boy up who was sleeping on a couch in the lobby. He was sleeping so soundly, I had to poke him on the shoulder, standing well back immediately in case he got the wrong idea. I needn't have worried. He got up in a daze, shuffled to the door and, still half asleep, unlocked it. Out I went into the newly-washed dawn – it was still quite dark – splashing through the puddles down the street and onto the coast road, turning right and peddling eastwards along the ribbon road I had seen the day before from the café with a view. It was heading in the direction of Sinop.

The line on the map running eastwards from İnebolu had turned red and continued red all the way to the border with Georgia, another five hundred miles away, eight hundred kilometres. I was ten days into the trip and had covered nearly four hundred miles. The question was as always how good the red road would turn out to be. Looking at the explanation of the symbols in the map glossary, the Turks were hedging their bets. The redness could mean the road was 'existing, under construction, projected, or sealed/unsealed.'

There were no dramatic plungings up and down that day. I fairly flew along the line of the coast, cycling easily as if on a switchback through the rolling hills dotted with houses. From a distance, the houses looked large, square and substantial, whether they were built of wood or brick. But when you got up closer, you could see that the windows were eyeless or had been patched with cardboard or anything else that might have come to hand; doorways were boarded up, there were holes in the roofs and walls were crumbling. It was often difficult to tell whether the houses had been abandoned and were standing empty or, despite their appearance, were in fact occupied. Often, cabbages and corn were to be seen growing in neat rows laid out in the middle of the wilderness of an overgrown garden. Sometimes, a red geranium grew in a pot carefully balanced on a rotten window ledge. I passed one home which was boarded up, but when I turned back to look, I could see smoke drifting out of a chimney. Despite the beauty of the countryside, there was an air of desolation, which was sad and disconcerting. It was obvious that many people in the past had packed up and gone elsewhere to make a living. To İstanbul or Europe. When I did see anybody, they were generally elderly men and women, the latter wearing headscarves and long skirts, bowed over, shuffling along, overseeing their cow and one or two calves in the lanes or haymaking in the fields, sometimes alone, sometimes with an aged husband, till death us do part. Most stared silently as I passed by, an intruder from another world and I refrained from any shouted greeting feeling it would sound brash and discordant.

The countryside felt remote and so did I that day, mentally wrapped in a cloak to repel the stares and shouts from the handful of disbelieving, fantasising drivers who passed by. I stopped in the small, seaside town of Abana and found a tea house on a corner in a street set back from the sea. I sat outside at a table next to a couple of Turkish policemen who were having a tea break in their busy morning. The tea house owner was understanding and efficient. He didn't ask me the usual questions about where I came from and where I was going and why I didn't have a husband. He just got on with bringing me glasses of water and tea and showed me where the very reasonable public toilets were up a hill behind the tea house. Abana seemed a nice, sensible town and I sat for a while reading a chapter of my book, briefly immersed in the sophisticated, rich, nineteenth century world of Henry James, with its allusions and shadows, so different from the one I was sitting in. I thanked the tea house owner profusely – he refused to accept any money for the glasses of tea I had drunk. On the way out of town, a pide house was already up and baking, its furnace oven red-hot. I bought a couple of fresh pide from an efficient young lady at the till, her hair done up in a pony tail. She sliced them up and made them into a packet for me to eat later on that day. It would make a change from stale bread, squashed tomatoes and rancid sheep's cheese.

I cycled on through Çatalzeytin, which looked small and pretty (my İnebolu hotelier had dismissed it as of no consequence), and continued on through Türkeli which he preferred, although I can't remember anything about it except that it seemed big and noisy. His judgement summed up the difference between the rich, northern European who wants to get away from it all and find somewhere quiet and quaint and the average Turk who is fed up with being quaint and poor and wants to go somewhere with shops, facilities, opportunities and crowds.

I made it to Ayancık, about sixty-two miles or a hundred kilometres east of İnebolu, comparatively easily. It was half that distance again to Sinop, too far for me to do in a day. I was unsure what to do. Ayancık was not exactly prepossessing, the buildings on the outskirts sprawling new and ugly on both sides of the estuary. I cycled into town over a concrete bridge and began to look for a hotel. I asked various people but was unable to understand their Black Sea Turkish or their directions. I made my way through the central square trying to ignore the silly, leering young men who shouted when they saw me and laughed and pointed. I pedalled slowly down the road to the sea, which was, as usual, concealed from the town by mountains of rocks tumbling over the front. Maybe it was another fish barrage or maybe it was a sea defence. A row of rotting, semi-derelict houses stood along the coast with their backs to the sea. It was unprepossessing and depressing and I was still being laughed at by groups of people hanging around. It was a quick and easy decision to make. I would catch the bus to Sinop. Immediately.

I returned to the square where I had already noticed the mini buses lined up along one side, some of them with sensible roof racks. I went into the bus office and bought a ticket to go to Sinop. The next bus was waiting; it would leave in just over an hour's time and had a roof rack!

The bicycle was carried away to be loaded onto the roof. I rushed to the back of the bus and scrambled up the ladder, not caring that my unexpected action caused an immediate sensation throughout the town square. I made sure the bicycle was lying on her left side, the gear mechanism facing upwards rather than downwards so that it would not be smashed against the roof of the bus as it jolted over any bumps. The man secured the bicycle tightly with rope and I added some of my elasticated, hooked luggage straps for good measure.

I went off to buy a large chocolate and vanilla ice cream cornet from the 'dondurma' seller across the square. He was so sour and unfriendly, I felt like squashing it back in his face. Now that would have caused a sensation. He had also overcharged me because, stupidly, I hadn't asked the price before buying it. I couldn't bear to walk round the town and so went back to the bus office, carried a chair outside, positioned it next to the bus and sat down to empathise with the bicycle tied up on top. I felt horribly pleased that I was going to be driven out of this town and all the young men, who had laughed at me, had to stay behind.

A boy selling simits, the Turkish twisted rings of sesame seed bread, wandered up to stare at me, his mouth open. He hovered close by, watching my every move. I began to burn with irritation and fury. In the end, I couldn't stand it any longer and, jumping to my feet, yelled at him to clear off. The Turks came running. They hate it when there is a fuss, especially involving foreigners. The simit boy was shooed away and his smile of triumph, as he loped off among the cars, was almost enough to send me into a murderous frenzy. I felt like running after him and knocking him to the ground together with the tray balanced on his head loaded with the simits which I was sure were stale anyway. The men urged me to sit inside the office out of sight to wait for the bus, and somebody brought me a glass of tea. I didn't have the energy to resist. I knew I was, as usual, breaking all the rules of their society, riding a bicycle, climbing up bus ladders, shouting and unaccompanied. Generally I tried not to care, but if it was going to involve street battles, it was time to give in for an hour or so. I put a lot of sugar in my tea and sipped it thoughtfully. Suddenly I noticed that the bus was driving off, the bicycle strapped like a victim on top. Apart from the driver, the bus was empty. Where was it going? I jumped up in panic but the ticket man told me it had gone to make a special journey to pick somebody up and it would soon return. Which it did. Phew!

There were only a few passengers heading for Sinop. We got in and arranged ourselves over the empty seats. The bus pulled away. No doubt the people of Ayancık were as pleased to get rid of me as I was to leave their town. The bus took a slow detour through the busy back streets, hoping to pick up more passengers. The fare was 250,000 TL, about £1. This was expensive and the passengers kept querying the amount. The person the bus had gone to pick up was a woman. She was sitting on the front seat next to the driver and was obviously furious about something. From the rapid conversation, I got the idea that she had asked an earlier bus to go and pick her up from her home, maybe because her luggage was too heavy to carry down to the square, but the driver had forgotten and set out towards Sinop without her. So she had had to wait for the later bus. The woman told her story several times to our driver, who listened and nodded sympathetically. In the end, she calmed down and began to chat normally with him in that impressive way Turkish men and women do, even if they have never met before, exchanging information about where they come from and about their extended families. They were by now good friends and when she left the bus she smiled. It hadn't been his fault and she didn't blame him for anything, she said.

Initially, the road to Sinop ran along the top of the cliffs overhanging the sea and then wound back inland. The countryside flattened out and the trees disappeared. I was, for the time being, leaving behind the hills and forests tumbling into the sea and getting a glimpse of the fertile plains around Sinop where tobacco, wheat, corn and flax were grown. Sinop has a colourful history. It was founded by Greek colonists in the seventh century BCE. According to legend, the town took its name from the water nymph, Sinova, daughter of a river god, who caught the eye of Zeus. He promised to give her anything she wanted in return for her favours. Her cunning request was to remain a virgin for the rest of her life, and, graciously, Zeus allowed her to do so. She may – or may not – have lived to regret it. At Sinop, Hercules battled against the Amazons, who lived along the coast. One of Sinop's most famous sons, Diogenes the Cynic, was born there, either in 412 or 404 BCE, making him about four years old or a boy of twelve when Xenophon and his men sailed into Harmene, Sinop's port, where they were presented with 4,000 bushels of barley-meal and 1,500 jars of wine.

Everybody went to Sinop, the Greeks and the Persians, the Black Sea Pontic kings, who made it their capital, the Romans and the Byzantines. The Selçuks from Central Asia, who were the first Turks into the Black Sea area, used Sinop as a port in the thirteenth century, after which it remained largely under Turkish control. The battle of Sinop in 1853, in which 4,000 Turks died at the hands of the Russians, led to the beginning of the Crimean War.

I had always wanted to visit Sinop to see its massive fortifications, which are based on foundations built around 2,000 years ago by Mithridates the Great. Because of Sinop's spectacular position on the coast, balanced on a peninsula and jutting out into the Black Sea, I foolishly expected great views as we drove into town. The key to successful travelling, however, is never to expect anything and then whatever comes is a bonus. It was a lesson learned from bitter experience. And indeed, Sinop was, initially, a disappointment. The approach was through the usual, urban, ribbon development with glimpses of monstrous apartment blocks towering up outside the town. These were painted in extraordinarily bright primary colours a child would choose from a cheap paint box. The first sight of the citadel walls was of a crumbling and desolate section on the west side that the town had decided to use as the bus station.

The bus driver had forgotten about the precious cargo tied on top, so I climbed up onto the roof myself to untie the bicycle and somebody helped me to lift her down. As I was strapping the bags back on, I noticed that one of the connections on a spoke holding the rear mudguard in place had sheared off and the mudguard was resting on the back tyre. I thought wistfully of Amca's repair shop in Ağva a few hundred miles back down the road. It was down to me to do something practical for once. I cut a piece off my washing line and tied up the spoke and mudguard in a neat bow to keep it from brushing against the wheel. The string bow was to be a perfectly satisfactory arrangement and last for hundreds of miles over horrendous non-roads. I arranged my belongings comfortably over the bicycle and cycled into town, passing another chunk of citadel which looked as if it was being used as a prison. I was still hoping to find a harbour and a View and, instinctively, I turned right and shot down a steep hill to the east side of Sinop to find them both at the bottom.

The reason I had had no real impression of the citadel was because the way in from the landside led directly in to the heart of it. The streets and buildings largely obscured any sight of the walls enclosing the town. The best way to get the walls into any kind of perspective was to see them from out at sea. This I would do a few weeks later when Sinop looked what she was, one of the most spectacular, walled, sea side towns in Turkey. That afternoon, as I cycled through the huddle of back streets behind the port looking for a cheap place to stay, I got a jumbled impression of massive, stone gateways, battlemented towers and high, imposing walls. I found a seedy pension in a side street leading down to the sea and took a room. It was stiflingly hot and had a peculiar smell. It was also too small to squeeze my bicycle inside unless I tilted her up on the back wheel, swung her in, shut the door and put her down again, effectively locking myself inside the room. I did this later on when I went to bed.

There were still a few hours of sunlight left to explore as much of Sinop as I could. Outside in the street, I was struck by the number of shops and stores selling alcohol. The shelves groaned under bottles and cans of imported spirits, wine and beer. When the Soviet Union collapsed, Sinop became one of the major Black Sea ports from which food and consumer goods were exported from Turkey to Russia and the former Soviet Republics. Close by the pension, I found a shop selling ships in bottles. The ships were made out of plastic, wood and shells. Cuttings from newspapers and magazines about the artists were pinned on the wall. The cuttings were in a variety of languages, although I didn't spot any in English. The shopkeeper had stuck large, plastic flowers for an eye-catching joke among the shrubs planted in buckets outside on the pavement. There was another smaller place across the road with a few dusty ships in bottles in its window, but the shop was closed and looked like it hadn't been open for some time.

There was a sad feel about Sinop despite the restoration work going on in some of the mosques, tombs and monuments crowded into the old town. The town council was trying to improve the municipal park close to the sea. One man was hitting something with a spade while three others stood around watching. There were a few flower beds dug out but it was obviously going to be slow progress. I thought what a shame it was that the two prime sites in the citadel were occupied, one by the prison and the other by the smelly bus station.

I realised just how vast the prison was as I walked past the dockyards and underneath the southern walls. It was still hot and I felt like a tortoise plodding along, trying not to slip on the stony, rough track, choked by the clouds of dust thrown up by the lorries tanking past. The bored soldiers, guns slung over their shoulders, peered over the battlements and towers, which were festooned with barbed wire and searchlights. They whistled as I passed by. It seemed incredible to have such a prison slap bang in the centre of what should have been a busy, tourist town and occupying what should have been one of the major attractions.

I reflected on the inmates inside festering in their stone cells. I wondered if they were able to look out over the docks and see the skeletons of the fishing vessels taking shape and the open sea beyond. Turkey had a poor human rights record. Torture was routine. There were many writers, journalists and intellectuals in prison, some of whom had been locked away for years. I had interviewed a woman publisher earlier in the year in İstanbul. She had been in and out of prison because she published controversial books about Turkey's Kurds, the massacres of the Armenians at the end of the nineteenth and early twentieth centuries and the treatment of the Greeks at the turn of the twentieth century. She laughed wryly as she told me how she was locked up with murderers, drug dealers and fraudsters. It was all rather interesting, she said with admirable understatement, puffing on numerous cigarettes as we discussed the possibility that she might return to prison later in the year, a plump, gentle, grey-haired woman, wrapped in her grey, baggy cardigan sipping her tea, deemed to be a threat to the Turkish state.

The prison in Sinop cast a long shadow. I turned back to the town centre and took refuge in an empty restaurant where I had a kebab and a salad. Afterwards, I went down to the harbour to consider drinking a beer. The waiters were prowling like wolves outside their territory overlooking the harbour. All the restaurants jutting out over the water were curtained off and secluded under their own heavy canopy. Inside, it was a bit like being confined in a padded prison cell, unable to get any view or perspective. I looked at the couples holding hands and gazing into each other's eyes, considered the price of the beer and went to buy my own from the loaded shelves at a shop round the corner.

The pension in which I was staying that night spread itself down long and narrow corridors over the third and fourth floors of the building. My smelly cubby-hole was the penultimate room with a small window on the seaward side. The room next to it was the one with the View overlooking the harbour. It was a spacious, high-ceilinged room and painted white with long, wide windows on two sides. Light from the sun and the sea poured through the windows, bathing the room with a dazzling brightness over which the shadows rippled. There was a balcony directly over the canopies of the restaurants down below, and this took in the panoramic views they lacked. The room was empty apart from some dilapidated chairs and I took up position on one of them, drinking my can of beer, cracking pistachio nuts and eating sweet peaches, the juice of which ran onto the dirty floorboards making them sticky. The peaches were an antidote to all the greasy, stodgy food I was constantly consuming. I sat and stared, feeling as if I were at the theatre and had a seat in a box.

The harbour at Sinop was busy, packed with fishing boats which had either finished for the day or were about to go out for some night-time work. Bigger vessels bound for Russia were being loaded up with melons, fruit and vegetables. This information was obligingly supplied by one of my fellow residents, who was also using the balcony for a grandstand view. He worked in the trade. He told me that when the Soviet Union collapsed, the harbour at Sinop could hardly cope with the amount of work as the Turks and ex-Soviets queued up to ship out food and goods over the Black Sea to ports in Ukraine, Georgia and Russia. It was an unregulated, black market trade and brought wealth and prosperity to the good folk of Sinop. But trade had dropped off since the local council had begun to 'control' it. Sinop was now less busy and many of the merchants had gone elsewhere.

The man was fat and jolly with a red face and bad teeth. He was accompanied by a large woman with blond hair. She was no longer young and the skin under her wide blue eyes was beginning to bag and wrinkle. She had once been beautiful and was still striking-looking, especially when she smiled. She spoke Turkish with a slightly foreign accent and I asked her where she came from. Her family were originally Azeri, she said, and she had grown up in Baku. She was now living in Sinop and married to the jolly man, who laughed and cuddled her and called her 'his gorgeous, kissable eternal delight' and 'his peach'. They asked me if I were married, whether I owned my own house and how much money I earned every month. I told them that I didn't have a full-time job and didn't earn very much money. I preferred the freedom to choose what I did. They looked at me in astonishment. I must have seemed extremely rich to them, riding around Turkey on a bicycle, my house waiting for me back in England. Their reaction reminded me of the response of a Syrian boy years before when I told him that I wanted to study Turkish and Arabic. 'What for?' he asked. 'I only want to learn to speak the super power languages.' The amazement of the couple sitting on the balcony that evening in Sinop, living together full-time in the small room next to mine, echoed his wonder at my choice of life style. Oh the rich, super-power luxury of choosing to be 'poor'!

They were a nice couple and evidently very much in love. Richness, I thought, didn't necessarily consist in having loads of money. I saw them later going out for the evening, he, squeezed into a smart suit, she, exotic and handsome in a brightly coloured, slinky dress, heavily made up and wafting perfume. I wondered where they were going in Sinop. Maybe they ended up at the party that seemed to go on for most of the night until around four o'clock in the morning near the pension, the sound of laughter and singing coming in through my window, which I had left open because of the heat and the smell. I thought I could detect Russian voices shouting and singing above the rest. It would not have been usual to hear Turks making such a drunken row into the early hours. It would have been considered a big disgrace. But I must say the party sounded rather fun.

It was not a good night. Apart from the stifling heat and the party, I was bitten by mosquitoes, which attacked me just like I had attacked the peaches earlier on. My anti-mosquito device had not connected properly when I had first plugged it in and the blue tablet was cold and useless. I managed to get it to work, although by then it was too late and I was covered in itching mosquito bites.

I got up feeling as if I had just gone to bed, manoeuvred the bicycle out of the room, wheeled her along the corridor and carried her down innumerable flights of stairs tucked under my arm, trying not to knock her against anything in case something else fell off. She was doing so well on the roads and yet I picked her up as if she were a baby and growled at anybody who even put out an inquisitive finger in her direction. I treated her well so she would look after me, but also because she was a very gentle bicycle. I leaned her against a wall and strapped on the bags carefully. I was hurrying as usual to beat the sun, which was already tingeing the sky with streaks of reddish pink. This was my favourite moment of the day, breathless with suspense, chasing away the shadows and the uneasy dreams of the night. Chords of Beethoven played in my head.

I headed back through Sinop the way I had come in, past the prison grim in the half-light. The town was awash with soldiers. They spilled like ants through the gates, ready for their tedious, daytime guard duty. I felt ashamed for mankind as I pedalled past in my relative freedom. The bus the day before had sped down a long, treeless hill into the bus station. I now had to cycle laboriously back up and continue on, past the turn to dreary old Ayancık, and head out eastwards towards Samsun around 170 kilometres or a hundred odd miles further along the coast. I knew I wasn't going to be able to reach Samsun in a day and wondered where I was going to spend the night. My first tea/soup stop came at Gerze twenty miles down the road from Sinop.

Gerze was an organised town, off the main road but set well back from the dangerous sea, with a town square and wide avenues radiating off it. The former town hall occupied the main corner of the square. It was a massive, picturesque, Ottoman building, but it was so wrecked, it looked as if it had been bombed. I wondered why the town hadn't had it pulled down. It looked extremely dangerous, as if it might collapse at the slightest puff of wind, certainly at the first major winter storm. On the other hand, if it were renovated, it would have been one of the most magnificent, historic buildings along the coast. The squat, concrete municipal buildings, which the town was no doubt so proud of, had been built almost opposite on the main avenue. I found an early morning soup house close by and went in for something to eat. Behind me in the restaurant sat a man who happily slurped his soup as if he were a baby with an enviable indifference to public opinion. He was enjoying his food so much it would have been a shame for him to have had to pretend otherwise.

With my soup slurping around heavily in my stomach, I returned to the square to ask the taxi drivers how the land lay ahead and what the towns further along the coast were like. 'Why don't you stay in Gerze?' one of the men asked. 'We have everything you can want here.' It was indeed a lovely town, I replied, and one of the best I had ever seen, but I wanted to cycle further on that day. What, I wondered, was Alaçam like? 'Don't go to Alaçam, it's a horrible place,' he said. Was there anything at Yakakent which was just before Alaçam? 'Pooh,' he sniffed, 'it's only a village, there's nothing there at all.'

They looked most unhappy I wasn't going to stay in Gerze, but I made my apologies and began to cycle back up the hill to rejoin the main road, passing a pide house. I propped the bicycle up on the high kerb outside and went in to order a large cheese and tomato pide to eat on the road later. I complimented them on how clean the town was and asked if I could use their toilet. A helpful little boy led me round the back to the dirtiest of dirty toilets. A slug was wandering around in the wet and ooze on the floor. It was the hugest of huge slugs. I balanced over the hole in the ground and tried to ignore it, hoping it wouldn't get in the way.

Back on the road, the plains disappeared and the trees and hills returned. Looking back over my shoulder, I could see Sinop sticking magnificently out into the sea on its headland and still visible after many miles. It was a beautiful sight and a beautiful day. The countryside was green and golden and I felt as if I were a bird flying along, wheeling and circling over the tiny houses and haycocks below. The hills crowded closer and closer together. Now the villagers raking in the hay far up on the heights above looked as if they could slip off the edge and tumble down on top of me. The land was cultivated in small patches and looked like a chessboard. I wanted to be a queen but I was only a pawn – or maybe even a prawn. I had a long way to go and many squares to cross before I could become a queen. My legs turned to jelly as I changed gear, pace and speed. I hung grimly on to the handlebars. The front light rattled like an old tooth in a dry, old socket. It didn't work any more; its wires had been pulled out when the mudguard broke. The bicycle was falling to pieces and so was I.

I kept running out of energy and had to keep stopping to re fuel as if I were a car, pouring into my system pide, chocolate, processed cheese, stale bread, black olives and water, gallons of it. There was endless, tiring disbelief and curiosity that day over the fact of a woman on a bicycle. I lost count of the number of dickmobiles, mainly lorries, which panted past, their drivers groaning out of the window. Fortunately, I could never understand what they were saying. I cheered myself up imagining. 'Mine's enormous, come and get it.' 'Come on darlin, fancy a quick one.' Sometimes a driver would pull over and stop just in front of me, his lorry juddering to an excited, abrupt halt, as, no doubt, any sex with him would have done. It would usually be on a hill or up a slope – I was convinced they deliberately picked the spot although in retrospect they probably didn't have the intelligence. There were just a lot of hills. I gritted my teeth, put my head down and pedalled painfully by, past the door they would always have hopefully open, trying not to run out of breath or stop. Often I would swing out, unconcerned about traffic coming in the opposite direction, hoping somebody would come by to rescue me, do something. I never looked at the drivers so I never knew what they looked like nor what they were doing. Nor what they actually wanted. I couldn't believe they really thought that I would stop there and then and have sex with them. They were living in a fantasy world, fuelled by foreign films and easily available pornographic magazines. It was on this road from Sinop that I cycled past one, its pages scattered over a particularly beautiful hedgerow of wild flowers. The explicit photographs appeared to be of blond, western women – of course. I cycled on feeling sick and apprehensive. I was probably more likely to be raped and murdered in Western Europe by a lunatic than in Turkey by those bored, frustrated men. Nevertheless, there was that fear of the possibility.

Towards Yakakent, the road snaked along high above the sea and, as I cycled around a bend, I came across a tea house in the middle of nowhere, built on the edge of a cliff underneath a clump of trees, with a long and shady verandah. A group of elderly men were sitting outside in companionable silence, watching the day go by. They politely tried not to stare as I cycled up, slipped off the saddle and leaned the bicycle against the railings. I said a general hullo and they responded enthusiastically with delighted smiles and welcomes, shouting to the man inside to bring me some tea quickly. I asked them about Yakakent. It was a reasonably sized little town with everything I might want there, they said. They laughed when I told them what the people of Gerze had said, loudly repeating it in case somebody in the group hadn't heard. I guessed my story would be one of the top tales of the week in their village. We were, at that point, only about twenty miles away from Gerze, but far away – or close enough – for local rivalries. I thought of Xenophon marching along with his men – not specifically here, of course, because they sailed by this part of the coast, but, generally, during his journey – and how the people of the settlements and towns they passed, which were not being plundered or threatened by the Greek mercenaries, must have hung on their every word, asking questions and making comparisons, going over and over the details about what they had seen and how they had been treated.

It was a lovely spot. I wished, for the thousandth time, I could stay a week and go walking into the hills around. I went to look at the sea view framed like a picture through the trees and the men liked that. 'It gets even better later on,' one man informed me. 'It will be more open.'

They paid for the tea. Those gentle, fine old men. They would have been so ashamed and mortified had I told them about the lorry drivers. I kept that story to myself.

As the man had said, the road did indeed dip down and run along the beach beside the sea, the cliffs crowding up behind, once again those incredible, cyclopean, rock formations. I was only a few miles from Yakakent when I passed a new pension set back from the road. It had individual cabins in a shady garden. It was opposite the beach and would make a good place to stay, rather than in a dump in an uninspiring town. I would be able to swim and sit in the sun. I went in to make enquiries and the obliging couple, who ran it, showed me one of the cabins. They were all equipped with shower rooms and had their own table and chairs allocated outside. If the cabins were unoccupied, the chairs were left leaning against the tables. Despite the fact that it was the weekend, it seemed very quiet although they told me they had one extended family staying who had been there for a week. I asked the price and it was reasonable, about £6. I said I would cycle into Yakakent down the road to get some things and return.

Despite what the taxi drivers of Gerze said, Yakakent turned out to be a busy and pleasant place, spread out along the coast and surrounded by fields. Its prosperity was based on tobacco and agriculture. Quantities of tobacco leaves were being sorted ready for drying. Along the street leading into the town off the main coastal road, entire families sat on rush mats outside their front doors with piles of shiny, olive green leaves in front of them. All the female members appeared to be involved, from mothers and grandmothers wearing headscarves and voluminous, floral patterned dresses, through to teenaged girls and toddlers. They were all occupied spearing the tobacco leaves onto long sticks. These were then hung up in rows to dry in the sun. Wherever you looked, you could see fence-like structures of tobacco leaves. As well as the tobacco, yellow corn on the cob had been laid out in rows on trestle tables and on low roofs. There was an active, prosperous air about Yakakent, so different from some of the other places I had been through. The street was dusty with building work going on. Shops and new blocks of buildings were going up everywhere. It was busy too. I had to keep pulling over to let vans and lorries pass by.

The road led straight into the town square overlooking the sea. There was a hotel on the corner. It looked rather pleasant. I balanced my bicycle against a lamp-post, crossed the street to a greengrocer's and stood admiring the boxes and crates of fruit: yellow apricots, plums, oranges, melon and red cherries, and the vegetables: smooth, green, chilli peppers, glossy black aubergines, salad cucumbers, potatoes and tomatoes and enormous bunches of fresh parsley. It was piled high in the shop and overflowed outside onto the pavement. Just looking at a Turkish food shop gives one a sense of well-being. I asked the greengrocer, as an expert, to pick me out a melon that would be good to eat that day. He was aloof and reserved but I knew he was pleased to be asked. The next stop was a general store to buy some shampoo, cream biscuits and a bottle of red wine. The store man nodded approvingly when I bought a handful of pistachio nuts. The Turks always eat nuts whatever they do and especially when they drink any alcohol, including, of course, rakı or arrack, the national aniseed drink, similar to the Greek ouzo or the French absinthe. The man carefully wrapped up the items in newspaper, paying particular attention to the bottle of wine to disguise it from prying eyes. Turkish shopkeepers do this as a matter of routine.

He added up my total on a pocket computer and showed it to me. It was absolutely correct.

'Where have you come from?' he asked

'From England but I've only cycled from İstanbul.'

He looked amazed and admiring, clear eyed and honest – another refreshing antidote to the memory of the pop-eyed, lorry drivers.

My bags were so heavy with the goodies that I cycled back slowly, wobbling slightly, buzzed every so often by boys on new, mountain bikes, who darted in front of me like swallows. They wanted to make sure I knew they were going a lot faster than I was. I ignored them but I felt that, unlike on some occasions, they were not doing it maliciously, merely out of high spirits. I had good feelings about the industrious people of Yakakent.

Back at base, I unpacked my stuff and went to use the bathroom. No water could be coaxed out of the shower. The woman showed me a bigger room with a double bed and went into the bathroom to try the shower there. Water came out although it was tepid. She looked at me anxiously. 'It'll be fine,' I said, and her face visibly relaxed. (I did not complain later when I discovered, on flushing the toilet, that water poured out from the back all over the floor.) I was very happy opening the window to let the sound of the sea slip inside, arranging my things, washing my cycling clothes in a deep, old-fashioned, white enamel sink in the room and opening the bottle of wine, coughing carefully to cover up the sound of the cork popping out. I had to go into the restaurant to ask for a glass. 'It's for water,' I said, lying through my teeth, and skipped back to my den.

I sat outside my room at my table to read, carefully arranging the three other chairs, which went with my room, into their proper sitting position, instead of leaning up against the table. It looked more comfortable that way, less solitary. It was still relatively early in the day. I was rich with oceans of time. The bottle of wine and the glass were still inside the room, fortunately, because at that moment, the man of the establishment walked up and sat down opposite me, uninvited. I wondered if he was checking me out (Natasha!?), and how long he intended staying. My oceans of time were not to be wasted and my glass of wine needed drinking. His eyes looked slightly shifty. The eyes as ever tell all. If only people knew that. He asked me the usual questions, where I was from, where I was going etc. And then it was my turn to ask a question – on behalf of two of my friends in Ankara. They had been operating as a couple for years, although the girl did not dare tell her parents about the situation. She always asked me to check out possible places where she might be able to stay with her partner. It was very difficult for unmarried Turkish lovers to go away and stay together in one room. There were understanding pension and hotel owners but they were few and far between. Foreigners could do anything they liked, of course. After all, they were not Muslim (largely) and therefore beyond redemption, although if one of the pair were Turkish, the same difficulty could arise. I thought I would try out my pension owner.

'I have some friends in Ankara who would possibly like to come and stay,' I said. He looked enthusiastic. 'They aren't married,' I went on. His face fell and he shuffled his feet under the table.

'This is a family pension,' he said. 'It would be difficult.'

'They've known each other for years. They're very respectable. They're both professional people.'

He thought for a bit. 'I'll do what I can if they come,' he said, and handed me a business card. He looked embarrassed and I knew he didn't mean it. I never passed on the card.

As soon as he had gone, I made lunch, cutting into the melon, which was ripe and juicy and immediately attracted the ants for miles around. I arranged the olives and cheese and put the beaded glass of Buzbağ winking at the brim out of sight on a chair. There was nobody else about. The bicycle snoozed inside the room, propped up against the wall under the window. After I had finished, I hung the melon up from a hook inside the room, hoping the ants couldn't climb up to get it, concealed the bottle of wine in a dark corner in case anybody spied through the window, and went off to the beach over the road. A couple of women and children were bobbing in the sea but otherwise the beach was empty. The white, plastic tables and whirly umbrellas looked rather forlorn and miserable, like unused, theatrical props gathering dust back-stage. Sadly, it was clouding over but I arranged myself over the stones, trying to keep out of sight of the road. One driver had a quick yell as he thundered past, a white-hot blast from the hungry furnace, before the door slammed shut again.

I joined the people in the sea – they welcomed me smiling – and admired the panorama of the green hills stacked up along the coast. But it wasn't long before the rain started, the drops plopping warm into the water. I missed the sun. I remembered my clothes hanging up to dry on the washing line in the garden and hurried back. The bottle of wine came in useful that afternoon, with the weather unable to make up its mind whether to rain or shine. I sipped my glass slowly, sitting outside under the overhanging roof of the cabin, reading my book and keeping an eye on the ants.

There were no other customers that evening in the restaurant and I sat in isolated splendour at a table set up for me at my request on the top of the roof with a panoramic view over the sea. There was not much activity there either. Apart from a few fishing boats and the odd tanker on the horizon, the Black Sea was not a busy sea, at least off the Turkish coast. I got film star treatment from the young boy in charge of the lack of customers that evening. With slavish devotion, he brought me the inevitably greasy balls of meat, lonely on a large plate underneath a garnish of parsley, and a tired salad. He watched my every move. It was horrible. When I went to look at the jungle-like tangle of trees magnificent on the hillside rising sheer from the back of the restaurant, he was there in my footsteps like a small ghost. When I gazed out at the horizon turning orange in the setting sun, his eyes occupied my eye space. He almost held my fork while I ate the meat balls, except that at that point, I told him I wanted to read and he could go and do something else somewhere else.

Downstairs, as I paid the bill, I noticed a poster advertising Tuborg beer pinned up in the restaurant. The lady in the photograph doing the selling was a topless, voluptuous, blond European. I remembered my conversation earlier that day with the shifty owner about how his pension was for 'families' and his worry about the effect on the family atmosphere if my unmarried friends came to stay. What a moral confusion.

Back safely in my cabin and away from prying eyes, I finished off the wine, washed out the glass to conceal any traces of red and wrapped up the bottle to take with me in the morning to be disposed of elsewhere. I wasn't going to contribute any more than I had done already to the 'confusion.'

9
Yakakent to Samsun

When, however, he reflected that no man can tell what the future will bring, and that for this reason there was a risk of losing even the reputation which he had won already, then he became uncertain what to do.

The alarm bleeped at 4.15. I leaped out of bed before I could get depressed, untied the melon and finished it off outside, dripping the sugary juice onto the tired shrubs struggling in the rock-hard ground outside the cabins. A couple of lorries roared by, their driver cabs and sides glowing with rows of lights. Emerging out of the dark of the night, they looked like many-eyed monsters from the ancient Greek legends. They were going fast and I hoped I wouldn't be squashed before dawn would come and make me more visible. A little way down the road was a dustbin and I deposited my empty, wine bottle inside feeling like a criminal.

I fairly flew along, past Yakakent and the fence-like structures of drying tobacco leaves and on eastwards into new territory in the direction of Samsun, the largest town on the Turkish Black Sea coast. It was nearly fifty-five miles away, eighty-six kilometres, but I felt confident I could easily cover the distance in a day. According to the map, the road cut through well-watered plains, the foothills rising to mountain heights further inland. I cycled through field after field of tobacco plants, the dense masses of olive green leaves relieved by the pretty, pinky white, trumpet flowers. People were already up and picking. Most people smoked in Turkey but even the Turks were becoming more health conscious. Smoking had been banned on transport within towns – something that would have been considered impossible just a few years before. Even the big, long-distance coaches now had no smoking areas downstairs, although the driver usually chain-smoked leaning out of the window. Many government offices had 'no smoking' signs up and some even meant it. If smoking ever did become a minority habit or was even banned altogether, the economic consequences in the Black Sea area of Turkey could be profound, although there were alternative industries. I lost count of the number of flour, rice and sunflower oil mills I passed that day.

The road was flat and uninspiring with bad surfaces, smashed and holed. The traffic was very busy. Lorries pounded along in both directions, belching out poisonous fumes from their obscenely enormous exhaust pipes. I thought wistfully of the beautiful, empty countryside I was leaving behind me. In no time at all and with thoughts of a tea stop, I reached the turning to the town of Alacağım. A barely legible sign pointed from the crumbling crossroads to what

I was sure would be a depressed city centre. I carried straight on to Bafra.

'Welcome to Bafra, welcome to our town of Bafra', shouted the signposts proudly as I cycled in over an iron bridge spanning the Kızılırmak, the Red River, the Halys of antiquity. But my brief passage through Bafra was not a happy experience. It was a drab, crumbling, rubbish-strewn town. There were half-built concrete apartment blocks everywhere and the roads were mounds of melting tarmac. It was difficult to look around because I was so busy trying to keep my bicycle from slipping off the whorls of tarmac and under the wheels of the lorries. 'Get me out of here,' she muttered. The main road up the steep hill out of Bafra was being re-surfaced. I stood at the bottom, the bicycle leaning weakly against me, or the other way round, and we stared upwards, literally upwards, at what was in effect a long, steep ramp. The workmen had poured quantities of shiny black, glutinous tarmac over it. This had made the new surface at least a foot higher than the old. It looked more like a ski slope than a road. There was no question of even trying to cycle up it. I clambered on to the slope, lifted the bicycle up beside me, and tried to walk to the top. The tarmac was melting so badly it was as if I were walking through sticky glue. It was a bit like being in one of those nightmares when you try to move but your feet are weighed down by a sinister, magic force. It was impossible to negotiate. The other carriageway was as yet untouched by the workmen, so I lowered the bicycle down onto it and stepped down beside her. I then picked her up, tottered over to the verge on the far side and began to push her up the hill, hoping the oncoming traffic wouldn't swerve and come crashing into us.

A quarter of the way up, I was aware of a young man on a bicycle on the new bit of the road. He was looking over at me to see if I was looking at him. He was pedalling madly, showing off to the foreign woman who had been unable to cope. I could see that his wheels were sticking and that it was getting more and more difficult for him to move forward, although he was desperately pretending otherwise. Suddenly, it was too much for him and he fell ignominiously off the edge of the road. Oh happy, happy moment. He dismounted and, without looking round, continued up the ramp pushing his bicycle. His hunched back looked embarrassed and discomforted. He could scarcely even walk through the glue-like tarmac. He was like a fly stuck in a web. I wished a spider would come and eat him. Towards the top, I got back on the saddle and, slipping into my lowest gear, gleefully cycled upwards, over the hill and away, leaving him far, far behind.

I stopped to celebrate my victory at a tea house attached to a petrol garage, sitting down at a table outside along with a group of lorry drivers. They plied me with tea and asked the usual questions. I told them I was English.

'I know your Prime Minister,' said one. 'It's Mrs Tatcherrrr,' and he laughed uproariously.

'Not any longer,' I said quickly. 'We've got somebody else now. It's Tony Blair.'

'Is it a man or a woman?' he asked.

'A man,' I said.

'And what about Diana,' he continued with an even wickeder smile, 'Olay kadın!'

Those two words said it all in Turkish, although it needed a much longer phrase or sentence to translate it into English. He had called the Princess of Wales something like 'that phenomenal woman', or 'the woman to whom many things happen'. 'The event-filled woman'. It was my turn to laugh. It was such a good description of Diana. I didn't know it then, but the biggest and saddest 'event' was just a month or so away.

'I'll write that down,' I told the man. 'It's the best description I've ever heard of her.'

He beamed with pleasure and bought me yet another glass of tea. They looked rough men but they were extremely kind and polite and I decided that none of them were among the ones who had roared at me like bulls on heat from their lorry cabs. They waved me off towards Samsun.

'Don't forget. Olay Kadın,' said my friend.

It was about another thirty-five miles to Samsun and I cycled fairly easily along the uninspiring road, which hugged the coastline. I lost count of the assorted small boys whose eyes lit up when they saw me passing by, small knights who whizzed out of the bushes on their steeds to match theirs against mine and then, no doubt, rushed back home to tell mum all about their adventure and that funny, old, foreign woman.

I wondered what Samsun was going to be like. I had a vague recollection of passing through years before when I had a four-hour wait at the bus station. I recalled trying to walk down to the sea but getting lost in a confusion of unfinished buildings and smashed roads. Back at the bus station I had been entertained by two men having a monumental argument. Their voices were loud and furious as if they were about to murder each other – until one of the pair caught my rather frightened eye observing them and, winking at me, he burst out laughing.

Samsun had grown since those days and the busy suburbs and peripheral roads appeared to stretch on forever. It seemed to take longer to reach the heart of the city than it had to cycle there from Bafra. When I finally arrived, I found they were still building Samsun's roads. The entire city was a nightmare of construction work. Every major route had been torn up by giant earthmovers; raw roundabouts loomed like giant mole hills and squares and entire pavements were being re-tiled. I got off the bicycle, wheeled her through mounds of rubble and queues of overheating cars and lorries, and slipped into a quiet, back street which, I guessed, would lead towards the centre and the hotel area.

It was a relief to get out of the dust and the din and the angry traffic jams –
the Turks are furiously impatient drivers. The shops in the narrow street all
seemed to sell spare parts for motor vehicles, men-only stuff. I was sure that no
woman had walked down that street for years, if ever. An elderly, bearded shopkeeper closed his eyes in dismayed horror and sighed 'Allah, Allah,' as I passed
slowly by, pushing the bicycle. I ignored him. I stopped a bit further up to ask
about the hotel potential and was waved onwards. The first hotel I got to wanted
quite a lot of dollars for a room with a shower, a cable television and breakfast
the next morning. Its card declared it was 'the first name for comfort'. Another
hotel round the corner, Otel Sandıkçı, 'your home in Samsun', offered me a room
with a double bed, a television and a clean shower room. (I later discovered that
I couldn't sit on the toilet properly because the wall got in the way and for most
of the time the water was cold, although Samsun was so hot and sticky, hot water
wasn't really necessary.) The charge was £6 and they didn't mind when I carried
the bicycle upstairs to park her safely in the room. I had covered the flat journey
from Yakakent in a few hours. The whole day stretched ahead, plenty of time to
explore.

Samsun started out as ancient Amisus, dating back more than 2,500 years.
The town was regularly besieged, captured and sacked and in the fifteenth
century the Genoese burned it to the ground rather than hand it over to the
Ottoman Turks. My copy of *Johnston's General Gazetteer*, which was printed in
1877, described Samsun as a sea port in Asia Minor with a lighthouse fifty-six
feet high and a population of 2,000. The town, it wrote, was an entrepôt for the
copper, timber, wheat, barley, tobacco and agricultural produce from the
interior, which was exported to Constantinople. It also recorded the fact that the
packet steamers of the Austrian Danube Steam Navigation Company sailed
backwards and forwards between Samsun and Trebizond (Trabzon).

Samsun's claim to twentieth century fame occurred when Atatürk sailed in
to the small, dusty port on 19 May 1919, (the date became his official birthday),
to begin organising the Turks into a national resistance army which, against all
the odds, would go on to liberate the country from the occupying Western forces.
The start of Turkey's war of independence was counted from that important day.

In 1997, Samsun had a population of more than 300,000 and it seemed as if
they had all gone down town that morning to go shopping. I had taken a shower
to wash the petrol fumes out of my hair and off my skin. It was an all-pervasive
smell, tasting unpleasant in the mouth and acid on the lips. I went outside,
stepping from the shade of the hotel lobby into the white heat of the day, which
hit me over the head and stabbed me between the eyes like a mugger leaping out
from behind a corner. The narrow streets were jam-packed, a big Turkish city
going about its business. I felt overwhelmed, like a country cousin visiting the
flesh-pot metropolis for the first time. The food markets were close by and I took

refuge in a börek place on the corner, down the steps inside, tucking myself up on a bench at a table so I could look up and out of the window at the food shoppers buying kilos of potatoes, tomatoes and onions and stuffing whole bunches of parsley into plastic carrier bags. Displayed in the window were mountains of fresh börek, the pastry flaky and golden brown. The man was slicing it up with his spatula and handing it out to customers at an incredible rate. He sliced up a big plateful of minced meat börek and placed it before me, shrugging when I told him it was far too much. It was hot and delicious and I ate it all. I had lost so much weight, I felt as if my body needed something substantial to work on. I drank glass after glass of water, unable to quench my thirst. The börekçi was handing out glasses of lemon and he brought one for me. It was ice cold and not too sweet. Sublimely delicious. A telephone rang constantly in the shop. The calls were from customers ordering platefuls of börek. These were neatly packed up and dispatched off. I had obviously picked a popular börek house. This man was running an empire, apparently single-handed, from this tiny hole-in-the-wall corner café. He charged me virtually nothing for my lovely breakfast.

Outside, the stallholders were in desperate competition. The sun was overhead and it was almost the hottest hour of the day. They wanted to sell as much as they could before everybody went home for the afternoon. The bargains were fast and furious, peaches and cherries at give-away prices if one bought enough of them. I invested in a kilo of cherries and began to eat them despite the mounds of börek I had just consumed. I was heading for the main square in Samsun, Cumhuriyet Meydanı or Republic Square, from where I was sure I would be able to locate Samsun's assorted Atatürk museums.

I walked slowly, enjoying the Turkishness of the streets and the Turks themselves. These extraordinary people, originally from the steppes of Central Asia, outwardly cool and reserved, inwardly intensely emotional and sensitive, eternally optimistic and energetic, curious and proud. Their imagination springs from the Thousand and One Nights, a creative force which they share with the Persians and the Arabs. Anything and everything is possible. The magic was visible everywhere in the most down-at-heel streets where an ordinary stationer's shop was 'the writing palace', a furniture shop sold 'diadem furniture' and a sweet shop was a true 'emporium of delight'. If they did not sell whatever you wished for, they would jump on their magic carpet, hand-made in Kayseri, special price for you, and fly to the ends of the earth to find it – at a price, of course.

On the way to Cumhuriyet Meydanı, I passed a Turkish Airlines office and went in to ask the price of a ticket from Trabzon back to İstanbul. The cost was around £40. I thought of the Austrian Steam Packet and remembered one of my friends in İstanbul reminding me before I left about the ships that still sailed along the Black Sea coast and provided a passenger service back to İstanbul. The girl in the office said there was a service once a week although she didn't have the details. At least, I thought, I could get back to İstanbul somehow. I told her about the bicycle and she laughed and shouted across the office to tell her colleague.

'Aren't you frightened?' she asked.

'A lot of the time,' I said. 'It's the lorry drivers. They shout at me.'

'They don't just shout at you,' she said, 'they shout at women who drive cars too.' We laughed conspiratorially over the stupidity of men. It made me feel better.

Cumhuriyet Meydanı was just round the corner, an enormous crash-box of a square around which streams of traffic screamed and hooted. There was a caravan in the middle of a small park. It called itself 'Tourist Information'. The windows and doorway were draped with thick, impenetrable, net curtains and I walked round and round feeling rather silly. In the end I screamed through the net door and a woman emerged. I asked her where Atatürk's museum was. She flapped her hand behind her in the direction of the sea and disappeared inside again.

I made my way through the inevitable roadworks, crunching over the unfinished pavements. It smelled as if the workmen had smashed up the drains as well because the stench of toilets and their unpleasant contents filled the air. It was hot, dirty and uncomfortable and my gloom deepened when I located the museum complex, a group of long, low buildings, in what looked like a rubbish dump. Two women were sitting on a bench in the middle of it all. They looked totally unconcerned about the mess lapping round their feet and even seemed surprised when I mentioned it. They're re-landscaping everything, they told me, and invited me to sit down and talk to them. The museum had shut for lunch and would re-open after an hour. I asked the women about another museum in Samsun that I had read about. It was a house that had belonged to a Greek family. On his arrival in Samsun in 1919, Atatürk requisitioned the house and stayed there during his momentous visit. The ladies told me it was shut for renovation work.

They were elegantly dressed women with immaculate make-up, probably middle-aged although they looked younger. They asked me where I had come from and why I was alone. I told them I was from England and wasn't married. They laughed appreciatively. Did I have any problems travelling alone? they asked. I told them about the lorry drivers and about being stared at so much in the streets. 'They are the men with moustaches,' said one, and she drew an imaginary, thick line over her lips with her finger, pulling a face at the same time.

She was depicting the clichéd image of the heavily moustachioed and traditional-thinking, Anatolian Turk, whose wife wears a headscarf and has a lot of children – anathema to the modern and independently minded women of Turkey. The arabesque singers of Turkey, like the golden-voiced İbrahim Tatlıses – oooh my soooul, my love, my passion, 'canım', 'aşkım' – all sported enormous, black moustaches. It is so easy to generalise, we do it all the time, although I am uneasy about negative generalisations. But the two women, who were obviously enjoying this chance encounter on a park bench in Samsun that lunchtime, looked so mischievous and naughty as they laughed at the picture that had been painted that I laughed too. Just then one of the curators inside the museum, who had a large moustache, hammered on a glass door and made drinking motions with his hand. He was offering to bring us some tea while we waited for the museum to open. This, I observed, would never happen in England. 'This is Turkey,' said the woman who had made fun of the traditional Turkish man. 'We are very kind to each other, because we like each other.'

There was still some time before the museum opened so I went to look at the sea, which, as far as I could make out, was close by across a road. It turned out to be a hot, uncomfortable and dirty walk, negotiating my way through a vast parking area along a sea front crowded with taxis and the ubiquitous Turkish dolmuş, which are a cross between a shared taxi and a mini bus. Even after that, the sea was still invisible, hidden behind high, ramshackle fences and concrete walls. This appeared to be the closest point to the sea from the heart of the biggest town along the Black Sea coast and you couldn't even see it, let alone get to it. I managed to find a low fence to peer over. The sea beneath looked and smelled like a sewer, not so much washing up against the shore as gurgling up, brown, thick and evil. Just twenty two years before, Fodor's *Turkey 1975* had described the Samsun coastline as 'one long sweep of beach, with fine white sand.'

I sweated back through the rows and rows of dolmuş, sizzling hot in the sun, ignoring the curious stares of the bored drivers, and decided to make a circle back to the museum. This was a mistake given the position of the sun overhead and the quantities of dust and filth in the air from the road works. However, I did get to see from a distance at least Samsun's Culture Palace, the town's new arts centre for ballet, concerts, theatre and opera. It was the most extraordinary building constructed in enormous, circular slopes near the waterfront. The *Lonely Planet* very neatly described it as a 'celestial ski jump'. It was probably this building, more than any other in Samsun, which gave a clue to the complexion of the city's administration. The town hall was run by the Republican People's Party whose national leader was the good-humoured and fiercely ambitious Deniz Baykal. His was a left of centre, staunchly secular party. This explained the mountains of roadworks in the town centre and the renovation work being carried out on the house once used by Atatürk.

It was a relief to slip out of the sun and into the museum, which had finally opened its doors. My two lady friends had disappeared and I had the place all to myself apart from the curator, who was delighted somebody, and a foreigner at that, had come to look round. He directed me into a room off the entrance hall. It was crammed with massive pieces of solid furniture, heavy, mahogany tables with carved legs and antique leather chairs. The seats were bursting open, the stuffing inside spilling out. This was some of the furniture from Atatürk's town house while it was being renovated. I was able to run my fingers over the polished table tops and, if had I wanted to, the proud curator would have let me sit down on the chairs. It was extraordinary. Being an Atatürk fan, I was overwhelmed. I had fallen in awe years ago, smitten by the image of a strong, intense, clever man with vision and energy, who could drink, talk and make love all night and still begin working early in the morning; a man who united a country out of the pieces of a centuries-old empire and outwitted and outfought his enemies who wanted to carve up Anatolia to their own agenda.

There were two particularly precious books in my bookcase at home. They were collections of British government documents on Atatürk (at that time still known as Mustapha Kemal) written in 1919 and 1920. I found them on the shelves of a tiny, second-hand bookshop in Beyoğlu in İstanbul. Atatürk flitted through the pages like the Turkish incarnation of the Scarlet Pimpernel, misunderstood and underestimated. Just seven months after he raised his standard in Samsun, Sir J. de Robeck, an admiral and a British High Commissioner, had written to Earl Curzon in December 1919 from Constantinople:

'I have the honour to inform your Lordship that although the National movement under Mustafa Kemal has overrun the whole of Turkey, it has in certain districts met with determined opposition on the part of the inhabitants . . . It is to my mind clear the Nationalists have at present no strong support in the general population of Anatolia.'

The British opinion of Atatürk had certainly changed by 1948. The former British Ambassador to Turkey, Sir Percy Loraine, paid glowing tribute to him in a broadcast on the BBC on 10 November 1948 to mark the tenth anniversary of Atatürk's death. He was 'a very remarkable man', said Sir Percy, fearless, with absolute integrity, self-discipline and a clear vision. His military career had been 'brilliant'; he had liberated the minds of the Turkish people and the view of him as a dictator was 'mistaken and misleading'.

Sadly, the museum in Samsun could not match the ones in Ankara. There were the usual photographs and lists of what Atatürk did and when. Some of his personal effects were displayed in glass cases, crisply starched and embroidered shirts, gleaming leather shoes and a large shaving box complete with bottles and brushes. And that was it. I had hoped for photographs and mementoes of that momentous visit to Samsun seventy-eight years previously. I wanted pictures of 'the rickety wooden jetties, striking out through the shallow water, which were the small port's apology for a quay,' as described by Patrick Kinross.

I skipped the Archaeological and Ethnological Museum next door with its Byzantine and Hittite remains and went back to Cumhuriyet Meydanı to collapse in the park on a red and white painted bench in the shade, appropriately opposite a statue of Atatürk astride a rearing horse. A pigeon perched on his peaked cap. Bold pigeon. The day was extremely hot and my fingers were swollen like extra pork-filled sausages. The park was crowded and people were queuing up to drink from the water fountains. Entire families perambulated past. Some of the women wore headscarves, long skirts and coats. How hot they must have been, I thought, although they looked comfortable enough. Others were dressed in jeans or summer dresses. Old men, crammed together tightly on park benches like kippers in a tin, shook their heads over the way of the world in the safety of the shade. Shoe shine boys prowled for business and street cleaners swept furiously at the dust. There were people selling a variety of snacks, pink, sugar-spun, candy floss, ice-creams, freshly-boiled corn on the cob and speckled simits. The tea boys walked around rattling their tin trays. Several men carrying old-fashioned cameras under their arms wandered around looking for willing subjects with money. One cool cat in shades, wearing tight, black jeans and a black shirt, posed in front of Atatürk's statue. He crouched down so the photographer could find an angle to get the whole of the statue into the background of the picture. He obviously wanted the teenaged girls, self-consciously tossing their long hair and wandering past arm in arm, to look at him. He removed his sun glasses to laugh over the photograph with his friends and suddenly the cool cat turned into a fresh-faced boy who was very pleased with himself. No doubt he would give the picture to his mother later on and she would put it up on the sitting room wall with the other family photographs. I noticed several beggars, who included an old woman dragging herself around the benches and a distraught young man who talked to himself and laughed aloud. Later, I saw a deformed man balanced on a street corner, apparently with no arms or legs. The Turks are generous and usually give small sums of money unostentatiously.

I made my way back to the hotel, passing Atatürk's house at the top of the square. It was an elegant, double-storied building that had been freshly painted. A sign outside announced that it was being restored. It stood out, like a ghost from the past, among the concrete blocks and shops of new Samsun. In Atatürk's time, it would have faced straight down to the sea. I flitted like a ghost in and out of the shadows down the streets back to my hotel, stopping to buy an ice lolly which I ate along with what remained of my kilo of cherries. After that, I collapsed on the bed for the rest of that hot, lazy afternoon. It wasn't so much a sleep as a dip into unconsciousness. This was becoming a regular occurrence. I emerged from the depths with the usual roaring in my ears that gradually subsided as everyday noises took over. It was a phenomenon that seemed to happen when I was in big cities or had been cycling long distances along busy roads. The poisonous petrol fumes no doubt had something to do with these sudden complete losses of energy.

When it was cooler, I thought I would give the sea front at Samsun one last try, and made my way back down to the sea, through some of the oldest alleyways in the city. The narrow lanes were shaded with leafy vines which had been trained over wooden trelliswork and tied on with string and wire so that they covered the street in the summer. The vines filtered the sunlight and only the odd wink or sparkle could get through. I explained to a helpful tea shop owner that I wanted a view, an open view, of the sea from Samsun. He told me to go to the port. I could get a dolmuş just around the corner. It was only a five-minute journey. I decided to walk. It was still very warm and I found myself picking a rather unpleasant way through more dug-up roads and bus parks and past a tangle of railways and sidings which seemed to go on for miles. As I got closer to the port, I passed shops and offices stacked with crates and sacks stuffed with goods that were either to be exported or distributed in Turkey. In one ancient warehouse, boxes of brown eggs were piled to the ceiling.

The man at the barrier across the unimposing port entrance wanted to see my passport and then, unexpectedly, asked me which university I had attended in England.

'York University,' I said, wondering why on earth this was significant. He thought I had said 'Yok' which is an all-purpose negative in Turkish.

'So you didn't go,' he said.

'No, I went to York,' I said.

'Yok?' he said and looked puzzled.

I felt hysterical. It was like a Morecambe and Wise double act. All I wanted to do, I said, was to go and look at the view. He smiled – ha, a very crazy foreigner – and waved me through the gate, after I had handed over my passport in case I decided to smuggle myself onto a container ship on the way to Georgia. I went down to the sea front, feeling dwarfed and squeezed by the port buildings on all sides, and peered out from the water's edge at the sludgy sea and the grey storage depots and grey cranes and felt like Shirley Valentine had when she sat on the beach and watched the sun go down: a bloody fool. I stood there admiring the non-view for a second or two, trudged back to the barrier to collect my passport and scuttled back into town.

The streets of Samsun were packing up business for the day. Earlier I had seen dozens of small restaurants dotted around the food market area but now I couldn't find one. As I walked backwards and forwards, I was excruciatingly aware of curious eyes following my every move. One shop keeper said 'bicycle' and 'on her own' to another. Obviously my movements had been tracked all day. I became painfully self-conscious. Whenever I looked, they looked. I stopped, they stopped. I mused, they mused. I smiled, they smiled. I stopped outside a restaurant. It was empty and dark, the spit in the window on which the lamb turns was motionless and bare.

'What are you looking for?' said a sharp waiter, coming outside.

'I was hoping for an İskender kebab,' I said.

'We can do that,' he said. 'Come in.'

I went in dubiously, wondering whether there were still bits of spitted lamb somewhere which they could work on. I was glad to get off the stage, away from the eyes watching me. The waiter began to put a great deal of effort into chopping something up and I went to look, still doubtful about how it could magically turn into a delicious, sizzling İskender kebab. He was chopping up a tiny amount of flabby chicken. I wouldn't have given it to a cat.

'İskender kebab!' I said, furiously. "With lamb!"

He looked unruffled. 'With chicken,' he said.

'Chicken! Yok!'

I left him still chopping and headed back to the hotel where I asked the man at the front desk to recommend a restaurant. He told me exactly where to go, back to the food markets, close by the clock tower and wrote down the name on a piece of paper so there would be no mistake. Tell them you come from the Otel Sandıkçı, he said. I retraced my steps for the nineteenth time and found the restaurant as he had described. There was no spitted lamb but they could offer an Adana kebab. This is a good alternative to the İskender dish and comes with strips of lamb, a dollop of yoghurt and tomatoes, but without the bed of pitta bread. After they had taken my order and then served me, I was completely ignored. This suited me fine. Everybody was busy listening to an almighty row between the owner, who looked like the godfather, and a white-faced young man who had obviously done something seriously wrong. The godfather was shouting too quickly and loudly for me to be able to understand exactly what. He was making gestures with his hands while the young man sat in front of him with his head hanging down. I think family honour was being invoked and money could have been involved because the godfather kept picking up notes from the till and throwing them down again contemptuously. And then, suddenly, it was all over. The godfather had had his say and the young man had grovelled and kissed his hand respectfully and promised never to do it again.

The storm inside the restaurant had blown over, but the one outside was brewing up. It was stiflingly hot and the sky had turned a threatening, thunderous black. I could smell the rain coming. I was getting used to these swinging Black Sea moods, sunny one moment and in a towering temper the next. Even as the clouds came over, it began to rain, quickly turning into a torrential downpour. In no time at all, the road outside had flooded and the passing traffic threw up sheets of water which further soaked any unfortunate passers by. I looked sadly at the sandals I was wearing. I stood in the doorway hoping the storm would ease, taking in the fresh smell of the rain and the cool wetness of the air. I made a dash back to the hotel, darting in and out of shop doorways and under overhanging roofs, jumping like a kid over the puddles. It was fun. By then, I didn't care who was watching.

Back safely in the room with the bicycle tucked up in a corner no doubt dreaming of lovely green hills and smooth road surfaces, I felt practically at home. I leaned out of the window, listened to the rain beating on the shop canopies and watched the cars inching through the swirling floods. Later, I watched the news on Show TV, which was, as usual, a breathless, American-style romp through all the unpleasant things that had happened in Turkey that day: fatal car crashes, gas explosions, police raids, the latest political scandal, all interspersed with tasters for more sensational news coming up. It was like a kaleidoscope of horrors, shake the tin and rearrange the pictures. Turkish television did not hold back from showing the most graphic scenes. On the car crash stories, the cameraman was right there thrusting his lens through the window into the face of the smashed up, possibly dead person, who was being cut free. There was something mesmerising about those pictures. It was very difficult not to stare in fascination and so I went to bed that night with death, doom and destruction.

10
Samsun to Ünye

So he brought two victims to the altar and made a sacrifice to Zeus the King, who had been declared by the oracle at Delphi to be the god whom he ought to consult.

The calls to prayer from the mosques nearby were particularly loud in Samsun, so I was awake before the alarm clock went off. Outside, the floods in the road had largely subsided and I felt that familiar sense of urgency and excitement as I got back on the saddle to shoot off like a Greek arrow through the dark streets, easily negotiating the roadworks at that early hour, heading off eastwards. I passed the bus station slightly out of town. I was sure it was in the same place as when I had visited some years before. Was I still there somewhere waiting for the bus? My younger, former self. The derelict area of land opposite across the road beside the sea was being planted with palm trees. Their little heads were silhouetted against the sky in the glimmering dawn, tiny beacons of hope. The city council was building a park out of the wasteland.

My destination that day was the small town of Ünye. It was about the same distance away from Samsun as I had covered the day before. Looking at the map, the road cut directly across the widest part of the Black Sea coastal plains, crossing over the Yeşilırmak, the Green River – the river Iris as it was known to the ancient Greeks – and catching up with the coast again a few miles before Ünye. We sped along out of Samsun over a wonderful, brand-new, three-lane highway, smooth and easy, the bicycle transformed into a white charger out of the legends, galloping along, its mane streaming in the wind – until the new bit of road ran out and we hit the old. It was a disaster, a crisis, a bike-breaking, shuddering, juddering horror. The road melted into sticky, gluey tarmac, some of which had lapped up against the sides and was hardening into lumps and mini hills over which I crashed and slipped, pulling sharply on the brakes to try to control the sudden drops down. In places it could hardly have been called a road, more a stretch of bubbling blackness spilling over the ground like volcanic lava and shining with a dazzling brightness in the early morning sun rising directly ahead. There was no point in anybody keeping to the rules and driving neatly in line on the right. It was every vehicle for itself, the drivers weaving a way around the obstacle course, trying to keep their wheels out of the potholes.

It was difficult to believe that this was the main road along the coast of the Black Sea and not just some unimportant, unused, back route. The traffic was by now a steady stream of lorries and cars, all going as fast as they possibly could, travelling nose to tail, furious and impatient with the conditions, incredulous at seeing a foreign bicycle in the middle of such chaos. I kept breathing in as they passed to give them more space, as if that would have made any difference. It was purely involuntary. Had the surface been reasonable, I could at least have kept close to the side but the uneven and unpredictable road made that impossible. Sometimes I took a chance and swung out to avoid a particularly bad chunk, sometimes I slowed down, almost stopping, to be able to guide the front wheel gently down over a ski slope or two, and sometimes I stopped altogether, sweating and shaking and waiting until there was a break in the traffic. The hooting and shouting and the noise of roaring engines was incredible. Another problem was the impact of the slipstream, which hit me in the face and on the side of the head, like a physical blow.

And then there were the manic, barking dogs. There had already been a few unpleasant short, sharp encounters with dogs up in the hills. One had chased me up a slope at the crack of dawn, running away when I threw stones, only to creep back silently as I started to pedal away again. A sixth sense had made me turn round and there he was, jaws gaping, about to launch himself at one of my bicycle bags. He was a particularly sneaky animal, otherwise the dogs in the hills were not too much trouble. They barked furiously but were fairly easily scared away. On the plain, however, they were a constant pest. They charged head down, like bullets, out of gardens and from behind fences, snarling furiously, teeth flashing, eyes swivelling, big dogs, small dogs, any dog, tumbling over themselves in their eagerness to get at the strange thing on wheels that had appeared on their territory. As soon as I stopped and shouted at them, they would usually screech to a halt, almost like a Tom and Jerry cartoon, and if I made a movement to pick up a stone, they would gallop off before I could shout 'bone'. But as soon as I got back on the saddle, most came charging back barking death and destruction. I was always worried they would snap at my legs or cause a pile-up. I knew I could never out-cycle them so I had to waste valuable time and energy stopping to look for a stone or a lump of tarmac to hurl.

Almost as bad as the dogs chasing me were the boys and men in the towns cycling to work. They managed to keep pace with me, cycling on apparently indestructible, old, flat, rubber tyres squeaking over filthy tracks covered in nails and broken glass. The tracks ran parallel with the main road through the town. They grinned and stared and rang their bells. It was no doubt fabulous fun for them and they meant no harm. There was no malice or ill intent. It probably livened up their entire day, but it was impossibly intrusive and infuriating for me. Unfortunately, much as I wanted to, I couldn't stop and throw stones at them. My imaginary machine gun and Amazonian battle-axe worked overtime.

The handful of towns I passed through that day appeared grey and featureless, stranded on the plains of the Black Sea coast, places to pass through to get somewhere else. I had been keeping an eye out for one town in particular which appeared on the map a few miles after Samsun. It was called Dikbıyık. This literally meant 'stiff moustache'. I'm afraid, schoolgirl-like, I found the name smuttily amusing. It reminded me of the two women laughing in the museum garden in Samsun. I wondered if all the men in Dikbıyık would be particularly macho and bristling. But Dikbıyık must have blended into the other grey towns because I didn't notice anything really special.

I longed to see the sea again as if that was going to make any difference to the rolling, rippling, furrowed mess of road. I felt guilty that I was making life even more difficult for the drivers. How dared I arrive in their place, a stranger, an intruder, breaking the rules and expecting to be accommodated, just as the Greek mercenaries did 2,500 years ago. I could feel the resentment and impatience, see the angry faces of the drivers edging past in their cars. There was a crisis when I reached a bridge over what I think must have been the Yeşilırmak, the River Iris of antiquity. The road over it was particularly narrow and traffic streamed across in both directions. There was no leeway along the edge for a bicycle. As I stopped to contemplate the situation, a passerby screamed at me.

'Yeter, yeter,' he said. 'Enough, enough.'

I assumed he meant that I should stop and catch a bus or preferably go home back to my husband. I was so enraged that all feelings of guilt and embarrassment disappeared. I had every right to be there. It was a free world and it was their fault for not building and mending the roads properly, as Xenophon had demanded. They should have been pleased that anybody even wanted to visit such a horrible place. And I launched off over the bridge, careless of the lorries and buses. Happily, I got across without further incident, but I did reflect that maybe I should have sailed along this part of the coast as the Greeks had chosen to do. Xenophon described how they were warned about the impossibility of crossing the mighty rivers across these plains without boats, including the Halys and the Iris.

After a couple of hours or so, I had crossed the plain and was back close to the sea and tucked in once more amongst the pine trees, which smelled green and cool and helped to absorb the petrol fumes in the air. I pulled in to a picnic spot from where I could glimpse the sea, pale-blue through the trees, and the inlet of a river, the Kocaman Çayı, the 'Enormous Stream'. A marvellous name. If it had not been for the traffic thundering past, it would have been a lovely spot. The boys in charge looked at me with disbelief. I asked if there was a place to wash my hands and they showed me to a clean basin in the open outside the restaurant. I washed my black face and hands and swilled out my mouth, which tasted of bitter acid. The wash made me feel a little better. I sat down at a table under the trees. This was a 'buy your own food and we'll cook it' kind of place. It was a popular business along the Black Sea coast. There were many of them along the major routes with their chilled display cabinets facing the traffic so that passing motorists were able to see the entire animal suspended inside on skewers and be tempted to stop and order a banquet.

It was still quite early, so the boys by the Enormous Stream were getting ready for the day ahead, preparing the charcoal on the barbecues set up beside their display cabinet. The thought of a chunk of sliced-off iced lamb made me feel extremely ill. I asked if there was any tea ready. Of course there was, and a steaming glass, sugar lumps dissolving in the hot drops spilled in the saucer, was rushed to my table. I pulled some bread and cheese out of my bag and immediately one of the boys disappeared to find me a large plate and a knife to use. I felt horribly guilty about my earlier uncharitable thoughts about the male of the species and salved my conscience by smiling as winningly as I felt I could, given my unprepossessing appearance, filthy clothes and greasy hair. The boys came to examine and admire the bicycle leaning by my side. They asked politely where I had come from, the usual questions. When I pulled out my diary to make some notes, they went back to their preparations, but kept an eye on me so that when I finished one glass of tea, they could hurry up with another. They began cooking fresh sardines on the barbecue for their breakfast and gave me one to taste. They offered to share them with me but I was keen to get back on the road. I wanted to get to wherever it was I was going as soon as possible. I guessed the roads would become even busier as the day went on. There was only another hour or so to go before I would reach Ünye, which, I had decided, was as far as I was going that day.

Along the road, I could only get glimpses of the sea through the trees before it was hidden altogether by the holiday homes built along the edge of the cliffs and down onto the beach. I kept my eyes open for a pension and found one situated on a small hill off the road. It was set in beautiful gardens, a riot of colours, shrubs, trees and flowers, a garden to dream about. The owner had to be nice, I thought. I wheeled the bicycle up the path and leaned her against a wall, trying to avoid crushing the bougainvillea. There were two immaculate, detached, new houses that would not have been out of place in Sussex. A Turkish family was sitting having breakfast outside at a comfortable table in the shade of a vine. I rang the bell of the house nearest the path and an elderly woman emerged. She was wearing a floral patterned dress and a frilly apron, the sort of landlady who expected you in by ten o'clock at night and no washing your clothes under any circumstances in your room. She looked at me disapprovingly, especially when she saw the bicycle, as if I were a rather nasty smell under her miserable, wrinkled, old nose. I gave her what I hoped was a dazzling smile. Never let the side down. I complimented her on her garden – she didn't blink – and asked her if she had a room for the night. She shook her head. 'Yok.' The young wife from the family at breakfast said something to her and the old bag – because that's what she was – suddenly remembered there was a room vacant in the house opposite. She went ahead and I trailed behind, glancing at the wife, who looked at me sympathetically.

It was a truly beautiful house inside, big windows allowing in lots of light, natural wood everywhere and a stunning wooden staircase leading up to the bedrooms. The woman showed me into what must have been her smallest and plainest room. There was just a double bed, still rumpled by the night's occupants. She wanted two million Turkish liras, around £8, for the night. She led me back down the stairs and suddenly, through a window, I saw one of my favourite trees. I had seen them in the park in Samsun. They have very green leaves and golden flowers which emerge like the feathery crest on the head of an ibis. They are common along the Black Sea and Andy later told me their name, *Albizia julibrissin*. I asked the woman what they were called and she told me the name in Turkish. For the first time she gave a small smile and took me into the kitchen to show me a fridge I would be able to use if I stayed. She even opened the door to let me see inside. It was loaded with mouth-watering, pink water melon and I nearly leaned it to take a slice. The woman suddenly seemed quite enthusiastic. It was too late. The room was very small and the price too high. I had been staying in hotels with my own shower for that price – and in any case, she had scowled at the bicycle. I asked her if there were any other pensions before Ünye. 'Yok,' she said firmly.

There was one right next door together with a pizza house and a small shop with an ice cream sign outside. I wheeled the bicycle in through the gate and propped her up against a table. There was a good atmosphere, very different from that created by the old icicle in her apron next door. I went into the shop and asked the man behind the counter if the pension belonged to him. It certainly did and what could he do for me. Did he have a bed for the night, I asked, and told him about his unpleasant neighbour, who had informed me that there were no other places to stay before Ünye. 'She looked at me as if I were a smell under her nose,' I told him. He burst out laughing. He obviously knew his neighbour well. I was in luck, he said. Normally his place was let to university students, girls; a party had just left. I could have any one of the beds in any one of the rooms and the charge was £3.

I went in through a side entrance and up the stairs. It was a big place with high, old-fashioned ceilings and wooden floors and was gloriously flooded with light. There were four large bedrooms equipped with bunk beds, yellow, foam mattresses and piles of blankets lying neatly on top. There were tables and chairs, a kitchen and a bathroom area. The girls had pinned up love poems in the bedrooms, and in the bathroom there were bars of half-finished soap, bottles of shampoo and plenty of jugs and bowls to pour water over oneself, Turkish-style. The large, central hallway had been made into a sitting room and it was comfortable with big sofas. A balcony opening off it looked out over the road to a belt of pine trees, the sea beyond. The door was open and a light breeze blew in. It was all mine. I was going to be a queen for the night. I went back downstairs to the shop. The man was busy sorting out his tins of tomato paste and ice creams. He asked me whether I was going to take a shower – he was still laughing to himself over the idea of the nasty smell under his neighbour's sharp nose.

I cycled in to Ünye to have a look round. It was a lovely ride in. I had left my bags behind and without them the bicycle felt light and free, skimming over the road, flying over the ruts and potholes and easily dodging the lorries. There were many holiday pensions built on either side of the road. Because of the ribbon development, the sea was hidden and only the occasional, enigmatic wink glinted through the pine trees and up the tracks in between the houses. The saving grace of these new developments in Turkey was that any gardens that were planted grew rapidly. The vines and bougainvillea, fiery red, pink and luscious purple, soon draped themselves over buildings, running up balconies, arbours and fences like multi-coloured waves of fire. If the buildings were low-rise, they quickly blended in. It was the high-rise blocks that were so extremely ugly, scarring hills and promontories.

The road was now even busier. There were more and more lorries speeding by on what was only large enough to be a country road. It was difficult to see how the situation could be improved. The road could not be widened into a dual carriageway because of the buildings springing up on either side. With the hills and mountains rising up directly behind the long ribbon of the coastal strip, there were few alternatives, unless the Turks moved all freight movement onto the sea. This was most unlikely. Here were major bottlenecks stacking up for the future.

Ünye lay picturesquely in the sweep of a bay. The town council had jumped on the bandwagon and laid out a park amid the pine trees along the sea front. As I slowly cycled in, a car overtook me, pulled over and stopped. The driver, a young man, leaped out, shouting and waving me down in a self-important way. I couldn't believe that anybody would dare do such a thing in the centre of a town. Automatically, I pulled out and shot past him. My heart pounded and my legs turned to jelly. I was furious with the unknown driver and furious with myself for reacting so badly. Seconds later, I spotted Ünye's tourist information centre and took refuge inside. The office was being manned by a couple of teenaged boys. They could speak some English and were thrilled to see a tourist. I was just asking for a map when a car drew up outside and a young man – the young man – came rushing in.

He introduced himself in gunfire English as the tourism officer for Ünye. He had seen me cycling along and tried to wave me down to tell me his office was near by and he could give me any information I wanted, but I had ignored him and cycled past. He had only wanted to help. I turned on him like one of the dogs snapping at my bicycle. I told him exactly what it was like to cycle as a single woman through Turkey, describing the bulls roaring through their cab windows. I would never, ever, I said, acknowledge any man who shouted at me anywhere anyhow in the street. He would never ever have done that to a Turkish woman. How could he possibly think he could do it to a foreigner?

The poor man. He was so embarrassed and shuffled his feet. He wanted to put an end to the unexpectedly unpleasant line of conversation and got out a book of photographs of the different hotels and pensions in the area and told the boys to practise their English on me. The teenagers were students, who helped out in the tourist office at weekends hoping to meet some foreigners. One of the boys took me to look at the photographs on the wall and began to explain what the pictures showed. He pointed to one and informed me that it was the famous castle of Ünye. It looked like a rather splendid, craggy rock. If it was a castle, it had been severely eroded by the harsh Black Sea weather.

'Here is castle in Unye. It is seven kilometres from town. You take taxi,' said the boy sweetly. He was adorable and I hung on his every word.

The tourist officer interrupted. 'We have A castle in Unye and you can take A taxi,' he said officiously.

I had had enough of the man. 'He is doing Very Well,' I said. 'He speaks Extremely Good English.'

The boy flushed red with pleasure and continued to point out the wonderful sightseeing potential of Ünye. I didn't like to say that I didn't have the energy to go sightseeing and what I really wanted to do was head back to my nice pension out of town and go and find a beach. However, one of the photographs caught my eye. It was of a street lined with picturesque, Ottoman houses snoozing in the sunshine. I asked where it was. It was somewhere in the town and the other boy could take me there, past a Byzantine church which had been turned into a hamam. He had a bicycle too. Off we went, through the streets and alleyways of Ünye. The shopkeepers lounging outside their stores and the townsfolk stared at the unusual sight of a foreign woman on a bicycle apparently playing follow-my-leader with a Turkish teenager who kept glancing back over his shoulder to see that she was still there.

We wove our way through the town and my young guide stopped outside an brick building tucked away in a side street. The circular roofs indicated that it had indeed once been a church. The Turks might have thought they were perfect for the circular domes characteristic of the Moslem bathhouses. My guide muttered that he thought it was a shame a church was being used as a bathroom. I wondered whether he said this because he thought it might have been what I was thinking. Maybe there were western tourists who had expressed their horror at the idea of people taking their clothes off and bathing inside what used to be a place of worship. I thought of the Ottoman mosques that were destroyed in

Bosnia when the former Yugoslavia disintegrated and of the mosques I had seen locked up and derelict in Bulgaria where the people continued to remember the Christian massacres under Ottoman rule. People getting their own back, ancient hatreds, nothing forgotten. The poor church at Ünye was a physical reminder of the historic bitterness that continues to poison the relations of so many countries today.

'At least it's still in use in some way,' I said diplomatically.

Around the corner from the church/hamam was the old street we had come to see. It rose steeply up a hill. It was too steep to consider taking the bicycles with us so we left them outside a tea house on the corner, asking the man inside to keep an eye on them.

It was like stepping back in time. The street was still paved with uneven cobbles and slabs of stone, rounded and slippery, made smooth through generations of use. The houses of wood and stone set in lovely gardens, some of them walled, had no doubt been built for rich Greek families. They were large and airy establishments. Some of them jutted out onto the hillside having been constructed on several levels. They had magnificent views over the bay. Some of the doorways were made out of ornate, Byzantine, stone columns. These could have been recycled from somewhere else in the town. It was an exquisite, magical street and my young guide was pleased with my pleasure and thrilled that I was enjoying his home town so much. As we walked back down the hill, we passed a bent, old granny under the trees in the shade minding a group of brown calves. They were fluttering their long eyelashes and daintily chewing away at the grass with their pink tongues. I stopped to admire them. The old lady said something to me, which I couldn't understand. As we walked away, my student told me she had invited me to go and pat them. I think he would have liked to have shown me round the sights of Ünye all day but I wanted something to eat and I was too tired to continue walking in the sun. I needed to get back, find a beach and lie on it. We shook hands and I complimented him again on his town and his command of English. I told him he was my 'abi'. The word means older brother but is also a commonly used term of respect. He thought this was very funny. I was his 'abla', his older sister, he replied. He cycled off and I went to find a soup shop in the town centre. It served delicious, steaming bowls of ezo gelin soup, made from lentils and rice, my favourite of all the Turkish soups.

I cycled back, past an enormous mosque being constructed like a science-fiction rocket launcher, and into Ünye's square where there were some food stalls. I bought a melon and admired some woven baskets for sale, filled with mauve berries that looked a cross between raspberries and mulberries. The elderly lady selling them said they were freshly-picked that day. I also saw my second lot of foreigners of the trip, a couple from Scandinavia with their teenage son trailing along behind. He looked extremely bored. Back towards the sea, a plaque on an ancient, mossy wall nearby claimed the site was the only remnant of a medieval fortress. Maybe the stone columns incorporated into the houses on the hill had originally graced its rooms.

Back at my place, I chose my bunk, organising the foam mattress, which I was looking forward to sleeping on. Foam is cheap and dangerous if you happen to set fire to it but it can be deliciously comfortable, especially when your body and muscles are particularly tired. I found some scratchy, cleanish bits of linen I could use as sheets, selected some blankets and arranged the bed. It was great to have the whole place to myself, the sea and the sun blowing in through the balcony door, voices drifting up from the garden down below. I felt half asleep, in a timeless, dream world. A man, a different one, came up from downstairs to see how I was getting on. He was a member of the extended family running the business, he said. He had called somebody to come and connect up the gas so there would be hot water later for a shower. I was sceptical that this joyful occurrence would come to pass and decided to go and find the beach.

It was on the opposite side of the road, behind rows of holiday homes and restaurants. I made my way past the waiters, who waited disconsolate amid the empty chairs and tables, and slithered down a grassy bank through the trees and bushes. The beach turned out to be a narrow strip running between the high ground and the sea. There was a lot of litter lying around; the sand was dotted with oil and I could smell the sickly-sweet smell of sewage. There would be no swimming in the sea here. The beach, however, was busy with families eating, sunbathing, playing and larking around in the sea despite the rocks, weeds and general murkiness of the shallow water. I found the least oily bit of beach I could and made myself comfortable. Two girls were sunbathing together close by, smoking and reading. They were amazed to see a lone, foreign woman and were even more excited when I told them I had cycled from İstanbul. I mentioned the state of the roads along the Black Sea coast and how difficult it was to get anywhere. They snorted and told me about the tax paid to the councils specifically to repair the roads, which, they said, remained shattered and smashed. Where did the money go, they asked rhetorically. They were both socialists, they announced, and, as far as they were concerned, most Turkish people were fascists. Unlike most of their contemporaries, they liked to think and read controversial things like the work of the German philosopher, Nietzsche, and Turkey's left-wing newspaper, *Cumhuriyet*, although their school had actively discouraged them from doing so. They were going to university, one to study social administration, the other psychology. They also wanted to learn English.

I listened in fascination. These girls would probably have ended up in prison in Turkey or worse, twenty years previously. They smoked and laughed and told me their families were very understanding, that they certainly didn't want to get married and that they were together all the time because there were so few other people they could talk to. They went off to swim, good-looking girls in their early twenties, independent and free. I admired them. It isn't easy to be different in a traditional society.

It was hot in the sun and I began to burn. I said goodbye to the girls and went back to the pension to find that while I had been out, the plumber had come to fix the gas, somebody had washed all the floors and the fridge had been switched on. Oh naughty me for doubting these wonderful people. I put my melting cheese, tomatoes, melon and water bottle into the fridge and took a wonderful, long, hot shower. What luxury. From the balcony, the ever-changing Black Sea looked like a silver mirror with tiny ripples across the surface. I lounged and read and drowsed on a comfortable sofa and wondered whether I would get to the border with Georgia in the time allotted. I had covered nearly a thousand kilometres, around six hundred miles, in less than two weeks. It wasn't so much but, given the hills and the potholes, I felt relatively pleased with my progress. I was collecting my miles like pieces of gold. They were piling up, clinking roundly, fought for and won in battle. I went downstairs to have a beer to celebrate.

The garden was awash with hydrangeas. These gorgeous shrubs were flowering everywhere along the coast, exquisite blooms in subtle shades of sky blue, pale pink and mauve, colours never to be found in any paint box. They were so perfect they looked like paper flowers and I had to touch them to make sure they were real. Two couples were sitting at a table in the shade eating platefuls of freshly-cooked pizza, and a small girl and boy raced around in a cart. The garden gate was shut to stop them racing outside under the wheels of a lorry. The boy occupied the driving seat while his sister skipped good-humouredly behind. I ordered a beer, which had to be cooled down first in the ice cream cabinet, and asked for a pizza to follow. It arrived, as usual in a long boat-like shape. It had been cooked in butter and dotted with the best feta cheese and spicy Turkish sausage. The pastry was crumbly and delicious but I suddenly missed anchovies and mushrooms and . . . I tried not to think about it.

Back upstairs, the man, who had kept his word and wonderfully organised the gas, was putting clean sheets and pillow-cases on my bed. He indicated that the linen I had found earlier to use would be far too scratchy and uncomfortable. He told me a family would also be staying the night in one of the other rooms, so I shouldn't be alarmed to hear noises later on. He asked me my name and then told me his. It was Savaş. I stared and burst out laughing and he laughed too. 'Savaş' means 'war' or 'battle' in Turkish. He was indeed a big man, unusually well-built for a Turk, with powerful shoulders, a craggy face and strong features. He looked the part.

'So you're a fierce man,' I said.

'Yes,' he said, '<u>very</u> fierce,' and he laughed again, this very gentle giant. He was enthusiastic about the idea of cycling along the Black Sea coast and asked me all about the bicycle and the journey. I had partly done the trip, I explained, because I had begun to feel so ill in England, tired and aching all the time. I thought the exercise would be good for my muscles.

'And for your head,' he immediately added, pointing to his own.

The Turks are reflective and intense people, quick to empathise with moods and emotions as if they have their own special window onto the inner soul. Savaş had hit it in one. I had indeed embarked on the trip in order to give myself time to think, although I wasn't sure what conclusions, if any, I was going to come to. I looked at this extremely nice Turkish man, putting on my sheets and pillowcases with his big hands as deftly as a nurse. I had offered to help, but he waved me away. When he had finished, I put my hand out to shake his and kissed him goodbye on the cheek, twice, like you do in Turkey to a good friend or a relative, definitely an 'abi'.

11
Ünye to Giresun

They cut off the heads of those who had been killed, and showed them to the Greeks
and to their own enemies, dancing at the same time and singing to a sort of tune. The
Greeks were badly upset by this.

The foam bed was comfortable, absorbing me like a sponge, but what with the
noise of the lorries thundering past all night and a party outside the pizza house,
I slept fitfully. I got up just after four o'clock. I was awake anyway. The garden
lamps were still lit and the chairs and tables left higgledy piggledy as if the people
who had been sitting there had only just left. It looked like a stage set, the actors
poised, waiting unseen in the wings for their cue. I ran up and down stairs
carrying the bicycle outside and then the bags, strapping everything into place,
checking the tyres to see if they had gone down for any reason overnight,
snapping on my gloves – I felt exhausted even before I had begun. I cycled off
towards Ünye, enjoying the freewheel downhill, familiar after the previous day,
past the park along the sea and then the tourist office, closed up and silent, and
out eastwards into new territory. The next destination was the town of Ordu
seventy-eight kilometres, fifty miles, away.

I had memories of Ordu, having briefly visited fourteen years before in
June 1983. I remembered a wide expanse of a mud/sand beach in front of the
town, which I had gone to take a look at, vaguely considering the possibility
of swimming and sunbathing. I had stood looking out to sea, completely alone
on the beach and suddenly realising how conservative the Black Sea region
was. I could no more have taken off my clothes than I could have flown to the
moon. The only beach on which I could possibly have sunbathed alone was
on the Mediterranean hundreds of miles away and over several mountain
ranges. I had turned round, disappointed, to discover that I was standing in a
semi circle of men who must have followed me down, silently, onto the beach.
They were staring in unselfconscious, child-like disbelief at this creature from
another world, who had arrived from nowhere in their town and was
apparently about to walk into the sea. As I looked at them, they scratched their
heads and looked away and pretended they were anywhere but where they
were. Man was but an ass, a patched fool, if he went about to expound this
dream. It was past the wit of man to say what dream it was. I walked back into
Ordu and found a tailor in a back street, who kindly sewed on a vital button
that had come off my shirt. He, too, could not believe his eyes when I walked
into his shop. After that, I abandoned the Black Sea, found the nearest bus

stop and stood there until a bus arrived to take me back to İstanbul via Samsun.

All the memories, not only of Ordu but of trips past to Turkey, came crowding through my head as I cycled out of Ünye. I think we leave bits of ourselves behind wherever we go and whatever we do, a sort of fifth dimension of hopes and dreams and expectations, so intensely do we live our crowded, little lives. The dark sky was acquiring a layer of pink trembling in the east and, even as I watched, flushing a bolder red. The sun, a giant ball of fire, appeared as if by magic on the clear horizon. I hardly dared to blink in case I missed its smooth and stately progress upwards, as if it were on the end of an unseen piece of string held in an unseen hand. The daily, greatest illusion. I was never surprised that people bowed down and worshipped the sun at dawn. We look for miracles, signs and portents and there they are, happening every day. The sea that day turned the nearest it had got to a proper blue, an unearthly, deep, metallic turquoise.

It was another head down, keep going sort of a ride. The pancake-flat road skirted along the coast but the sea was often hidden by houses and ribbon development. The mountains loomed up further inland in the distance. There were lots of plots of land up for sale. Buy me and make my dream come true. The road was horrible, a stony, slippery surface and much too narrow for the volume of traffic. I had to keep edging off it into the even worse ruts alongside so that the buses and sweating lorries could squeeze past. Much of the time the road was higher than the level of the ground on either side, too high for me to drop down safely. Then I had to stop and get off the bicycle, leaning away from the traffic as it roared past. Sometimes it got to the point when I would watch for an empty stretch of road and then pedal hard until a new line of traffic came up behind me when I would quickly get off and wait until it had all shot past. The lorries were kinder to me than the cars. The men behind the big wheels were better drivers. They tried to give me as much space as they could, probably aware of the impact of their slip stream and also possibly worried about the consequences if they squashed a stupid, foreign cyclist along the way. Although it was Sunday, the traffic was just as heavy as it was during the week. The dogs were also out in force, relentlessly territorial, even though they sometimes just missed being run down by a lorry as they chased the bicycle. What with the stinking fumes of the traffic, it was not a cycle ride to be recommended or ever repeated.

Despite the obstacles, I covered a lot of miles very quickly. I sped through the depression of Fatsa to arrive at the tiny harbour village of Bolaman. There, a magnificent, castle-like structure overlooking the sea and some fine old buildings nearby brought me to an excited halt. To my great pleasure, the site was being restored. I leaned the bicycle against the wall of a stone mosque opposite (obviously a former Byzantine church) and went to have a closer look. It wasn't really a castle, more an enormous, ancient, Byzantine citadel built of stone out of the living rock. A wooden house had been constructed on top at a later date.

Parts of the house were made out of entire tree trunks. A sign announced that the 'konak', or mansion, had been built in the nineteenth century by the powerful Hazinedaroğlu family and was to be rebuilt. The scaffolding was already in place. It was Turkish-style scaffolding, made out of planks of wood and the trunks of young trees. It could be seen throughout the country, whenever there was any building work taking place. It was almost as picturesque as the ancient monuments. I hoped to find a soup shop or a börekci in Bolaman, but it was too small to consider catering for travellers and at that hour in the morning was still fast asleep. All I could do was eat a biscuit or two and carry on.

The scenery improved and suddenly the forests and the mountains returned and I was back toiling up hills instead of pounding along on the flat. It was a relief to see trees and the countryside again but I could have cried at the state of the road. The ride would have been so easy had the surface been a good one instead of disappearing under piles and heaps of stones. By then, I was so fit I felt I could have cycled up anything, but instead I was having to get off and coax the bicycle up the slopes, slipping on the stones, almost unable to stay on my feet. At least it slowed the buses and lorries down too. There was plenty of warning that they were coming, a desperate grinding and crashing of gears being changed as the sweating, cursing drivers struggled to control their vehicles.

Emerging out of the mountains, I dipped back down and into the small sea-side town of Yalıköy. This was a busy, active place and, most important of all, it had a soup restaurant just off the main road, which was in full steaming swing. I leaned the dusty bicycle up against the window. She was doing so well with her rear mudguard tied on by a piece of washing line. I looked at her with love and devotion, unpeeled my gloves and went in to sit slumped at a table facing the window. I read some more of my Henry James, reflecting that I didn't actually like any of his characters but that he wasn't writing them to be liked. He was trying to portray the complexities and subtleties of human relationships, the loneliness of the human condition. I almost fell asleep, lulled by the hum from the monster fridges and the machines in the kitchen. Le patron brought me a bowl of chicken soup and I ate it slowly, dipping in endless pieces of fresh bread until I had consumed almost an entire loaf. The soup was excellent. The man periodically shuffled to the door and yelled, 'buyurun, buyurun', at anything and anybody who passed by. He was a handsome man with white hair and a white moustache. His head was massive and heavy, his dark eyes expressive and his nose strong and shapely. Classic features. He looked more Greek than Turkish and this was hardly surprising, given the historic mix of cultures in the area. He offered me a cigarette, calling me 'bayan' as they do in Turkey. It means 'woman' and I always think the word has a biblical ring to it. There aren't words like that in English. It is an insult to call somebody 'man' or 'woman'. 'Miss' was what you once called somebody in a shop, and you can't go round calling people 'Ms'. In

Turkey, you are a woman when you are no longer a girl. Religious families make their daughters wear headscarves from the age of about ten.

The road after Yalıköy improved for a while and turned into a switchback rolling along above the sea. It was one of the prettiest areas of the stretch of coast line from Sinop, with lots of small and secret bays hidden from the road by its bends and curves, only seen if one stopped on a steep corner and hung over the edge to peer back and down through the trees. Semi-circular harbours had been built up and out into the sea from formidable chunks of stone to give shelter and protection to the small boats of the fishermen, who were busy puttering in and out over the glassy water that day. They were well-kept, attractive, little ports. Saplings had been planted along the stone walls at regular intervals, protected from the weather in boxes. This was a part of the Black Sea coastline which would be best seen by hiring a boat and chugging gently along, hat on against the glare of the sun.

The beauty of the bays emphasised the ugliness and disappointment of the town of Perşembe, which means 'Thursday' in Turkish. There, the sea front was an earthquake of earthworks and blocks of stone. It was depressing and I felt depressed, a feeling not helped by the overwhelming number of invitations I was getting that day from bored drivers who pulled off the road and opened their car doors and shouted and roared and hooted their horns to get my attention. I wasn't frightened. The road was too busy to worry about anything unpleasant happening. It was just irritating and made me feel slightly sick. I spent a lot of time trying not to resent the whole of the male species and mentally running through all the very nice men I had ever met, who would have been horrified at the situation. I put my hat on, which I had stupidly left off that day because it didn't feel so hot, with the result that my forehead was badly burned, and tried to disappear inside. I felt like cloaking myself in a veil, enveloping myself in black to disappear altogether. There was something to be said for the strict Islamic head to toe dress – but it would have been difficult to cycle in.

I recognised the sweep of beach as I cycled in to Ordu and wondered if the kind tailor was still sewing away in his shop in one of the back streets or maybe it was run by his son now, and whether the men were still waiting for me on the beach, which was as muddy and empty as it had been all those years before. Moreover, there were major earthworks taking place along the sea front where yet another enormous fishermen's barrage was being built. In the mid nineteenth century, Ordu had an image problem then too. My Gazetteer reported that the climate was unhealthy and the town deserted during the summer, despite the fact that three steamers, Russian, French and Turkish, stopped off every week.

Around two and a half thousand years before, Xenophon and his men stopped off at Ordu, which was then a Greek city and a colony of Sinop and called Cotyora. They camped outside the city's fortifications for forty-five days.

Xenophon liked Cotyora so much, he considered founding a new city nearby. In his account of the journey, he described the reluctance of the Cotyorans to sell them food or to take the sick men inside the walls. As a consequence, there was much plundering and ravaging of the nearby Paphlagonian settlements. Ambassadors from Sinop arrived, anxious to find out what was going on. They advised Cotyora to give the Ten Thousand the ships they needed so that they would sail off westwards along the coast. As Xenophon so simply and sweetly wrote: 'One of the results of power is the ability to take what belongs to the weaker.'

The Greeks went west. My direction was eastwards. I cycled on through Ordu and out the other side, now determined to get to Giresun. It was only another twenty miles or so, thirty odd kilometres. I had stayed in Giresun in 1983 and remembered it as a pleasant town with the remains of an ancient fortress scattered over the hill above. I stopped at a petrol station along the way to refill my water bottle. It was a big, business-like garage, drive in, fill up with petrol, wash the car – the Turks wash their cars and coaches incessantly – eat something, drink something and speed off again. They were very different affairs from the small, personal garages in Turkey just a few years previously, when every petrol pump was manned and hordes of men waited, eager to help wash the car and change its oil and tyres.

I wheeled the bicycle in, ignoring the stares of amazement, and asked if there was a water fountain. There wasn't – a sign of the times – and was directed round the back to an outside sink in the middle of a field close to the toilets. The garage still had a lot to do on the toilet facilities front. As I hesitated, wondering about the logistics of getting to the sink, a woolly lamb wearing a bell round its neck pushed past and tinkled its way busily and with a self-important air straight into the men's toilets. It was so unexpected and essentially Turkish that I screeched and pointed with delight, looking round for somebody to share my pleasure with. I suddenly realised that nobody was looking at the lamb at all. They were all looking at me, as surprised to see a woman with a bicycle, apparently laughing and talking to herself, appearing from around the corner, as I was to see a fluffy lamb going into the toilets. Oh the mirrors that are suddenly swung round and held up for one to look into, the unexpected perspectives and angles, when one looks and does not recognise what one sees. This wasn't me. I was nothing special. Except that I was, here.

In his *Anabasis*, Xenophon described the various tribes of the Mossynoeci the Greeks encountered as they marched from Giresun to Ordu. The tribes fought viciously against each other in ways that astonished the Greeks. They were also the most extraordinary people the mercenaries met during their journey. The boys were specially fattened up on boiled chestnuts and became obscenely fat. They were also tattooed all over with colourful designs of flowers. When they were in a crowd, they acted as men would act when in private, including having sexual intercourse, and when they were by themselves, they used to behave as they might have done in company, talking and laughing to themselves or stopping to dance wherever they happened to be.

Along the Black Sea, I often felt like I was being observed by the Turks as the Greeks regarded the Mossynoeci, although I didn't have any tattoos nor did I have sexual intercourse in public, or in private come to that – although I often felt they hoped I might. The lamb at the garage episode was one of those occasions. I couldn't reach the sink and I held out my bottle in silence. A man came forward, took it and went over to the tap to fill it for me, also in silence. I wondered what the lamb was doing.

Back on the road and it was a question of hanging on and not getting killed by the lorries and the buses pelting past. The rest of the journey was obviously going to be a flat, straight run into Giresun. In all, I was going to cycle seventy-five miles that day, around 120 kilometres. It would then be a similar distance from Giresun to Trabzon. I could easily do it, although it wasn't going to be very pleasurable. I wasn't enjoying this part of the Black Sea coast. The traffic was overwhelming and I missed the beauty of the mountains. I decided that at Trabzon, I would reassess what I was doing.

I woke up suddenly from my thoughts. I had arrived at a long, narrow bridge, high over the wide bed of the Turnsuyu river running down into the sea. The bridge was so narrow that there was no room for a bicycle if there was traffic in both directions. I had to consider how to get across the bridge without causing a major accident. The best thing to do was to wheel the bicycle across. I was half way over when a scene happening down below made me stop, oblivious to the traffic bearing down on me. In fact, I wanted the traffic to stop too, to share in the shame of the spectacle. An old man was beating up a woman who I assumed was his wife. It was summer so the bed of the river had partially dried up. Only a few rivulets of water ran along. The couple were standing in the middle of the riverbed. A small heap of clothes lay on the ground close by next to one of the stretches of water. It looked as if the old man was bullying the woman, ordering her to get into the water and wash the clothes. He kept pushing her towards the clothes and into the water, shouting and hitting her. She was resisting, ducking away from his grasp and feebly trying to run away, only to be caught by him once more, and hit and pushed back towards the clothes.

I was horrified. The couple were too far away to hear me if I shouted. I couldn't move easily because of the bicycle balanced against the kerb and the lorries thundering past me rocking the ground. Even had I tried to get down there, turning off onto the bank and making my way down the dirt track, it was going to be difficult to locate them through the bushes and trees along the side of the river. I was convinced anyway that somebody would intervene. But nobody did.

The people on the riverbank probably couldn't see what was going on. Only a couple of young boys and I on the bridge were able to see what was happening. The boys leaned over the railings and watched in amusement. I felt distraught and useless, ashamed to be a spectator. The fight went on, the man was carrying a heavy stick. Although he raised it to threaten the woman, he didn't actually use it. It looked as if she was begging and pleading with him to stop. She kept slipping over and the scarf on her head fell off. The shame of it all, she struggling to tie the scarf back on, automatically trying to maintain her dignity even as she ran away from her husband, falling down and scrambling back up and running again. They looked like marionettes on a string, acting out a Punch and Judy routine, except that this was real life.

I stood and watched, feeling powerless and ashamed of having seen them. It was as if I had opened a door and caught two people doing something so shameful, they would have died if they had known that they were being observed. I wondered if the woman would even have wanted somebody to go to help her, so complicated are we in our emotions and traumas. At last, the man got too tired even to raise his arm holding the stick and he gave up. He stopped shouting and hitting the woman and she managed, finally, to put her headscarf on. The pair walked away, he in front, she behind, nevertheless together. The pile of clothes was left beside the water. The old woman had won, at least for the time being.

I cycled into Giresun feeling extremely relieved to have made it in one piece. The town was built into the sweep of a bay and climbing up into the densely forested hills behind. It had no doubt expanded since my previous visit and I couldn't recognise the town at all, although I had a dim memory of all those years before when I had sat on the grass high up on the citadel hill behind the town and tried to talk to a group of teenaged girls, who were fascinated to find a lone, foreign woman in their out-of-the-way town that day. I was determined to get up to the citadel once again, despite my tired muscles.

There were several hotels in the streets radiating off the central park area, which appeared to be the focal point of the town. Giresun still felt as if it were a small place despite the sprawling suburbs. The first hotel turned out to be one of the most expensive in town, but the man behind the desk good-naturedly told me that the cheapest was just around the corner. I found the Otel Bozbağ (Hotel Grey Vineyard) up a side street. (Many place names featured the seemingly dull adjective 'grey'. I was later told that in the Black Sea area, the word conjured up a pleasant feeling of a gentle mistiness and moisture in the air, as opposed to just being 'grey'.) There were no steps up to the door of Otel Bozbağ, so I began to wheel the bicycle straight into the tatty reception area. A grim-faced woman behind the reception desk screamed at me to take her out. At once. There was no argument. The man sitting beside her rushed out with a key and hurried me up the street, unlocked a door and showed me a filthy storehouse where, he said, I could leave the bicycle while I looked at a room. With extreme reluctance, I balanced her against a grimy wall and went back into the hotel. The harridan looked grimly at me and the man took me upstairs to show me a room.

The hotel was seedy and deserted, the long corridors dark and claustrophobic. My imagination was working overtime. It was as if time was standing still inside that hotel. What secrets were behind the silent, locked doors? The man had difficulty getting the key into the lock to open the door into the room. Inside, there was a double bed and a small shower room. The room's wide windows were heavily net curtained to keep out prying eyes. It was very cheap, just £3 a night. But I was tired and felt uncomfortable. Unusually, I couldn't make a decision. The hotel was so bleak and empty and I was worried about the bicycle. I also didn't like the man, who had jet black eyes and stared at me with a lean and hungry look. It felt, once again, like the hotel in the film, but it wasn't so romantic being in it rather than just watching from the safety of a cinema seat. I muttered something about looking round the town and possibly coming back. I didn't want to cancel my options. I rushed to extricate the bicycle from the darkness of the store room.

The next hotel looked much more respectable but the youths manning reception refused even to consider letting the bicycle sleep next to me in a room. I don't know why I was so insistent on having her under my nose in Giresun. She had stayed in all kinds of places. I began to walk up a hill and passed a posh, five-star hotel which I didn't even bother to consider. The people in the street were staring at the stranger in their midst, who kept walking backwards and forwards through their town. I felt, not for the first time, like a bloody fool. My precious time was ticking away. I turned round and went back to the Grey Vineyard. The harridan had, fortunately, disappeared leaving the man to look after the empty hotel on his own. He suddenly seemed to be an old friend. His eyes were now kind rather than darkly manic. He dwindled from being a mass murderer into an innocent provincial, staring with awe at my British passport, so rarely had he seen one. He allowed me to install the bicycle just off the lobby in a desolate sitting room area next to the television. The woman, he said, wasn't coming back that day.

It was such a relief to have made a decision. I liked my room. I bounced on the bed, which was deliciously comfortable, and experimented in the shower room. The plumbing was impressive. Although there was only half a chain, the Western-style toilet flushed like Niagara Falls and there were no leaks. Although there wouldn't be any hot water until the evening, how could I have even hesitated over such a bargain. I went outside into the fiery heat of the afternoon to find the castle.

It was directly behind the town, up a stiff climb winding through streets of old, stone houses tucked into corners, busy, new apartment blocks built to fill in the gaps and small, dark, grocery stores selling cherries and melons. Half way up the hill was a park shaded by mature trees and overlooking the sea. It had been built in Ottoman times, like the town's wonderfully ancient courthouse opposite. An inscription written in the flowery and flowing Ottoman Arabic script was engraved into the stone lintel over the park entrance. It would have looked as foreign to the children of Giresun as it did to me, even though their great grandfathers might well have been able to read it. From the park, one continued up an even steeper spiral of a road, passing underneath a lighthouse where everybody stopped to gaze at the panoramic views over the Black Sea. The traffic thundering by on the coastal road down below was reduced to children's toys.

The hillsides directly underneath the castle were dotted with single-storey homes, which were almost hidden in their well established, lushly green gardens. It looked as if the town had started life on the hill, gazing over the sea from a safe distance and, slowly moving downwards through the centuries, dipped its toes well and truly in the water in the twentieth century. I stopped frequently to admire the view and to give my legs a rest. I was finding it hard going after the day's cycling. A Turkish family walking up at the same time nodded and smiled at me, asking me where I came from. They ooohed and aaaahed about the steepness of the climb and laughed over how long it was taking us all to get up to the top.

The citadel was Giresun's crowning glory. It covered a wide area and was being well cared for by the Turks. The mossy stone walls and surviving medieval ramparts were well preserved. There were signposts for paths leading to even more splendid views and to caves in the hillsides. I knew, however, that I couldn't go any further. I was just able to manoeuvre my legs to the nearest café overlooking the sea and, collapsing into a chair, ordered a beer. A thrilled youth brought me an ice-cold glass of Turkish beer and a heaped plateful of hazel nuts. 'The nuts are without charge. They are from Giresun,' he said proudly.

I had never tasted such delicious hazel nuts in my life and I ate them all slowly, one by one. It wasn't until I had done some serious food pricing in Trabzon a couple of days later that I realised the plate of nuts the young man had brought me would have cost about £5 had I bought them in a shop. Hazelnuts are a valuable commodity. The gift in the citadel was a very generous one. I was eating the historic wealth of Giresun, which began its life as the Greek city of Cerasus, famous for its hazel nuts and fruits. Cerasus means cherry tree in both Greek and Latin and is the root for the English word 'cherry', the French 'cerise' and the Turkish 'kiraz'. A delicious name for an illustrious city. Jason and the Argonauts sailed past the site of Cerasus on their journey to the kingdom of Colchis (Georgia) in search of the Golden Fleece. The fierce Amazons built a temple dedicated to the god of war on an island just off the coast. (The Amazons with their battle-axes knew a thing or two about keeping men in their place. They would have eaten the lorry drivers for breakfast, spitting out the stones.) Xenophon and his merry band of plundering mercenaries stayed in Cerasus for ten days when a count took place of the number of men that had survived the march over the snow-covered plains and mountains from Persia. By then, Xenophon wrote, owing to the freezing weather and the bloody battles, many men had died or been killed and there were only 8,600 left. (By the time they reached Byzantium, they were down to 6,000, although history ignored the detail and has continued to refer to them as the 'Ten Thousand'.) A couple of hundred years after the Greek mercenaries travelled through Cerasus, a new town was founded on the same site called Pharnacia, thought to have been built by Pharnaces, the grandfather of Mithridates the Great. After the Romans conquered the Kingdom of Pontus, the town resumed its former name of Cerasus. The story goes that General Lucullus was so pleased with the unfamiliar and delicious fruit, he took some trees back with him to Europe.

The citadel was busy that Sunday afternoon, packed with families having picnics, brewing up their endless pots of tea on charcoal fires. I love Turkish tea pots. They are in two parts, one pot sitting comfortably on top of another. The water is boiled in the bottom pot. The tea leaves are spooned into the top pot which is half-filled with water to make a sort of liquid tea concentrate. The traditional, slim, Turkish tea glasses are then half-filled with the tea and topped up with the boiled water from the bottom pot. The Turks drink tea all day, a teapot cosily puffing steam into the air never far away. A Turkish friend once thoughtfully and slowly tapped his teaspoon against the side of a glass to make that special ringing sound only Turkish tea glasses make. 'That is one of my favourite sounds in the world,' he said, gently tapping the spoon against the glass and smiling to himself.

There were many memories that afternoon as I walked slowly round the top of the citadel, trying to blend into the background but failing conspicuously, the Turks staring curiously at a pair of dangerous, blue eyes walking past in a blue dress. I was followed by a group of schoolgirls, who tittered and giggled behind me, wondering who I was and where I had come from. I felt too tired to speak, but in the end turned round and told them. They were amazed I could understand what they were saying. There were more sniggers and giggles when they heard I had visited Giresun thirteen years previously – could anybody be as old as that apart from their mothers! – until they got bored and drifted off to find other entertainment. I was half asleep on my feet and stood and watched the children playing on the swings and roundabouts in the playground set up in the dazzle of the shade of the trees. The ropes of the swings creaked and groaned rhythmically, backwards and forwards. Shut your eyes and listen and the years dropped away and everything blurred into sunny, swinging memories. It occurred to me that some of the younger children playing there could have been the sons and daughters of the teenage girls I had met in 1983.

I creaked and groaned back down the hillside, stopping to look at the road rolling eastwards to Trabzon and wondered how tough the trip would be. I would spend, I thought, at least a couple of nights in Trabzon. The idea of being able to stay in bed and not have to get up at the crack of dawn seemed rather an attractive one.

Back at the bottom of the hill, I began to think about the eating possibilities in Giresun. I was hoping to find a restaurant as splendid as the one I had discovered in Ereğeli. I was still savouring the bubbling hot İskender kebab I had eaten there. It was only eleven days before but already it felt like an ancient memory. I had spotted a fast food takeaway selling greasy kebab sandwiches near the Hotel Grey Vineyard, but I was hoping Giresun could offer something better than that. And sure enough, returning to the main park in the town centre, there it was waiting for me, a large, square, substantial establishment strategically built on a corner, next to the town hall and opposite the park.

I pushed through the door. The restaurant was like a cavern inside, enormous with wide picture windows and a high ceiling, light and airy like the most fashionable of French brasseries, but unsophisticated and unpretentious. This was the best kind of traditional Turkish restaurant, a veritable food factory. I sat down at a shiny clean table and savoured the scene. There were roast chickens, crisp and brown, basting on spits in a glass-fronted oven. A display cabinet was crammed with Turkish meze: white cheeses, cold beans in oil, purple puréed aubergine, stuffed vine leaves, olives and yoghurt dishes, a feast of colour. An ayran machine in a corner moaned and groaned and churned out glasses of the white stuff for the thirsty customers. Ayran is a salted yoghurt drink. I don't like it, but the Turks drink it until it comes out of their ears. It looks delicious, like pure cream, but tastes like, well, sour yoghurt. In the window was the *pièce de resistance*, an enormous spit of lamb, the deliciously greasy juice running down and hissing as it fell onto the coals underneath. It was a hunk of lamb to dream about, enough for a thousand different kebab dishes. The man in charge of the spit was busy slicing away with a murderous knife, cutting off chunks of meat into a shovel. He weighed these expertly on a pair of red scales. At the same time, he continued to stoke the glowing coals under the spit. It was a brow-mopping work of art. It is an underrated skill to slice up spitted lamb. It also takes stamina to stand in front of a burning hot lump of meat all day. I could have watched him work for hours, savouring the smells and anticipating the taste in my mouth.

I slumped happily into my chair. The restaurant was very busy with Sunday families. Unusually, like me, they were sitting downstairs in the main part of the restaurant rather than upstairs in the quieter, gloomier area, which is traditionally reserved for families or women unaccompanied by a man. I blended into the general background and nobody stared at me. The waiters ran backwards and forwards carrying loaded trays of food in their arms as carefully as if they were carrying babies. I ordered a kebab, and when it arrived, the meat was sizzling and the yoghurt was cold, just like it ought to be. The blend of hot and cold in the mouth was a truly wonderful experience.

The hotel still seemed completely deserted when I got back and I sped upstairs and down the long corridor trying not to think of the awfulness of the empty rooms behind the locked doors. I scuttled inside my room, turning the key in the lock behind me. I had so much to do. I tested the bed, so springy and comfortable, arranged and re-arranged the contents of my bags, wrote my diary, consulted the map for the ninety-ninth time, rejoined Maggie in *The Golden Bowl* for a while and then went to sleep. How blissful life could occasionally be.

12
Giresun to Trabzon

They put on board ship the sick, and those who were over forty years old, and the women and children, and all the baggage which it was not essential to have with them. The rest travelled by land, the roads being now in a good state of repair.

My face was a mess in the morning, burned red and sweating. I crammed on my greasy sun hat and considered the reflection in the mirror. I really needed a scarf around my neck as well. The effect of hours of exposure to the sun and sea air was catastrophic. It was just enormously uncomfortable to wear hats and scarves, the sweat trickling down inside like an insect pricking its way over the skin. It drove me into a frenzy of fury and irritation which ate away at my precious energy levels. There was no an answer to this. Either one covered up or sunstroke struck.

I cycled out of Giresun, underneath the citadel hill and past the town's museum situated in the former Greek Orthodox church of St. Nicholas. The church was, predictably, closed for restoration. I was looking forward to seeing the museum church of St. Sophia in Trabzon. Carefully wrapped up in my bag was an article from the Turkish Daily News, Turkey's English-language newspaper. It said that the local Welfare Party, which controlled Trabzon, wanted to take over St. Sophia and re-open it as a mosque (as it became after the Ottoman conquest), even though it had become one of the most famous tourist sites in Trabzon. It sounded like a row to me, a clashingly good row, once again emphasising that the concept of history being history was a foolish one.

The road continued to hug the coastline and the scenery was becoming more beautiful again. I saw many of the 'ibis' trees with their spectacular golden crests of flowers. They were growing in people's gardens as well as springing up wild along the verges. Somebody had placed a wooden bench underneath one of them so that passers by could sit down and take a rest in the shade. I stopped to take in the beauty of the picture that had been created. It looked like an oil painting or a scene from the endless, ongoing play I seemed to be taking part in, sometimes as an actor and sometimes as a spectator. Here, I wanted to sit on the bench and become part of the picture.

The mountains were densely green and were now within smelling distance. I looked at them longingly; they were cool and remote and far away from the traffic. By now, this was horrible, the driving manic and hysterical, nose to tail, mustn't slow down for one second, shake, rattle and roll but without the fun. I cycled over bridges getting glimpses of spectacular gorges leading into the interior and houses dotted amongst the trees and perched high up on the edge of precipices. I remembered Andy telling me I should try to go up and along one of the rivers inland away from the sea. It would have been fine with a four-wheel drive but less practical with a bicycle. For the time being, I had to make do with looking from a distance and dealing with the mayhem around me.

A lorry shot past and braked sharply in front of me, skidding to a halt. The door opened and the driver leaped out, waving his arms and shouting at me like a lunatic. I hid under my hat and scooted past, only to be overtaken by another lorry whose driver had seen what was going on and who, likewise, stood on his brakes and swerved the vehicle to kangaroo to a stop on the side. Could you have believed it? What fevered imaginations! It was mass hysteria. The whole of the Black Sea coast was going to be littered with my rejects. Although I knew I didn't look like one, however desperately the lorry drivers roared, I began to feel like a pop star. I wondered if I should stop and offer them my autograph. It was almost funny.

Moments later, I passed a family standing by the side of the road, the parents and a troop of children. As I cycled by, the man appeared to lose his head and erupted into bellows and howls, frantically waving his arms around and pointing at me. I wondered what on earth he was saying and what his wife and children must have thought. Maybe they would blame me for the apparent temporary madness of the head of the household. My nerves were on edge after two weeks of constant exposure to looks and stares and astonishment. I was now seriously thinking of murdering the next person who asked me why I wasn't married. I was looking forward to getting to Trabzon where, hopefully, I would be able to disappear into the crowds of a big city which would be used to the Natashas from the east and wouldn't bother with a middle-aged woman with greasy hair and a burned, red nose.

Although there were supposedly picturesque villages and ruined castles along the road, I didn't spot any castles at all and the villages and towns looked very much like each other, grey and depressed, with the inevitable fish barrage dominating the sea front. None of them were making anything of their sea views. I was beginning to feel overwhelmed by the number of new mosques being built, with collecting boxes positioned outside inviting passers-by to make a contribution. I couldn't help contrasting the bustling activity surrounding these mosques with the lack of activity at the numerous roadwork sites. The road menders were still throwing down sticky tarmac, splat, stick, glue, in ripples and waves, as if there was no real point in making a decent job of it because the weather would just rip it all up anyway and, in any case, everybody would emigrate to Germany. In contrast to my journey, those among the Ten Thousand, who opted to travel westwards on foot on this part of their journey, found the roads in good condition. This was owing to their leader's gently menacing suggestion to the locals along the coast that it would be a good idea, a very good idea, if they mended the roads. 'They will do what we ask,' Xenophon told his men, 'both because they are afraid of us and because they want to get rid of us.' It was a request they could not refuse.

As I reflected on the desirability of having power, I passed a chocolate factory belonging to the Ülker group. I could smell the sweet cocoa and almost taste the crunch of the hazelnuts they add to the bars as I lingered by. Ülker chocolate was deliciously smooth and creamy and – I thought – easily competed with Swiss or Belgian chocolate, which was four times the price. Ülker had connections with Refah, the Islamist Welfare Party. Earlier in the year, the military, which took pride in defending the secular principles of Atatürk and had just ousted the Islamist prime minister, Necmettin Erbakan, had reportedly told its personnel to boycott products made by businesses close to the Islamists, including Ülker. The story had made front page news in the Turkish press. After I passed the Ülker factory, I went into the first shop I could find to buy a bar of their hazelnut chocolate.

I stopped to use the toilet at a vast, empty resthouse along the way and the man in charge invited me in for a particularly awful glass of dreggy, stale tea. He was kind and enthusiastic about my journey. His nephew came to talk to me – in French. He was a taciturn, gloomy little boy. He told me he lived in Paris with his parents and had come back to Turkey for a holiday. He was pleased to find somebody he could speak French with. It was obviously now his first language. It was strange to hear a Turk speak French. I was more used to hearing them speak German or English. I found I had forgotten many French words and more easily used the Turkish, which made us both laugh. I wished for the umpteenth time that I could speak many languages fluently like so many of the people I had met abroad, especially the Dutch and Scandinavians. It is the curse of being English. We just don't have to make the effort. The boy's uncle listened with rapture, proud that his nephew could so easily communicate with a foreigner. A woman – a cousin or an aunt – came to collect the boy and she gave me some freshly baked cakes to eat. Uncle was leaving to catch the bus into town. He looked out through the picture window over the sea and studied the clouds.

'There's going to be a storm,' he said. 'It's going to be a big one. Be careful you don't get caught in it. I'm worried I'll get wet even before the bus comes.' He spoke with all the authority of a man from the Black Sea.

Outside, I looked at the clouds and decided he had been exaggerating. After all, I came from England and also knew when it was going to rain, didn't I? I was sure I could outride any storm that was coming. I waved goodbye to him as he stood observing the sky like a human barometer at the bus stop and set off, speeding down the hill and into the town of Akçakale. Half way down the street, I could sense the clouds thickening overhead and suddenly I could smell the rain coming. The atmosphere was hot and electric. Exciting. My bicycle once again turned into a winged steed. I felt as if we could cycle on for ever, soaring over the sea and the mountains. I shot by a tea shop and had second thoughts, wondering if I should pull over, see what was going to happen and wait until whatever it was had passed by. The old men sitting outside under the awning watched me cynically. Pooh! I was sure I could beat the storm. I pedalled even faster, out of town and along the coastal road. There were no buildings along the shore, and the sea, flat and with a sinister stillness, stretched out alongside and ahead of me. Thunder cracked and rolled overhead and lightning forked down. The town was literally disappearing behind me under a purple fury, the bruised clouds billowing and rolling down, enveloping the houses, the mosques and the old men sitting drinking their tea. It was a stupendous, beautiful sight. I had never seen anything like it. It was Sodom and Gomorrah, the wrath of an angry god punishing mankind for its sins. I stood on the edge of the storm and began to understand how myths, legends and gods were created.

Now I knew I could never run before such weather. This was going to be cataclysmic. I pedalled furiously looking for shelter and, just before the town dribbled to a halt and the open countryside began, by a miracle I found a family restaurant with a covered terrace outside. I picked up the bicycle, bags and all, and ran onto the terrace. A girl, the daughter of the family, was washing the floor. She brought me a chair so I could sit and have a grandstand view of the storm. She invited me inside but I wanted to watch what was going to happen. The sea had turned a silvery blue, the seagulls were laughing manically from an island of black rock silhouetted against the sky opposite and the red ball of the sun was hanging huge and round in the east. The rain arrived and the wind blew the water under the awning. I retreated inside together with the bicycle, slipping and sliding over the wet tiles. I apologised for having brought the bicycle inside too, but the girl smiled a welcome.

I had made it just in time. With the rest of the family, I watched through the windows. I had only ever seen storms like this before on television. The trees, grass, even the hydrangeas were flattened by the gale which blew up. Everything disappeared in a white blizzard of pounding rain. It was impossible even to see across to the other side of the road. The cars stopped and put their blinkers on, and then vanished too. It was a white typhoon, a wall of water and wind. The water gulped and poured from the awning and roof, sideways, upwards, downwards, battering on the doors and windows. It felt like the end of the world. Had I still been on the road, I would have been blown away or drowned. This was high summer. What must it be like in the winter?

After a while, the world slowly re-emerged from the whiteness but the rain continued to pour down. There was nothing to be done except to wait until it stopped. I chatted to the family. The eldest daughter told me that the restaurant had just opened and proudly showed me a large tank at the back filled with enormous trout. Customers could select which ones they wanted to have for dinner. I asked her what business was like, on the edge of this small town. It was already good, she said, and people were coming to eat there. At that moment, her brother ran in, his arms filled with fresh loaves of bread. He sparkled with rain and looked like a young, handsome god. After the greyness of the towns I had come through, this vibrant, family restaurant was like a breath of fresh air.

It was only another twenty-five miles, forty kilometres, into Trabzon. Despite the road surfaces, I had come far and fast that morning. I could hardly believe it. Earlier on, there had been road signs to the towns of Erzincan and Sivas in the east of Turkey, and I had seen buses heading for the great cities of İstanbul and Ankara. Familiar names but it felt as if they were in a completely different country. As I set off from the restaurant, a bus came past destined for the lovely town of Antalya on the Mediterranean, Ak Deniz in Turkish, literally the 'White Sea', that sunny, sparkling, hot, sexy sea so different from the opaque, cold Kara Deniz. In July, by midday on the Mediterranean, it would be too hot to sit on the beach. And here was I adrift in the wet, north-eastern corner of what felt like a mythical land, wondering if it was ever going to stop raining.

I continued on. The road was wet and greasy. Again, I had to balance along the edge as the traffic sped along, most of the cars making no allowance for a bicycle. I could feel my wheels slipping away unsteadily down the sloping edges and off the road. It was a nightmare. I felt as if I were balancing on the edge of a tightrope. One slip and I was in the abyss and heading down to Hades. Again, I kept having to stop and wait for the traffic to squeeze past. What was I doing? Why wasn't I at home, respectably looking after my garden? Getting myself a husband? Settling down?

The sea had turned a milky white, an unearthly colour, concealing the monsters lurking in the depths. The clouds now looked innocent, like puffs of cotton wool, instead of swelling with the furious, billowing, black anger that had possessed them earlier. It rained some more but nothing serious, the drops falling on my face like individual, warm, globules of oil. The flood water, muddy, thick and yellow, gushed and spouted down from the rocks and hills into the ditches. Now I could understand why the road was built up, however roughly, the sides sloping down to stop the roads themselves from flooding. Except that I didn't want to fall down there too.

I thought at least there could have been a round of applause as I cycled in to Trabzon, Trebizond, the ancient Greek city of Trapezus, where Xenophon and his men at last reached the sea in their retreat from Persia and close to where they stayed for thirty days while they plundered and ravaged the surrounding countryside, so relieved to be off the mountains and out of the winter snows.

Nearly a thousand years later in 1461, Trabzon, the last outpost of the Byzantine Empire, which had been ruled by the Comneni family since the disastrous Crusader sacking of Constantinople in 1204, fell to the Ottoman Turks. It was overwhelming to see the sign: Trabzon, population 150,000. It was well over a thousand kilometres back to İstanbul, and I had cycled most of it, over hills, through storms and along horrible roads to get here. I felt like waving to everybody, although that feeling soon evaporated as the uninterested and uninteresting concrete suburbs of Trabzon closed around me. Where were the famous walls, the twin towers, Saint Sophia, aunt Dot with her camel . . . ?

It was a sweat of a journey in. I found Trabzon to be the hottest and most humid of all the cities along the Black Sea. I carried on through the concrete jungle along the sea and at last found a sign that pointed up to the city centre, away from the line of the coast. There were a lot of hills to negotiate and I kept asking people, desperately, where the city centre actually was, furious that it seemed to get further and further away. One woman I stopped in the street at first pretended I wasn't there. When I repeated the question, she pointed, reluctantly, straight ahead, although she refused to look or speak to me. I wondered whether she thought I was a Russian woman, a Natasha on a bicycle, because of course Trabzon was, at this point in its long history, the heart of the Natasha trade from the former Soviet Union. At last I was going to see the girls everybody throughout Turkey was talking about.

Further on, opposite an appalling, soulless, civic and shopping centre – please, please don't let this be the centre of Trabzon – I stopped at an ice cream and coffee store to ask for a drink of water. The man gave me a glass and, after a close look at my face, handed me a second. 'Just a bit further,' he said. I bashed on, up such narrow, one-way streets the cars had to allow me to pass in front of them for once. Despite having to concentrate on the traffic, I couldn't help but notice the enormous number of sleazy-looking hotels packed into the back streets.

Finally, I rounded a corner – and there was historical Trabzon waiting for me: magnificent, shining, black walls plunging down into a chasm crossed by ancient bridges, red-roofed houses lining the slopes and nestling down below in the valley, cobbled streets and squares and graceful Ottoman buildings, all resplendent in the sunshine. It was like another world, although the traffic was so heavy and the streets so congested that I had to get off and walk. The road led straight through to what was obviously Trabzon's central square, a crash box of hotels, shops, restaurants, buses and taxis. All I wanted to do was to find a hotel, preferably not like the ones I had just seen. I had stayed before in a hotel (not in Turkey) which had been frequented by prostitutes, and ultimately it had been neither a pleasant nor comfortable experience. The tourist information office was, wonderfully, right there on the corner. I leaned the bicycle against the glass and went in, immediately noticing the Russian/Turkish dictionary to hand in the middle of the desk. It was an efficiently-run office. A helpful woman recommended a hotel and suggested I should come back when I was less tired. As I was heading for the hotel, which she had assured me was close by, an excessively thin Japanese boy came up and pointed at my bicycle.

'I've got one too,' he said. 'Where have you come from?'

'İstanbul,' I said. 'What about you.'

'From Thailand,' he said.

'Gosh,' I said weakly. 'That's a long way.'

He was staying in the hotel next to the one I was heading for. I wanted to ask him a thousand questions but his English wasn't so good. We were standing on a traffic island with the traffic thundering by, shaking the ground, and a small boy was poking at the back of my bicycle. When I shouted at him to stop, he just grinned and carried on fiddling. I began to feel hysterical. 'See you later,' I said to the Japanese boy and pressed on. My hotel was a bit further on, down a small road leading to the port. I later discovered that I could have come straight up from the sea through the old markets but had, instead, laboriously followed the main road winding inland up and over the hills. No wonder the town centre had seemed so far away from the coast.

Otel Anıl was new, reasonable and apparently respectable, although the host of young boys who manned the reception desk were unsmiling and reserved and continued that way for the three nights I was to stay there – possibly they were taking no chances. The small cupboard of a room with a shower was stifling hot but it had a view overlooking the port. It was around £6 a night. I nipped next door to check the prices at the hotel of the Japanese boy, glimpsing his bicycle, which was as thin as he was, leaning in an exhausted fashion against the foot of a staircase. From Thailand! The hotel's rooms were slightly more expensive. The Otel Anıl it was to be.

I too had to lean the bicycle against the stairs in the hotel's basement stairwell. A less public spot would have been preferable. One of the boys had shown me into the basement storeroom, which was impenetrable, draped as it was with the day's wet sheets hanging up to dry. He didn't hesitate to push his way through the sheets, which wound round us as if we were corpses, to get to the boiler throbbing somewhere at the back. I didn't fancy leaving the bicycle among the clinging shrouds. I thought she might get upset in the night. So I tied her up to the bannisters, hoping nobody would fall over the back wheel, which was slightly sticking out into the passage and tied up with my washing line. She looked tired and dusty, just how I was feeling. Three nights in Trabzon was what we both needed.

I took a shower. There was hot water which I used, alternating it with the cold, to create my own blissful, mini sauna. From my window, opened as wide as it would go, I looked down into the port busy with storage silos, warehouses and rows of dock cranes. A ship was sailing in past the lighthouses on both ends of the harbour walls. The port of Trabzon was the largest along the Black Sea. Goods arrived there by sea and continued by road into Central Asia and Iran. I thought of the loaded lorries sweating along the tight, breathe-in coast road to the border with Georgia and decided to re-consider my original plan to follow in the same direction. The thought was filed away in my mental drawer marked 'pending'. There were three nights to go before any decision had to be taken.

Looking up from my window, Trabzon appeared to be enfolded among hills like a bird in a hand. Some areas of the hillsides were still green but most were scarred with concrete blocks and the tops of the hill bristled with antennae. Down below and underneath my window, the cobbled street was crammed with traffic jostling to get past the delivery trucks blocking the way. The noise was deafening, with people shouting, engines revving and car horns hooting impatiently. The buildings were ancient; some were practically tumbling down, their mossy, red tiled roofs sliding drunkenly towards oblivion. I was able to peer into the windows of the restaurant opposite. The top floor was a beer house and there were signs on the windows in Russian. Its name was Yudum. In Turkish, 'yudum' means 'sip, sup, gulp or swallow'. I thought the name summed it all up rather nicely. I wanted to watch to see who went in but realised what I was doing and pulled my head in abruptly. I didn't want people in the street down below or from the beer house opposite seeing the head of a foreign woman leaning, however uninvitingly, out of the window.

I always feel overwhelmed in a big city, unsure where to start first, worried that if I look for the 'sights', I will miss out on the people. I knew I wanted to visit Atatürk's villa, my hero's country retreat in the hills above Trabzon, and I also wanted to see St. Sophia and find out more about the 'row'. I decided to go back to the information office in the big square, get some maps and start from there.

I went back downstairs, leaning over the banisters to peer fondly at the bicycle in the basement, past the non-smiling crowd of boys lounging like well-fed young lions in the lobby, and out into the street. I walked slowly, looking around, absorbing what was going on. For once, nobody took any notice of me. It was wonderful. Trabzon was indeed a different city from all other Turkish cities.

The first bit of excitement was a newstand on the corner, which was selling copies of the *Turkish Daily News* from Ankara. It was my first sight of an English-language newspaper since getting on the plane at Heathrow airport.

'You're the first place to sell the TDN I've seen since İstanbul,' I told the dark-haired woman in the shop.

'They're here every day by the middle of the morning,' she said, smiling at my excitement.

In the tourist information office, one of the officers was dealing with a French family, handing out maps and brochures and speaking in very good French, while the other, the woman I had met earlier, was on the telephone. I sat down to wait for her to finish her conversation, pleased to get the chance. A cup of sweet Turkish coffee appeared as if by magic. The woman was efficient and practical. The buses and the shared dolmuş taxis to the different sites around Trabzon all left from the square, she said, and even told me how much the fares would be. (They were very cheap.)

'Can I still get into St. Sophia?' I asked tentatively, hoping she would say no. It would make the story so much better.

'Yes, of course you can.'

'But what about the report of the plan by Refah to close it and turn it back into a mosque?'

'That was completely untrue,' she snapped.

My heart sank further. 'I read the story in the newspaper.'

'There's a new government in Ankara now,' she said. And that was all I could get from her on that subject.

I turned to another burning issue. 'There are a lot of Russian girls in town, aren't there?'

'Quite a few.'

'It's funny,' I went on. 'Trabzon is controlled by Refah and yet they let the girls come in.'

'We are a free country,' she replied shortly.

I wasn't prepared to abandon the idea of doing a story about St. Sophia. I suddenly remembered that on my way in earlier, I had spotted a press club on the square, almost opposite a line of taxis offering trips to the former church. I walked back the way I had cycled in and found the club in a lovely old house with art deco windows. The real story was that the culture minister in the ousted Refah-led coalition government had started proceedings to have St. Sophia closed as a museum and re-opened as a mosque, as it had been on and off since 1461 when the Ottoman Turks had occupied Trabzon. Most of the people of Trabzon had protested against the plan and the new coalition government, which had come to power shortly afterwards, had stopped the process immediately. Why, I asked, had the people of Trabzon been against the plan and yet had voted in a local council controlled by the Islamists? Refah, the journalists told me, had got in with less than a quarter of the vote. In any case, the town realised that St. Sophia was a major tourist attraction and wanted it to stay that way. The worry was that if the Islamists regained control of the central government, they would resume their attempts to take control. I asked if anybody at the club supported Refah. Everybody grimaced and shook their heads.

Before leaving, I was shown round the building. There were yellowing, framed copies of former front pages hanging up the stairwell and large, panelled rooms with carved and decorated ceilings. The people in the club that day seemed delighted by a visit from a foreign reporter and I was briefly introduced to the most famous among them, the sports writer who covered the matches of TrabzonSpor, the local football club and one of the biggest and most famous clubs in Turkey. He honoured me by shaking my hand before dashing off somewhere. Sports journalists are all the same, places to go, people to talk to.

Back on the square, I took a different turning and discovered the labyrinth of the old markets (in Turkish, 'pazar' or 'çarşı'). It was huddled on the hills running down to the sea in a warren of narrow lanes, packed with shops, workshops, goldsmiths, wood turners and copper markets. There were ancient mosques, many of which had started out as churches, next to stone hans, ruined bedestens (covered market halls) and hamams. One whole area was made up of food halls with trestle tables crowded together and groaning under the weight of every kind of fruit and vegetable.

As I wandered happily around, it seemed to me that there was a satisfied, relaxed atmosphere in Trabzon. That gnawing, itching, male frustration, almost palpable in Turkey and in the Middle East generally, was just not there in Trabzon. The shopkeepers asked what nationality I was in a business-like way, as if they were simply adding to their own store of information for future use. I felt as if I were walking in European streets in the sense that nobody bothered me. I could walk, stop and look, secure in the knowledge that nobody cared and the usual thousand pairs of eyes fixing on me were just not there. I could only assume it was because of the influx into Trabzon of girls from the former Soviet Union. For me, it was great, a revelation. There should obviously be legalised brothels for men – and women, yes, why not – in every town and city throughout the world.

Emerging from the market at the bottom of the hill, I found myself back on the coast and in a street of warehouses. Inside, the piles of leather jackets, jeans and denim clothes almost reached to the ceiling. It must have all been worth many thousands of pounds. As I wandered past, eyes popping, the shopkeepers didn't even bother to invite me in. They could tell just from looking at me that I really was 'just looking' and had no intention of doing the bulk buying their usual customers did before transporting the goods back to Georgia, Ukraine, Azerbaijan or Russia to sell on for a profit. There were cafes, restaurants and hotels in every direction. Most of the signs were written in the Cyrillic script. It was obvious that this was the Russian business area. At last I had found it, but I was going to have to wait until the next day to explore. I crossed the road to pick my way through the usual filthy wasteland beside the sea, no hint here of any attempt to make a green park, and bought a kilo of bright red cherries from one of the fresh food stalls. By now I could hardly move one leg in front of another. It was a steep climb back up through the market, taking a detour through some of the main streets, to return to the town square, past the buses and taxis, noting the enormous number of restaurants and exchange money shops. I tottered down a side street. It should have been called The Street of Sweets. The shops were crammed and popping with beribboned boxes of Turkish delight, imported chocolate, nuts and sticky sweets of every kind. Like the piles of jeans and jackets down below in the warehouses, these shops were geared up for bulk buying, the goods destined to be bought and resold in the countries east of Turkey. I bought a bottle of red wine from a liquor store. The man wrapped it up carefully in newspaper and put it into a carrier bag.

Clutching my guilty secret, I returned to the hotel. There was no one in the lobby and, after a loving look at the bicycle, I staggered upstairs. The room was like an oven and smelled horribly of my sweaty canvas shoes. I opened the bottle of wine with anticipation, but after just a few minutes, it tasted like it had been heated up in front of a fire. I ran the cold water in the basin in the shower room and put the bottle in, hoping to cool it down. My face, which was so badly burned, seemed to catch fire; the skin was swollen and sweating. I felt terrible. I looked at the distorted creature in the glass and could hardly recognise her. I had just about enough energy to stand under the shower before collapsing on my bed, unable to move. Despite the tempting sight of the restaurants I had just passed, I knew I couldn't get to them. I had to make do with the cherries and remnants of bread and cheese from my bags. I fell asleep, despite the roar of Trabzon coming in through the window, and dreamed of a storm in which everything was swept away.

13
Trabzon

The people of Trapezus provided the Greeks with facilities for buying food, and gave them presents of oxen and barley and wine.

I got up at eight o'clock the next morning. Such luxury. It felt as if half the day had gone and it was already midday. I dropped in at a restaurant off the square for a breakfast bowl of rice and lentil soup and then crossed over to the stop to take a dolmuş to St. Sophia which was on the outskirts of Trabzon. There were queues of these ageing, spacious, saloon cars waiting for passengers and mine pulled off as I got in even though it was empty apart from me. Nervously, I asked the driver whether it really was a dolmuş. They generally waited until the vehicles were at least half full before leaving. I was worried he had decided to change himself into a taxi so he could charge me more to compensate for the empty seats. He nodded reassuringly, however, and I paid the dolmuş fare, the equivalent of about 30p. The car wound through the suburbs to drop me off close to St. Sophia. I was amused to see that along the road one of the signs called the church/museum 'St. Sophie'. A line from the musical *My Fair Lady* ran through my head: 'I'll go to St. James so often I will call him St. Jim.'

St. Sophie, Aya Sofya, Haghia Sophia or Church of the Divine Wisdom sat behind low walls on a promontory overlooking the sea. I walked down a track, past a tumbledown factory and some old buildings, to get an overview before going in. On the hillside all the way down to the coastal road were vegetable gardens. It was a lovely, peaceful place. People had worshipped a god of one kind or another on this holy spot for millennia. The Byzantines, as the pre-Christian people before them, obviously liked their important places of worship to be on a high place with a sea view. The churches at Ordu and Giresun had been built on similar sites. I imagined the area when St. Sophia was built around eight hundred years ago, way out of town and surrounded by orchards, gardens and open countryside. I retraced my steps and found a small souvenir shop just before the gates. It was already open despite the early hour. The shopkeeper looked lonely and forlorn behind his maps and guide-books, waiting for the handful of tourists who might come that day if he were lucky. I bought some postcards of some surviving frescoes but it didn't cheer him up.

I walked through the gates, bought a museum ticket from the kiosk and turned to look at St. Sophia crowned with a red-tiled, octagonal, tower dome. The stone carvings on the triple archway and supporting columns over the main open porch entrance had been attacked with hammers in the past and were sadly blurred and battered. I wandered round the garden enjoying the early morning freshness and the sea air, but there was something lonely about the place. There was a forlorn look about the scrappy hedges and the straggling roses. A gardener was sawing away at the branches of a tree, thinning them out, although I couldn't really see why.

St. Sophia was built in the thirteenth century alongside a monastery which had been constructed on the site of a pagan temple and an early Byzantine chapel. The rather forbidding-looking bell tower next to the church was built nearly two hundred years later. There are no remains of the monastery or the chapel. The Ottomans converted St. Sophia into a mosque after they occupied Trabzon in 1461, but the building was neglected and fell into disrepair. During the First World War, it was used as an ammunition store and a hospital before being turned once again into a mosque. St. Sophia was restored in the late 1950s and early 1960s when a team from Edinburgh was allowed in to save the remaining frescoes. The building was then opened as a museum. Was that why it felt so sad? A museum looks back to the past, to the glory that has been, not to the future.

The church must have been very splendid. The dome, arches, vaults and walls inside were covered with frescoes telling the stories of the Old and New Testaments. They were painted in warm reds and glowing oranges, rich browns and blues. On the floor were geometric mosaics in gold, silver and blue. Many of the faces of the holy figures had been obliterated and there were deep scratches and score marks across the lower paintings. It was incredible that any had survived at all given that the church had been used as a mosque for such long periods of time. The representation of human images is forbidden by the Muslim religion – as in the Jewish faith.

I walked around in the gloom admiring the wonderful Byzantine faces that had survived, those deep, melting, dark eyes, firm noses and strong mouths. I could have fallen in love with all of them. The narthex in particular was well preserved. There were scenes from the life of Christ painted in incredible, psychedelic colours and patterns that reminded me of the work of William Blake. One wall painting showed Christ walking on the water, calming the storm and feeding the five thousand. The cherubim and seraphim in one of the panels looked as if they were having a very good time at a very good party. Their experience was definitely turning out to be ecstatic.

For once, I wasn't alone. A couple from Scandinavia turned up to look round together with their extremely bored son and daughter. We all tiptoed round in reverential silence broken by the noise of the man's camera furiously flashing away at the frescoes and the sweet singing of the birds outside. I wondered if the craftsmen and painters had enjoyed their work in such a place, in peace and quiet far away from the din of the city over the hills, refreshed by the breeze and able to smell the sea. Did they stop every so often as they chipped away at the decorations in the stone or coloured in those magnificent eyes, probably like their own, to stretch their legs and admire the view?

Despite the summer heat, the building smelled disused and damp and I noticed a patch of water on the ground. I assumed it was rainwater leaking from the roof – although it could well have been something else. A small, deformed dog was hopping around inside accompanied by a woman pattering merrily over the flagstones behind it – until they saw my face and hopped and pattered respectively out again.

On my way out of one of the church doors at the side, there was a plaque on the wall with some words from the Koran on it. They were in English and Turkish: 'True temples belong to God alone and within them therefore shalt thou worship no other but God.'

Truly it was lucky some of the frescoes had survived.

I saw the woman with the dog again at the kiosk by the front gates. She was organising souvenirs, beads and postcards in a glass display case. She beamed merrily at me and was so happy, almost humming and dancing with good humour, I had to smile back.

'Come and have some tea and see what we've done,' she said joyfully and led me to an area off the square, which had been laid out as a tea garden for the visitors. A barn had been turned into a tearoom and a table outside was laid for breakfast. There were olives, honey, jam and cheese. Two girls, one of whom was the woman's daughter, were already tucking in. They fetched a chair and invited me to join them. I asked the woman about the threat from Refah to turn St. Sophia once again back into a mosque. She scowled and shrugged. 'They can't now,' she said dismissively. I asked her why she was so happy, virtually dancing in the church. She laughed. 'It's the atmosphere. It makes me very happy to work here. It's such a lovely place. I'm so lucky.'

I felt horribly guilty that I had thought for one second that the place felt forlorn and dead. For her it was alive and living. She was happy about everything, the fresh honey and eggs, her life, her job, her daughter. She was exactly the right person to be in charge of St. Sophie. 'Do you know how old I am,' she went on. She was a slim, pretty woman but I didn't dare guess in case I got it wrong. I estimated she was older than I was. 'I'm forty,' she said proudly. 'Aren't I lucky.' My mouth nearly dropped open. She was younger than I was! Thank god I hadn't said anything. The mirror swung round once again, creaking, for me to peer into clearly. I complimented her on her youthful looks and she beamed even more happily. She danced off to the kiosk to see to two more tourists, who were about to drive back into the town centre. They offered to give me a lift. Before we left, the woman asked me to write in the visitors' book. I couldn't resist. Before we (the English) criticised the Muslims for knocking the church of St. Sophia about, I wrote pompously, we should remember what we did ourselves to our own churches during the Reformation and visit, in particular, the Lady Chapel in Ely Cathedral. I could also have mentioned the rape, murder, pillage, theft and wholesale destruction carried out in Constantinople in 1204 by Western European, Christian Crusaders during the fourth Crusade. But I didn't. Nevertheless, I hoped I wouldn't get any hate mail.

Of the two tourists, one was a Turkish girl and the other a Norwegian man. I was curious to know if they were being allowed to share a room in the hotels. By no means. Because the girl was Turkish, they were having to pay for two rooms. The silly thing was they weren't even lovers, they said. They really were just good friends. They dropped me off at the start of the main square. It was still only mid-morning so I decided to carry on the sightseeing roller coaster. I bought a small pide from a bakery and made my way through the park back to the bus stops and taxi rank area, which was by now thick with the smell of diesel fumes. I was following the next set of useful instructions from the tourist information office on how to get the bus to Atatürk's villa. The bus stops were crowded and a girl took me under her wing. She would tell me when my bus arrived, she said. She asked me the usual questions and I admired the silver ship she was wearing on the necklace around her neck. It had been given to her by her eldest sister, she said, her 'abla'. She asked me whether I would like to have it. I had forgotten. Never say you like anything in Turkey because the person wearing it will automatically offer to give it to you. I was never sure what would happen if you said you wanted it. Part of the game was to decline politely and, of course, I did. The girl was pleased a foreigner had noticed and admired her beloved necklace and happily waved me off when the bus came along.

The woman in tourist information had said that the bus to the villa, which was a few miles out of town, would ride alongside part of the length of Trabzon's imposing, fortified walls before swinging out of the city and up into the forested hills. And so it did. I felt like a kid being taken out for the day for a treat, gazing at the views through the window, pleased not to be slogging up the perpendicular road on two wheels. Not so long before, the hills outside Trabzon must have been green with pine trees and empty of development but new houses had begun to creep up the sides, although the higher we went, the fewer they became. The road was so narrow the bus filled it entirely. This was alarming until I realised from the road signs that the traffic was one way.

With a great crashing of gears, the driver fought to manoeuvre the bus up and around the hairpin bends. It was lucky we didn't meet Xenophon and his men coming down the other way after one of their successful plundering expeditions during which they burned a whole city to the ground: 'houses, towers, palisade and everything else except the citadel.' (The oxen, barley and wine presented to them on their arrival in Trapzon had been swiftly eaten and drunk.) Loaded with their spoils and keeping a sharp eye out for angry reprisals, the Greek mercenaries found the way back to their camp dangerous and difficult. 'They were apprehensive about the return journey to Trapezus, as the road was steep and narrow', Xenophon confided. The villagers on board my bus with their bulging shopping baskets at their feet took it all completely for granted and sat unmoved throughout the hair-raising journey.

The bus stopped outside the large gates of Atatürk's villa to let me get off, the only tourist, and crashed on up the hills to higher villages. The villa was an extraordinary sight at the end of a manicured garden. There were bushes of hydrangeas and clipped hedges around tiny pockets of grass. With its red turrets and towers, the villa looked as if a witch in a steeple hat had flown in on her broomstick and conjured it up with a wave of her wand. The house had been built around the turn of the twentieth century by a member of a Greek banking family. The city council requisitioned the house two decades later and formally presented it to Atatürk in 1924. After his death, the villa became the property of the nation and was turned into a museum. I thought how sad the Greek family must have been to leave their lovely house behind. Even as I stopped to stare at the gate and savour the atmosphere, the sky began to cloud over. By the time I had got down the path and reached the front door, it had begun to rain.

Hurrying in through the door, it was like stepping back in time. It was as if the great man had just finished playing a game of billiards at the enormous table in the hallway and, glancing at the splendid clock loudly tick-tocking away on the mantlepiece, had ascended the wide staircase to dress for an evening engagement. The drapes at the windows, the sofas, the heavy, ornate furniture and the exquisite crystal in the cupboard were all as he would have wanted, sophisticated, elegant and very Western. There were photographs of him on the wall, those film star eyes, piercing down with that extraordinary, unearthly brilliance, as if seeing a different dimension, as if they were looking into your soul. Atatürk had the reputation of being a great womaniser. No wonder. He was devastatingly attractive. What woman could have resisted his charisma and power. I tried to imagine what I would have said if I had met him hurrying back down the stairs, doing up his cufflinks.

'Buyurun, Pasham, buyurun.'

Upstairs, there were many bedrooms and meeting rooms and a tiled bathroom with a gorgeously painted European toilet. French windows led outside onto wide terraces and balconies and were open that day despite the weather. The wind swept the curtains backwards and forwards and the rain pattered down like hurrying footsteps. It was at least another hour before the bus would arrive to convey me back into the city and the rain had begun to fall in buckets. The curator invited me to sit in the vast kitchen and have some tea. It was comfortable sitting at the large table. A man handed me a heavy, crystal glass of tea – one of Atatürk's glasses! Maybe he had even drunk from it! The enormous old range with its many cooking plates and ovens was still there, a wide, hooded chimney over it. I sat and sipped my tea, read my book and thought about Atatürk until it was time to catch the bus. The rain had stopped and by the time the bus had lurched and jolted back down through the hills, past the citadel towers and into Trabzon, the sun was shining again. This enchanting land of rain and storms and tempests, which stopped as suddenly as they began.

The bus terminated off a large square in a quiet street filled with Ottoman mansions. One had been turned into an educational establishment. I slipped in through the solid front door to admire the lofty, decorated ceilings and the great wooden staircase leading up from the hallway to the upper floors. The heat and the noise of the city outside had been left behind, dissipated and absorbed in the inner space and airiness created by those clever Ottoman architects. A world apart.

I decided I had done enough feeding the mind and soul. It was time to feed the body. I didn't normally eat lunch but I wanted to try one of the restaurants. Cycling burns up the calories and I was permanently hungry. I had lost so much weight, I could have justified going to the Street of Sweets and buying up armfuls of the sticky stuff. One was spoilt for choice for a restaurant in Trabzon. I had never seen so many restaurants and eating houses, in the main square, the surrounding streets, in the market and down by the sea. It was a gastronomic blow-out of a city. Obviously with so much business of one kind or another going on, people had extra large appetites.

Browsing along the main street in the central square, there were spitted roast chickens, lamb döner, every kind of soup, mounds of rice and green beans, vats of bubbling stew, golden chips, stuffed green peppers and deep-fried, little, Black Sea fishes to choose from. I selected a restaurant where the fattest of fat men was in charge of the lamb spit. He bobbed in and out of the door all day, calling 'buyurun, buyurun', in between frantic sessions of slicing through the meat with an electrically-operated knife (modern progress), collecting the strips in a plate-like utensil for weighing, before stuffing the meat into a plump, greasy and delicious kebab. He smiled a welcome from behind his moustache. I squeezed past to order a plateful of crispy fish from the man in charge of the food cabinet and sat down at an empty table.

There were two girls sitting at a table close to the window. They were both ravishingly beautiful. They looked as if they had just washed their long hair – one had black, the other blond hair – and blow dried it to get that effect you usually only see in shampoo commercials on TV, shiny, squeaky-clean, rampantly fluffy and utterly gorgeous. Their faces were exquisitely made up, lustrous eyes and glossy red mouths. They were wearing loose, well-ironed tee shirts and closely fitting jeans. Here in front of me was the secret of Trabzon's success, the reason why it was different from all the other towns. These girls were

'Natashas'. Nobody disturbed or bothered them. In fact nobody else appeared to be even looking at them – except for me. Had it been any other provincial village, town or city in Turkey, the whole place would have been sitting in shocked silence, everybody staring open-mouthed at the sight. The girls smoked, chatted to each other, ate something and left. They must have been in their early twenties but their faces already looked disillusioned and cynical, older than their years. The jolly hooker only exists in the films.

As I reflected, yet again, on the meaning of life and how lucky I had been in so many ways, my plate of fishes arrived, 'eat me' written all over them. After the fish, I ordered a piece of baklava which was still slightly warm, oozing honey sweetness through flaky pastry. Afterwards, I felt deliciously sick. The afternoon stretched ahead. I had done enough sightseeing. It was time to see life. Slipping on the cobbles, I made my way down the steep hill, through the markets and back to the Russian business area along the coast. I knew that somewhere in this area was the 'Russian Market'. I wasn't sure whether it was simply a street market, as I had seen once before over the other side of the Black Sea mountains near Erzurum. There, people had come over in busloads from Georgia to spread out on the ground everything from the contents of their kitchens back home to cheap trinkets from the Far East.

I discovered Trabzon's Russian Market housed under canvas on the sea front. The words 'European Market' were written up over the main entrance, probably to make it sound more respectable. It appeared to be highly organised and was manned by people selling tickets which were checked every so often by policemen. A sign said that Turks had to pay 20,000 Turkish liras (the equivalent of about 12p), while foreigners could enter for free and were welcome. It seemed rather unfair.

Inside, it was an amazing sight. There were two rows of trestle tables, piled high with goods, stretching as far as one could see and beyond, in the gloom of the vast, cavern-like structure. The place was lit by lamps which gave the place a magical, Arabian Nights feel to it. What made the market so unusual was that the stallholders were, without exception, mostly from the former Soviet Union. There were big, buxom matrons with dyed blond hair, bare arms and shoulders and plunging necklines. Had they been Turks, they would have been keen and attentive, ever ready to catch any potential customer's eye and point out the bargains on offer. Instead, these women with big eyes and high cheekbones virtually ignored the prowling crowds, plumply sitting behind their tables, puffing away at cigarettes and chatting together in Russian or Georgian or one of the other Central Asian languages. I noticed that they all seemed to be able to turn it effortlessly into Turkish, which they spoke with only a slight accent.

I met Svetlana right at the beginning of the market, a tiny, beautiful girl with her long, dark hair brushed up and back into a pony tail which hung down her dainty back. She looked like a ballet dancer. Her father was Turkish and her mother was Azeri, she told me, but they all lived in Georgia and she considered herself to be Georgian. She was living on her own in Trabzon, far away from her family, and she had come to earn some money. Svetlana was selling crudely painted boxes from Russia and cheap jewellery, tiny hearts to wear on chains around the neck. Her face was heart-shaped like the jewellery, the sort of face you could gently cup in your hands. Looking up at me with her glistening, dark eyes, she told me that business was difficult. She had to keep putting her prices up because of the strength of the dollar on the currency markets. She was worried that they were too expensive. Her jewellery pieces cost the equivalent of about 35p.

'What's life like for you in Trabzon?' I asked.

'It's not so good,' she told me. 'It's hard to be here on my own, without my family.' She lowered her voice to a whisper. 'They want sex you know,' she confided.

Every woman tarred with the same brush. If you were foreign, you had to be a Natasha and therefore up for sale. I asked her how many languages she could speak. She reeled them off without even blinking: Georgian, Russian, Turkish and Azeri and she could understand Armenian and Kurdish. I told her how much I wanted to visit central Asia. 'You must come and visit me when you come to Georgia,' she said. She broke off to watch an enormous lump of a girl who was pawing her jewellery and looked quite capable of slipping some of it into her pocket. Then, tearing a bit of paper out of a notebook, Svetlana wrote down her address, first in the Cyrillic script and then in the Latin script, to make sure I would be able to read it when I came. 'I shall be waiting for you,' she said, just as the Turks do.

I moved on down the line of stalls, my head swivelling in all directions. I tried to remember the goods I could see on sale. It was a bit like playing that party game for children in which items are brought in on a tray, the tray is then removed and you have to write down as many of the items as you can remember. Most of the goods seemed to come from the Far East: jewellery, Chinese toys, vases, tools, clothes, richly decorated Indian dresses, cloth, cushion covers, waistcoats, cheap make-up, tempting eye-shadow paint boxes, scissors, lamps, shoes, Russian dolls, gaudy samovars, watches costing the equivalent of 75p, perfume, underwear, jeans and sparkly, spangled hair decorations. I lingered over one stall heaped with colourful dresses, waistcoats and scarves from India and began to burrow through the piles. My heart sank when I unearthed a patchwork bedspread coloured a rich red, maroon and shades of pink. It was decorated with sequins, tiny pieces of mirror and gold embroidery. I knew I wanted it. The woman behind the table could see my interest. She unearthed a whole pile and began to unfold them over her table so I could compare and contrast. I continued to prefer the first one I had seen. I tentatively asked how much it was. The price was just under the equivalent of £20. 'They would be more than that in London,' she said.

I already knew that. For thirty seconds I agonised about the stupidity of increasing the weight of my bicycle bags. 'I'll take it,' I said. I couldn't bring myself to bargain. I didn't even want to. I didn't want to feel pity for these proud people. Pity is demeaning. But I felt sorry that they had been so cheated in their lives by their own regimes – and by the West, which could have done so much more to help when the Soviet Empire collapsed. I asked the woman if she would accept a £20 note. This was worth slightly more than the number of Turkish liras she had asked for and by the following day would already have increased in value. Nevertheless, she hesitated, calling over to one of her friends to ask what she should do. Somebody had a mobile telephone and they used it to ring up one of the money changers in town. They obviously didn't know the exchange rate for sterling. I watched in sheer amazement. These people behind the stalls in the Russian Market were not natural merchants. Any Turk in the smallest of shops knows the dollar, mark and sterling rates on any day of the week and can convert the currencies in his or her head as quickly as the fastest computer. The man got off the phone after an earnest conversation and said something to the woman. She turned to me with a beam of relief. She understood what I was offering. She rushed to get a plastic bag and some paper, folded up my glowing piece of Indian cloth and squeezed it into the bag. I walked away, clutching my naughty purchase.

The one aisle through the market divided into two and there were even more trestle tables further on and into the cavern, although there were no others selling anything similar to my bedspread. I reached the far end of the market and peered out of the entrance. The sky was grey and miserable and it was pouring with rain again. There was nothing to be done but to continue browsing. I stopped half way up to lean against an opening and, avoiding the raindrops trickling down from the overhanging canvas, looked up and down the street. Virtually every other building was a hotel. The signs were written in Turkish and Russian. I could see rows and rows of girls sitting on covered balconies gazing out at the rain. Most of them were wearing tee shirts despite the cold wind and the wet.

I had to keep stepping back to let people push in and out through the opening. Unusually, the Turkish men who passed ignored me. Suddenly there was a stir. Out of the gloom appeared a dazzling troupe of girls who were making their way through the market. They were an extraordinary sight: beautiful courtesans unexpectedly allowed out of the harem, a flock of rare and colourful birds touching down bringing with them a whiff of exotic places. No wonder the favourite mistresses in the harems of the Ottoman sultans were largely Circassian. The girls jingled and glittered along, looking disdainfully at the grey, common masses blocking their way. They whisked past me and vanished into the street, leaving behind a hint of perfume in the air. No wonder the Turks were ignoring dowdy, old me. These exquisite girls simply had no competition.

The rain was still pouring down. I decided to go and find a place to sit and have some tea. Emerging from the market into the street, I dived into the first restaurant I came upon. It was packed with girls. I asked the scowling Turk behind the till whether I could just have tea. He scowled even harder and shook his head. This was unprecedented in Turkey. I turned towards the door and one of the girls, blond, buxom and sisterly, rushed from her table to follow me out into the street. She put her arm around me and pointed up the road. 'Forget this place,' she said. 'There's a tea house a bit further up. My name's Suzanne. Tell Ali that Suzanne sent you.' And she dashed back inside, out of the rain.

I couldn't find Ali's tea house. Instead, I found the Georgia Restaurant, a long, narrow café with plastic flowers in vases on the tables and Swiss alpine scenes painted on the walls. It was filled with tables which were busy with people, Turkish men and eastern women. What a sight. I felt as if I had stumbled upon a fancy dress party. The women were wearing sparkling evening gowns, skimpy skirts with long slits up the side, plunging, see-through blouses and skin-tight jeans that looked as if they had been sprayed on. Necks, arms and legs were bare despite the cold and rain blowing in through the door. Their hair was mainly long and black or dyed blond, and luxuriant, decorated with ribbons and bows and extravagant hair slides. Their faces were heavily made up, large, lustrous eyes rimmed with black and shaded in greens and blues, and full, lipsticked red lips. The women were every shape, size and age, fat, thin, hard, innocent, flirtatious and bored. The men were old and young, plain, handsome and smirking. They offered the women cigarettes, glasses of tea and cups of Turkish coffee. It was like a scene out of a Shakespearean play, the Inn at Cheapside where the men were rogues and the girls jolly.

I sat down. Fortunately there was one empty table. The women were sizing me up, obviously wondering what I was doing there and whether I was one of them or not. I blessed the pouring rain outside which gave me an excuse, a reason, to be there, and although my fingers itched to make some notes, I didn't dare take out my diary. It would have seemed so rude and obvious. I ordered a Turkish coffee.

One of the women came up to me. She had the red lips and the bouffant hair of a pantomime dame. Her eyes were baggy and her bottle-black hair was tied up in a red scarf and decorated with an enormous, gold-coloured hair slide. The high-heeled shoes she was wearing made her even taller. She was dressed in a green, leopard-skin evening dress, sleeveless and low cut, tight across her body, revealing the fat rolls of her stomach in intimate detail. Had I been a man, I would have been terrified of her. As a woman, I was terrified. She picked up one of the plastic flowers and offered it to me. I politely declined. She suggested that she give it to one of the men who would give it to me. Saying it with flowers suddenly took on a whole new meaning. I declined again, and with a slightly puzzled look, the woman moved back to her group.

I sat at the table drinking coffee after coffee and trying to look like a tourist caught out by the weather,. I watched the scenes going on around me with fascination. The women moved around the café from table to table, as one does at a cocktail party, drinking endless tea and coffee, eating nuts and smoking cigarettes. Musical chairs, revolving beds. Anything had to be better than hanging around all day in the cheap, Turkish hotels they lived in for months at a time. I could imagine the beds crammed into the rooms to save money, the washing and ironing, wet clothes draped over chairs, the hair curlers and the face make up, the jolly camaraderie of a girls' dormitory, the necessary support the women would give each other. Imagine waking up each day to face the same old routine until you had made enough money to justify going home.

One man ventured to kiss the neck of the woman sitting next to him. He was a handsome man. Most of the men sitting around in the café that afternoon had fine features. The Turks are a good-looking lot, generally small, slim men and I thought the women were rather lucky in some ways. At least the men they were selling themselves to were not totally repulsive. As for the men, lucky, lucky them, sex on tap, theirs for the asking. All they had to do was cough up the cash and no more anguish, no more tortured burning and it would still be there available the next day.

It looked as if some negotiations were going on that afternoon, but it also looked as if many of the women were just whiling away a tedious, miserable day. One woman was sitting close to me on her own. She must have been in her forties or fifties. She had short hair and was wearing a minimal tee shirt and short skirt. She sat, hard-faced, smoking cigarette after cigarette, and waited. Nobody approached her or spoke to her and her face remained expressionless, so alone in the midst of so many people.

To add to the unreality of it all, a man suddenly came through the door. He was a dwarf and his arms were deformed. He had come to beg and he did so, proudly and impassively. It was the women who hurried to get their money out first, their faces filled with sympathy as they bent down to put the liras into his hand.

I could have sat there all afternoon but the café was getting even busier and the empty chairs at my table were needed. A man sat down opposite me and I thought it was best to go. I went to pay for my drinks and the man at the till waved my money away. I insisted on paying, and, with a shrug, unsmiling, he accepted the money. I returned to the hotel through the wet streets of Trabzon, exhausted after the different, emotional experiences of the day. A historical panorama of a day. I unpacked my purchase from the Russian bazaar and spread it out over the bed. It was beautiful even if it was going to fill up my bicycle bags. I threw out a pair of cheap rubber sneakers. They were too uncomfortable to walk far in anyway. It wasn't much but I felt better. I folded up the bedspread as small as I could and squashed it down into one of the bags. With the shoes gone and so few clothes in them anyway, the bags were still not over-heavy.

I was to spend one more day in Trabzon before returning to the road. I needed more time to consider what route to take. Life's like that, isn't it, a ceaseless search for the right path, the illusion of being in control of one's own destiny. As if one more day in Trabzon could have sorted that out. I pored over the map. No doubt the road along the coast to the border with Georgia would continue, narrow, hair-raising, smelly and tediously flat. But what if I turned inland from Trabzon and cycled up into the mountains, stopping off to see the Monastery of Sumela along the way and going as far as Bayburt with its fabulous citadel on its acropolis hill, before returning onto the coast. The map showed that there was a road from Bayburt marked in yellow, a scenic route even, which crossed over a mountain pass, Soğanlı Geçidi, in the eastern Black Sea Mountains at 2,330 metres, 7,642 feet, and dropped down to the coast via Çaykara. The road followed rivers along much of the way. It would be an exciting journey – and there was something else important about it. I would also be going over Zigana Geçidi. This was the pass Xenophon and the Ten Thousand are believed to have used to cross over the mountains on their journey to the Black Sea. I would be going in the reverse footsteps of the Greek mercenaries. I wondered if I would be able to do it and suddenly thought of the Japanese boy in the hotel next door. Maybe if I spoke slowly, I could ask him which route he had taken to get here and what the road conditions were like. I hurried next door. He was out, so I left a message.

The phone in my room rang a couple of hours later. He was waiting in reception. I hurried downstairs clutching my map and we went to sit in one of the hotel sitting rooms. He told me that he had started cycling from Thailand seven months previously and had made his way through India, Pakistan and the deserts of Iran into Turkey. He had either stayed in cheap dumps or, as in the Iranian desert, had slept next to his bicycle under the stars. He was going through to İstanbul and on to Europe. He was tired but the main problem had been the food. He laughed. 'I want Japanese food,' he said with a slow, burning intensity. 'That's what I miss so badly, Japanese food.'

His English was good enough to describe his eight punctures and four broken rear spokes, all of which he had mended himself. I listened in awe. I could just about fix punctures, although I had rarely had to do so. I had never even thought about broken spokes. I asked him what route he had taken to get here. He had come over the mountains on the main road from Erzurum via the famous Zigana

Pass. It had been hard but beautiful. The journey had taken just two days and he had stayed the night with a family because there had been nowhere else to stay. I asked whether there were many houses along the road.

'There's nothing much up there,' he said.

I shuddered, thinking of my pals, the lorry drivers, prowling like wolves thousands of feet up in the Black Sea mountains. I asked him how steep the climbs had been. He laughed again and made a flying motion with his hand. The main slopes had largely been on his side, however, and it had been downhill for him most of the time. I shuddered again. I would be going in the opposite direction – upwards. I wondered what he thought of trying to go over Soğanlı Geçidi from Bayburt. He told me that a man in Bayburt had suggested that very route down to the sea. It would be a good road to take, he had said, but the Japanese boy had not believed him.

'A very good road.' I was to remember that description a few days later.

From my oven room that night, looking out over the harbour, the lights of the ships shone out. One weighed anchor and slipped out of port hooting its goodbyes to Trabzon, lights ablaze, an unearthly multi-eyed creature moving slowly over the oily blackness. I wondered if it could be the passenger ship heading back to İstanbul. This reminded me that I still had to find out about sailing times.

It was my first job the next morning after I had bent myself back into shape following another night spent on the hard mattress. I was being slowly crippled by my bed and my muscles and legs were missing the copious amounts of daily exercise they had become accustomed to. In a perverse way I was glad. It meant I would be more ready to leave the following day. My hotel was situated on the hill that led straight down to the port. I forced my legs to carry me down the steep street to the main gate from where I was directed to the passenger enquiry office. The boat would return to İstanbul the following Wednesday from Rize in the afternoon, calling at Trabzon in the evening and then stopping at Giresun, Samsun and Sinop before arriving in İstanbul underneath Topkapı Sarayı on Friday, around three o'clock in the afternoon. Two nights on board. The friendly official gave me a price for a bunk in a two-person cabin. It was the equivalent of £28. If I were lucky, he said, I would have it all to myself because it was unlikely there would be another single woman traveller. He beamed. Bicycles went for free <u>and</u> there was a swimming pool on board.

I had always wanted to sail from the Black Sea into the Bosphorus. This would be my chance. The issue was solved. I would get the boat from Rize. That would leave me another day in Trabzon and then time to test my legs and nerves in the Black Sea mountains. I walked back up the street which was lined with ticket offices and travel bureaux organising trips and tours between Turkey and the former Soviet Union. All the signs were in Russian. It looked like there were regular passenger boats to the Russian port of Sochi in particular. After those wasted decades when the borders were closed, Trabzon was busily trying to regain its old position as a travel and trading centre in the area. What fun it would be to buy a ticket to sail to Russia . . . another time, maybe. It is always a good idea to have things you want to do. Alexander the Great was said to have wept at the thought that he had conquered the known world. He didn't have time to find out about the unknown one.

I myself was not going to conquer much that day, just the high hill bristling with antennae hanging over Trabzon. The sign pointed up behind the town to Boztepe. It was a steep climb up through the suburbs and people stared at me curiously, unable to imagine anybody making their way up there on foot. It was either too hot, pouring with rain, or many degrees below zero ever to walk anywhere here. Despite the torrential downpour twenty-four hours earlier, the weather that day was fine and it was pleasant to climb higher and higher away from the crash and din of the city. I stopped just before the top to see whether a ruined monastery spread out over a slope was accessible. It was locked and there were varying accounts from the people living in a street of old houses close by as to when and if the gate would be opened. It had obviously once been a huge place with heavily fortified walls enclosing it like a fortress. As I slipped and slithered around trying to see if there was a break in the walls, I was closely observed by an extremely knowing-looking boy. He could only have been about thirteen. He was smoking a cigarette and the way he was looking at me made me shiver. I enlisted the help of a man passing by to get him to clear off.

Climbing further up the slope behind the monastery, I was able to look over into the ruined interior. The walls were still absolutely solid and there was no way in. I wondered if any frescoes were left inside somewhere. I later read that the monastery had been founded in the fourteenth century and was in continuous use by the Greek Orthodox church until 1923. It was just one of many monasteries and churches that had been built on and around Boztepe. The site had always been sacred. Before the Christians built their churches, there were temples there dedicated to the Persian sun god Mithra (the root name of so many Pontic kings) and the Greek god, Apollo. Xenophon and the Ten Thousand regularly made sacrifices to the gods, including Zeus and Heracles (Hercules) asking for safe guidance. I wondered if they had done so on Boztepe during their stay at Trabzon.

In his *Anabasis*, Xenophon described a sports day held during the time the mercenaries camped near Trabzon. The setting in which it was held would fit Boztepe. After the Greeks had finished making their sacrifice, he wrote, they held athletic sports on the mountain on which they were camping. There was wrestling, boxing, running and horse racing. They made the boys 'mostly from among the prisoners' compete in the short distance race. The horse race involved galloping down 'a steep bit of ground' and into the sea where they turned round and raced back to the altar. It was hard going, wrote Xenophon: 'On the way down most of them had a thorough shaking, and on the way up, when the ground got very steep, the horses could scarcely get along at walking pace. So there was a lot of noise and laughter and people shouting out encouragements.'

The ghostly peals of laughter of the Ten Thousand rang in my head as I forced my solitary way, without encouragement, through the trees, bushes and brambles, to emerge in a park at the top of the hill. Few people were about, although there were several vans and lorries delivering supplies to the scores of tea houses, cafes and restaurants, which no doubt did a roaring trade at the weekends. I carried on, skirting a military base, and found a graveyard behind a wall. There were poems engraved on the headstones just as there were in English churchyards. I sat on the wall, ignoring the soldiers hanging curiously out of the windows of one of the military buildings behind me, and copied down the words from a couple of stones. I wanted to compare it with what was written on tombstones back home. I could understand bits of the Turkish but some of it was too difficult.

The Turkish service of BBC World Service Radio helped to translate it when I got back to England. One of the inscriptions read: 'I came into the world one day in spring. Was I a good son for my parents? I go with a prayer to the nest of heaven. Don't be deceived by the lies of the world.' Another inscription was written in the form of a poem and was in memory of Semahat Köşe, wife of Hacı Ahmet, who must have been a practising Muslim because the name 'Hacı' is used by those who made the pilgrimage to Mecca. His wife Semahat must have died shortly after they married. 'Like a rose bud I smoothly unfolded, only to go back again before I could enjoy my youth. Don't be deceived by the lies of the world. Be happy. Come to my villa in heaven.'

It doesn't matter what religion or culture the inhabitants might have belonged to, graveyards are profound, hallowed places. I sat on the wall, chewed my pen and considered the meaning of life for the umpteenth time and for the umpteenth time decided the only meaning was the one you could give it.

I emerged from my reverie to consider that the soldiers hissing and whistling behind me might tumble out of the windows onto their heads and hurt themselves. I continued on my walk. I was heading away from the sea and had a good view of the road I would take the next morning. It wound up along the river gorge out of Trabzon, ever upwards, and disappeared into the mountains looming in the distance. It looked blissfully quieter than the coast road. I imagined the thin Japanese boy crouched over his thin handlebars, whizzing headlong down from the Zigana Pass. I imagined me toiling up in the opposite direction . . . but I decided to stop imagining at that point. A vivid imagination can be a major handicap.

Leafy, green corridors of lanes stretched away from Boztepe and out into the countryside. The military camp sprawled over the hills for quite a way and, to my delight, what sounded like the Trabzon first battalion brass band was on a practice march, blowing away on its tubas and bashing away at its drums without a mournful, eastern quiver to be heard. I found myself marching in sympathy and trying to catch a glimpse of the band, but the belt of trees was too thick. It was pleasant being on two feet rather than two wheels, picking a way through the mud and skirting round the tracks still filled with rainwater. Two women sitting on stools outside their house waved and invited me to stop by for tea on the way back.

There was a great deal of development going on in every direction: new houses, apartment blocks and silver-domed mosques, their minarets pointing like fingers up and over the trees. If it wasn't being built on, it was being cultivated. There were extensive groves of hazelnut trees bursting out into fruit, little parcels of goodness wrapped up like exotic presents to hang on a Christmas tree. Market gardens on the edge of precipitous slopes were rich with corn, runner beans, plum trees, cabbages and onions. Away in the distance were the yellow-green slopes of pastureland. One could have jumped with a bound into their softness. A woman walking with her daughter staggered under the weight of a couple of shopping bags stuffed with leeks, potatoes and nuts. It was all freshly grown food, the woman told me, and gave me a handful of the hazelnuts. I went into a village store to buy some peaches and a bottle of water. The man looked at me as if I were from outer space and his small, bright son obligingly translated my Turkish into Turkish so his dad could understand.

On the way back, the two women were still sitting outside the house and they eagerly waved me towards a spare stool. The older woman was knitting an exquisitely patterned sock, while the younger, who was her daughter-in-law, was crocheting lace. They told me they sold their work in Trabzon to make some money. A bowl of small cucumbers sat on the ground in front of them. The mother-in-law quickly peeled a handful and indicated a dish of salt. 'We grow them in our garden. We grow all our food,' she said. 'It's cheaper and healthier.' I picked up one of the cucumbers and dipped it into the salt. Its sharp bitterness contrasted with the taste of the fresh cucumber. They were refreshing to eat in the heat of the day. The women were desperate for conversation, the two of them sitting there together all day, every day. The younger woman's husband worked in Trabzon. They asked me why I wasn't married. I tried to think of an answer. They both looked at my face as I tried to explain this alien state of being. 'Single life is hard, although finding a good man is hard too,' observed the mother-in-law. Unusually, they both seemed to sympathise with my reasons, whatever they were, and abruptly decided not to continue that line of conversation. The older woman told me that her son had married her daughter-in-law seven years previously. This time it was my turn to ask a personal question. 'Do you have any . . .', but before I could finish, the older woman quickly replied. 'No there are no children,' she said simply. 'She can't have any. There's a problem.'

I looked at her daughter-in-law, who bent her head over her crochet. This time it was my turn not to speak. Having children and grandchildren in Turkey is virtually the be-all and end-all of existence, central to the life of a family. We talked about Trabzon and, inevitably, the numbers of foreign women in the city. The younger woman couldn't contain herself. The problem was, she said, that the Turkish men left their Turkish wives for the Russian women. It was a disgrace they were there; it shouldn't be allowed. 'We don't want them here. We don't want them here at all,' she went on vehemently, no doubt fearful for herself and her own childless condition.

I left them sitting together, the mother and her sad daughter-in-law, reflecting together at the way things were, and headed for a bus stop at the end of the track. The two women, who had given me the hazel nuts earlier, were chatting in the garden of a friend close by and hurried up when they saw me again. The woman was plump with rosy cheeks. She was dressed in a long skirt and her head was covered with the traditional headscarf. Atatürk might have tried to get rid of the veil but he could not get rid of the headscarf. The teenaged daughter with her was the eldest of her four children.

'Do you have a husband and children?' she asked.

'No,' I replied.

'But that means you won't have any grandchildren,' she said, eyes wide with astonishment. 'In Turkey, they are the most important thing in any family.'

I asked the daughter if she wanted to get married and have children. Of course she did, she replied. Her mother listened with interest as I spoke about my travels to Turkey and the Middle East. 'Look at me,' she said. 'I'm forty and I've hardly been anywhere.' She lowered her voice confidentially. 'Do you know I can't even read. But things will be very different for her,' and she nodded towards her daughter.

Back in Trabzon, I whiled away the hazy afternoon in one of the city's open air tea places, strategically choosing to sit in the area reserved for families. A courting couple were sitting at another table reassuringly close by. I didn't want to be disturbed by any problems or misunderstandings. I had, I suppose rather stupidly, asked if they served beer – which I suppose might have created some. The blushing boy in charge, who looked about twelve, said they only served tea, coffee and soft drinks. Definitely no alcohol. I asked for a safe cup of Turkish coffee. I had bought a Turkish Daily News and read with gloom about the strength of the pound. It meant I would lose even more money when the German marks I occasionally earned were converted into sterling back home. A story on the foreign pages reported that the bookmakers, William Hill, had started taking bets on Diana's options (Olay Kadın): remarriage 6 – 4, becoming a nun 25 – 1 and joining the Spice Girls 1,000 – 1. How wrong they were.

It was lovely sitting and doing nothing, a whole week still to go and the biggest part of the trip was about to come. I still had not thought too much about how to re-organise my life, slamming the drawers shut before anything could jump out and demand attention. I was reserving that job for the two days and nights on board the boat back to İstanbul from Rize. I returned to the restaurant for a disappointing last meal in Trabzon. The electricity had failed and all the food was stone cold. I should have noticed when I walked in that the lamb spit at the door wasn't turning round as usual and the lights were off. My kebab swam on its plate, glutinously red, congealing at the edges, and the kadayıf – one of the many honey-sweet Turkish puddings, was stale. Ignominiously, I didn't complain. But I didn't leave a tip.

I went to buy supplies for the next day in one of the new supermarkets on the corner of the main square. I asked the man behind the fresh food counter for a few grammes of crumbly white sheep's cheese. He looked at me in astonishment. 'That's very little,' he said in innocent surprise. I had to stop myself from leaping over the counter and assaulting him. That was my business, not his. It was only a detail but I suddenly realised how tired I was of being such an oddity in this society, at having to answer constant questions about what I was doing and explain myself and my behaviour to the ever-curious Turks. If he had asked me what I was doing on my own and where my husband was, I swear I would have wrenched the knife out of his hand and stuck it through his heart. Fortunately he didn't.

I thought the deferred beer might be a good idea, so it was back to the liquor store via the Street of Sweets for one last, sticky look at the boxed and beribboned tons of nougat and candy. The beer was cold when it came out of the refrigerated cabinet but already hot by the time I got upstairs to my room. I drank it – it tasted greasy and flat – and looked out of my window at Trabzon, the port down below lit up in the night, a lone ship, its fairy lights ablaze and looking like an illuminated coat-hanger, gently rocking backwards and forwards on the water. Opposite, the sipping, supping Russian beer house was in full swing, and above, the antennae winked on the top of Boztepe where the body of Semahat Koşe lay buried, her soul hopefully safe in her villa in heaven, waiting for visitors.

14
Trabzon to Maçka

My friends, these people whom you see are the last obstacle which stops us from being where we have so long struggled to be. We ought, if we could, to eat them up alive.

The alarm went off at 4.45 am. The plan that day was to take the road heading steeply southwards away from the sea in the direction of the Zigana Pass, but only to go as far as the small town of Maçka from where a road branched off towards the Sumela Monastery. The Japanese boy had crossed over the pass from the other direction and cycled so fast downhill that he had enough time to turn off and take a look at the monastery before continuing on to Trabzon. I knew I would never be able to 'do' the monastery and cycle up to the pass in one day, so I was keeping my fingers crossed there was going to be somewhere reasonable to stay in Maçka. The town was only around twenty-eight kilometres, seventeen miles or so, away from Trabzon, but I wasn't sure how difficult those miles would be and in any case, psychologically, I still needed to start at the crack of dawn. It was all part of the routine.

As I swallowed down some breakfast, the telephone in my room rang making me jump. I had as usual told reception the previous evening I would be leaving at around five o'clock and they were providing me with an early morning call – without being requested to do so. I suppose this was fairly reasonable but I was furious, as ever hating any unnecessary interruption as I mentally geared up for the day ahead. I carried the bags downstairs – the bedspread didn't make too much difference to the weight – and dumped them by the door. The night receptionist sat in a chair, unsmiling. He was probably fed up too because he had had to wake up early to make the call. He watched my every move. It added to my irritation and I tried to ignore him. I went down to the basement to untie the bicycle and carry her upstairs. My fury increased to rage when I saw somebody had fiddled with the gear levers. Cyclists would sympathise with me over this. The main complaint from everybody taking their bicycle to a non-European country was that people always pulled and pushed the gear levers out of curiosity, putting an extra unnecessary strain on the gear cables. As I checked the tyres, I also noticed that one of the black caps over an inner tube valve had been spirited away. Fortunately, the valve itself had not been tampered with. The loss of the cap would not make a great difference and I even had a spare one, but it reinforced my dislike of having to leave my precious companion in a public place. I continued to ignore the receptionist, who was still sitting in exactly the same position in exactly the same disengaged way. It was a relief to get out of the door into the freshness of the morning, climb back on the saddle and bump down over the cobbles through the market street leading to the sea and the coastal road. The streets were deserted at such an hour. My spirits rose. I was on the move again.

I cycled eastwards wondering how far I would have to go before there would be a turning off to Maçka. I spotted two police officers sitting chatting in their police patrol car and nearly gave them heart failure when I tapped on the window to ask the way. They wanted me to follow their car straight up a short cut in the shape of a steep cobbled hill! This, they said, would take me out onto a roundabout where I could join the main road to the mountains. I declined their kind offer to follow the car and toiled up the perpendicular street at my own dead-slow speed to find that it was indeed a short cut to the river and the main road to Maçka.

Jocund day wasn't exactly standing tiptoe on the mountain tops as I began to cycle up the road. The glimmering dawn had given way to the full light of the day but it was a subdued light and suggested that inclement weather was to come. I was definitely climbing, but the ascent was slight and not at all difficult to manage. I was cycling directly alongside the river-bed. According to the map, the river would be joined by several tributaries around Maçka. One of them ran down from the mountains soaring nearly 10,000 feet, 3,000 metres above, through Altındere Vadisi, the Valley of the Golden River. Here, a Greek monk called Barnabas arrived in the fourth century clutching an icon of Mary the Mother of God. It was said to have been painted by Saint Luke. The strong-legged Barnabas found a cave on a ledge above a sheer rock face and left the icon inside. It is believed that the Sumela monastery was established there a couple of hundred years later, although the remains date from the thirteenth and fourteenth centuries when Trabzon was ruled by the Byzantine Comneni dynasty.

I enjoyed the cycling, probably enjoying it all the more at the idea that I wasn't going to go too far that day. It was all so beautiful. The steep sides of the valley, their rocky peaks jagged against the sky, were a delicious, lush, emerald green dotted with houses. These were widely spaced out and blended harmoniously into the countryside. There was beauty and room to breathe. The greenness was overwhelming.

I reached Maçka easily. It was still so early I wondered if anybody would be up. At the entrance to the town was a newly built government rest house. I wheeled the bicycle into the courtyard, leaned her against the railings and went inside. The tables of the long restaurant with picture windows were laid out ready for the coach parties from Trabzon. A man was hosing down the terrace outside. He looked as if it were an every day occurrence to have cyclists dropping in at the crack of dawn. The Japanese boy told me that he had left his bags there when he visited the monastery. I asked if I could leave mine. It wasn't a problem, said the man, and helped me carry them into the manager's office. I used the toilet – what luxury, clean tiles, soap, towels and hot and cold taps that worked. It was rather disconcerting to find the man waiting patiently for me outside the toilet door. He escorted me outside. It was seventeen kilometres (a mere ten miles) up to the monastery through the mountains south-east of Maçka, he said, and there were signposts. I asked him about the hotel potential in town. There were two and one was better than the other, he replied. What about the weather? Would it rain? He shrugged and smiled. It was impossible to tell, he said.

I cycled off into town and found one of the hotels overhanging the river, which flowed straight through the town centre. Despite its rather pleasant situation, the hotel was poor and rundown. A boy of about twelve was in charge. He told me to bring the bicycle right inside and into the tea house on the ground floor and then showed me upstairs. It was smelly and gloomy and the dirty rooms with their peeling walls were crammed with beds covered in dirty, rumpled blankets. The boy said I could have one of the rooms and he would only charge me about £2. I asked him what the other hotel in town was like. The same, he said. I told him I was going to visit the Sumela Monastery and might come back to stay the night. He nodded, his pale face impassive and detached. As we went back down the corridor, I noticed a balcony outside overlooking the river and went to have a look while the boy waited. As we went downstairs, I turned to him. 'Isn't the river lovely from the hotel. What a beautiful view,' I said. He smiled shyly, the smile lighting up his face, and nodded. 'Yes,' he said. 'It is.'

He was so pleased a foreigner should have found something pretty and pleasant in that grotty place which was, after all, his home. I decided it wouldn't be too bad to stay there if I had to later on. I asked him whether it would rain. It was hard to tell. What about a restaurant, would there be one open in the town at such an hour? I had to go back over the bridge, along the back street running parallel to the main road through the town and I would find a soup house. Which I did. I leaned the bicycle against the window so I could see her while I was sitting inside and went in to order a bowl of lentil soup. I ate it slowly. It was so early, there was no reason to hurry. The whole day stretched ahead. I felt rich with time. My bicycle, meanwhile, was attracting an admiring throng outside. Holding their hands firmly down behind their backs so as not to touch, they were gazing at my smooth tyres, worried about whether they were good enough for the bad roads. These very kind people. I had to reassure them that they were special tyres and extremely tough. I hadn't had one puncture, I told them. They listened transfixed, impressed that such tyres existed.

The soup men told me to go back down the road and rejoin the main street. This would take me directly to the turning to Sumela. It was seventeen kilometres to the monastery, they said helpfully. I cycled off, noticing some shops filled with burnished copperware, Turkish jugs and bowls and beautiful things gleaming invitingly through the windows. Fortunately, the shops were shut. The turning was clearly marked. It was a wonderful sensation to be cycling without any bags dangling from the bicycle. The climb was a steep one but I zipped along, past farms, houses and trout fisheries scattered along the banks of the river rushing down from the mountains. The road surface wasn't too bad and because the bicycle and I were so light, we could almost fly round and over the potholes. At one point, I heard a pinging sound, as if something metallic had fallen off the bicycle and dropped onto the road. I stopped and had a look, but I couldn't see anything missing. I assumed I must have gone over a nail on the road, but everything seemed fine.

I cycled on up the valley, the sides becoming steeper the higher I went, past a pension being built on the green slopes on the other side of the river. The two men working there that morning eyed me intently as I cycled by. They were probably multiplying me by a hundred in their imagination and hopes for the future. I passed an Ottoman, humpbacked, stone bridge, which didn't lead anywhere anymore, and swung across the modern bridge over the river. On either side of the banks was a fine collection of buildings, the new blending in with the old. It was a big establishment and included a trout farm, restaurant and a pension. I decided to stop on the way back down and have a look inside. I could always go and collect my bags and cycle back up. It wasn't far.

The climb became steeper and the scenery more and more magnificent, the sides of the valley turning into dramatic, jagged rocks and sheer peaks through which the road squeezed in zigzags. I felt dwarfed and overwhelmed by the giant rock formations literally towering over my head, the world closing in around me. The river turned into a swirling torrent, foaming down, carving its way through the rocks, which were polished smooth with time. It was awesomely beautiful, the stuff of myths and legends. I imagined the monks climbing up along the river, picking their way painfully through the rocks before there were any roads. Those incredible people, fired by their beliefs, clutching a picture of a woman who, they believed, would keep them safe from the storms and the landslides. Such is faith.

Although the bicycle was light, I was by now having to use all my muscles to persuade her up the steep road. One thing that kept me going was the anticipation of the ride back down later on, roaring through the rocky switchback, racing the river. The rocks and peaks widened out and disappeared behind impenetrable, evergreen forests. The monastery of Sumela was enclosed in a country park. There was an entrance at which you stopped and bought a ticket. I felt overcome by the ride up and the beauty of the place and avoided looking at the ticket man as I handed over my entrance fee. I did not want even to consider answering any questions about why I was cycling alone, why my father, brother, husband were in England and wasn't I worried that I would have no grandchildren. I leaned the bicycle against a shed and gobbled down half a packet of sweet biscuits trying to renew my energy levels. As I, locust-like, munched the biscuits, a car drew up at the ticket entrance and a man got out. Two women sat waiting inside. Tourists and foreigners! A wave of paranoia washed over me. I didn't have the energy or the inclination to go and say hullo. I was sure the man was English, what was more a writer, probably freelance, on my territory. I hated him. He didn't bother to speak to me either. Maybe he was thinking the same.

To my relief it was still so early there were no tourist coaches in the coach park. A small post office, however, was open for business, as were the souvenir shops and a cluster of restaurants built over the river at the start of the trail up to the monastery. Each restaurant was belting out its own Turkish music to attract the trickle of visitors arriving. It was the most incredibly awful and inappropriate noise. The monks must have been turning in their graves. Almost knocked over by the wall of sound, I tied up the bicycle to some wooden railings, concerned that I didn't have any ear plugs for her, rushed past the restaurants and began to climb up the path away from the river through the trees. The forests were so thick, the music was quickly absorbed and lost in the green and the brown. It was a stiff climb, zig-zagging up and round, higher and higher. Every so often, there were staggering views of the encircling mountains from ledges and promontories. Their slopes were likewise thickly covered in pine trees and the mist curled and swirled around the peaks like a pure, white curtain of foam.

I knew that the monastery had been built, literally, out of the sheer face of the rock and onto and into the ledge behind, and that the view from underneath was a splendid one. Even as I remembered this, I glanced up – and caught my breath. It was perfect timing. Through a break in the trees, clinging to the rocks was the monastery directly overhead. The walls and windows looked intact, even though I knew that what lay behind was, sadly, in ruins. What a piece of engineering. How on earth could anybody have built it, except maybe the Nabataeans with their experience of building on sheer rock faces in Petra in the south of Jordan. The Sumela monastery was, unusually, even more spectacular than the photographs I had seen.

The woodland trail continued. I could hear voices above me and realised I was climbing more quickly than whoever it was and would soon overtake them. It was, of course, the man, his two women companions and a small child which I hadn't noticed in the car. There was nothing to be done except push them over the edge as I passed by – or stop and speak to them. I chose the more civilised course of action.

'Hi. What a tough climb and what fabulous views.' It wasn't very original but it was the best I could do.

They turned and smiled at me. They seemed delighted to see a fellow countryman. I felt very ashamed of myself. We introduced ourselves. The couple were British; their companion was American. The women were teaching English in Ankara. The man stayed at home to look after the baby and was indeed writing a book, a novel set in India. I confessed what I had been thinking earlier and they were kind enough to laugh. The couple had been living and working out of Britain for many years and were loving Turkey. Next time it would be the wife's turn to stay at home and write a novel. What an excellent arrangement. I felt green with envy. I joined them and we climbed up through the trees to the monastery.

Restoration work was being carried out so visitors to Sumela had to wear hard, yellow hats and were allowed in for just fifteen minutes. One could see why as soon as one crept in through the narrow stone entrance. The interior of the monastery behind the walls, which rose up from the sheer rock, was relatively small and would be overcrowded with just one coach tour. We were lucky, however. There were so few visitors at such an early hour, we were allowed more time to look round. The frescoes in the inner cells and chambers off the central courtyard must have been stunning before they were vandalised, stolen and destroyed by graffiti. The paintings on the ceilings out of arm's length were better preserved. We ducked in and around the scaffolding looking at the remnants of the wall paintings, those rich, glowing colours and fine-eyed Byzantine faces, painted hundreds of years before. The monastery was occupied until 1923 when it had to be evacuated along with all the other Greek Orthodox places along the Black Sea. The original, precious icon of the Virgin survived and was deposited in a museum in Athens. These mountains in northern Turkey were once dotted with similar monasteries, some of them perched in even more inaccessible places. It was a shame that the Turks had not thought about their tourism potential before letting them crumble away, although something, it seemed, was at last being done to save Sumela.

We made our way back down the trail, which was by then echoing with the voices and laughter of groups of Turks who had come to see the sights. Many of them were amazed to find themselves successfully tackling such a steep climb. By chance, my three new friends happened to be staying in the pension by the bridge over the river that I had already earmarked as a possible place to stay overnight. The question was settled. I would return to Maçka, collect my things from the government rest house and cycle back up to join them.

The descent was fun. I got back on the saddle, pointed the bicycle's nose downwards and only had to control the steering and the braking as I sped back through the cool of the pine trees, along the path of the rushing mountain waters, keeping balance as we wound our precipitous way once again under, round and through the elephantine, colossal rocks. It had taken a couple of hours to climb up but it seemed like only a matter of minutes before I was back at the bridge and the pension. I decided to stop and check that a room was available and found the party ordering lunch which they were going to eat in a picnic area next to the river. They invited me to join them and we sat with the river at our feet admiring two tower-like, wooden storehouses nearby. Both were carved and decorated and each balanced on four pillars fashioned out of whole tree trunks. One of the storehouses was still in good condition; the other had been restored by the family. It was estimated that they were both at least two hundred years old. The man of the household took us to admire his trout farm, which teemed with big, black, slippery, shiny fish. With the vagaries of the weather and the pollution of the Black Sea, he said, the fish farms were a safer and more controllable way of fishing. We admired the business created by this industrious family, obviously proud of its achievements, taking care to restore the old and make sure the new fitted in to the environment. The pension itself was tucked away against the side of the valley, up a steep track in the middle of hay barns and orchards. It was cleverly constructed in a traditional, alpine chalet-style on several storeys. The building fitted in to the hill rather than obtruding on it and could hardly be seen from the road.

By the time I started off on the final two miles or so back to Maçka to collect my belongings, the temperamental weather was closing in and the rain clouds were rolling down below the tops of the hills. I sped back down through the valley, racing into the town centre where I slowed down, peering into the shops as I passed, hoping to spot one that sold alcohol. I arrived at the rest house to collect my bags. As I went to strap them on, I noticed that one of the baggage hooks to hold a bag in place against the rear wheel was missing. That had been the pinging noise as I had started up the hill. I was cross with myself. I had known it was loose but hadn't bothered to tighten it up. It wasn't a disaster, merely an inconvenience. I always carried several stretch luggage attachments which could be used to strap things on to the bicycle. I hooked two of these together, wound the length around the bag and attached the ends onto the rear pannier carrier. That would keep it in place. The man from earlier on that morning watched the performance anxiously, worried I didn't have a husband, brother, father there to help me. I reassured him I could survive and told him I had met some people with whom I would be staying that night. He waved me off and told me to ask for him the next time I came to Maçka. He would be my brother, he said, another dear abi.

Returning to the main street to go shopping, I started to look for a bottle of wine for the evening and the usual provisions for the next day. There was a general store with boxes of fruit and vegetable outside. I was hurrying even more by then. It was definitely going to rain and, as I got off the bicycle and leaned it against the potatoes and tomatoes, the rain started. Fortunately, the shop sold everything I wanted: a bottle of red Buzbağ wine, sheep's cheese, olives, biscuits, an enormous and expensive packet of delicious Turkish crisps, tomatoes and bread.

The grocer was delighted he was able to serve a foreigner with almost everything her heart desired, carefully writing down all the prices on a scrap of paper and adding them up as a grand finale. I squeezed the items into the cycle bags. By then, it was raining with a dull and steady determination. I rode off looking for a convenient tea house and found one around the corner where I was able to wheel my bicycle inside and sit watching the rain drops pattering down through the plane trees lining the street and the puddles turning into floods in the gutters. How extraordinary this Black Sea region of Turkey was, so different from the rest of the country, which would be baking in the heat of the summer in July. I felt cold, damp and fed up. I thought of the baggage hook that had fallen off. What would go next? The bicycle and I were deteriorating together. Things were dropping off from both of us at an alarming rate. At least she could have new bits screwed on. I couldn't. (In fact I could, as I was to find out just six years later.) I was so cold I had to burrow into the bottom of the bag to get my jacket right at the bottom. From then on, for the rest of the trip, I always packed my sweat shirt and my jacket at the top.

At last the rain eased off and I ventured back up the road. My feet kept slipping off the pedals giving me a nasty jolt. Cycling like that is positively dangerous, but I was unable to use toe caps because I was so frightened my feet would stick in them and I would fall off. I cycled slowly, concentrating on keeping my feet on the pedals. The good news was that the various dogs, which had barked furiously at me earlier, had all disappeared inside out of the rain. I was wondering whether I would spot my luggage hook lying in the road, but of course I didn't. It looked as if the day would continue rainy and overcast and I was pleased the trip to the monastery had been accomplished so early in the morning before the bad weather set in. I could drink the rest of the day away as soon as I arrived back at the pension.

On the way up, I passed the American woman off on a walk to photograph the old Ottoman bridge nearby, hoping the light wouldn't be too bad. The two others, she told me, were supervising their son's afternoon sleep. We would meet up later for a fish dinner. At the pension, I tucked the bicycle away at the back of a vast, indoor restaurant just off the road and the owner helped me carry my things up the hillside, trying not to slip on the wet grass, past the hay barns, creeping underneath the dripping fruit trees and into the pension. It had been built entirely of wood. Open, spiral staircases connected the various levels of platforms and corridors off which the rooms were built. The clever architecture disguised how spacious the pension was inside. I was given a lovely room with a low, sloping ceiling, a comfortable double bed and two windows. From one, I had a wide view overlooking the valley and from the other, a hay barn and an apple tree. A rug was thrown artistically over the floorboards. I unpacked my things – and remembered I didn't have a glass for the wine.

I went thoughtfully downstairs to take a shower. After a few hiccups, I managed to coax the hot water out of the tap. I tried to ignore the water as it rose around my ankles, assuming it would eventually trickle away. I was glad we seemed to be the only people staying. As I returned to my room, I bumped into the man in the corridor and told him about my dilemma over the wine. He went to get one of his son's plastic mugs that I could use as a wine glass. They were all going for a walk and we arranged to meet later.

I scuttled back up the spiral staircase, shut my door – and promptly found I was locked in owing to the idiosyncratic way the locks had been fitted. I leaned out of the window nearest the ground but decided it was just too high up and the apple tree just too far away for me to risk trying to climb out. In any case, everything was so wet and greasy from the rain that I decided it would be positively dangerous. Feeling like a princess in a fairy tale, I decided to ignore such a small detail, opened the bottle of wine and got down to some serious drinking. By the time I spotted the pension owner outside coming up the track, I could hardly speak. I hid the bottle in a cabinet beside the bed and called to him from the window. I was locked in, I said, trying not to slur. He came running and opened the door. He shut the door behind him and showed me that I hadn't been locked in at all. If I jiggled the key slightly this way, then another way, breathed in a bit, hey presto the door opened. Easy. I hoped he couldn't smell the wine.

The party continued later in my room when the couple and their friend came to drink beer and eat crisps. What a treat. I was so glad I had met them. How wrong my initial, misanthropic thoughts had been. Afterwards, I remembered that we all went downstairs to eat dinner outside along with a jolly group of Turks who had come to the restaurant for an evening out, and I remembered wondering in the damp of the night whether it would still be raining in the morning. And that's about all I could remember.

But I knew I had had a very nice time.

15
Maçka to Gümüşhane

They came to the mountain on the fifth day, the name of the mountain being Thekes. When the men in front reached the summit and caught sight of the sea there was great shouting. Xenophon and the rearguard heard it and thought that there were some more enemies attacking in the front, since there were natives of the country they had ravaged following them up behind . . . However, when the shouting got louder, and those who were pressing forward started running towards the men in front who kept on shouting, and the more there were of them the more shouting there was, it looked then as though this was something of considerable importance. So Xenophon mounted his horse and, taking Lycus and the cavalry with him, rode forward to give support, and, quite soon, they heard the soldiers shouting out 'The sea! The sea!' . . . Then they all began to run, the rearguard and all, and drove on the baggage animals and the horses at full speed; and when they had all got to the top, the soldiers, with tears in their eyes, embraced each other and their generals and captains.

Thus wrote Xenophon, describing how he and his men, early in 400 BCE, came from the south up to the mountains and onto the Zigana Pass from where they got their first glimpse of the Euxeinus Pontos – the Black Sea. Nearly 2,500 years later, I was going in the reverse direction on my bicycle and on my own, pedalling furiously up away from the sea to go over the pass and into the mountains. Xenophon didn't describe the weather at the time. His men were so busy fording rivers, thieving, burning, fighting and running away from the furious locals, they would not have had the time to notice whether it was overcast, raining or what. My preoccupations were not quite as grave as those of Xenophon and the Ten Thousand so, as I set out in the dark and early on the morning of Friday, 18 July 1997, I was able to observe that the clouds were low in the valley although the rain had stopped. I whistled back down the hill into Maçka, re-joined the main road and started up into the mountains heading south towards the Zigana Pass and the town of Torul on the other side. It was thirty-two miles to Torul, fifty-two kilometres, and it was going to be uphill all the way.

I could scarcely get along at a walking pace, ever up along the river. The lorries pelted past, loaded with timber and sweet-smelling hay, spewing diesel fumes into my face. The road played tricks on me. It looked flat yet I could scarcely move my legs, scarcely keep the wheels going round. I had to keep stopping and turning round to look behind me to reassure myself that I really was climbing and climbing steeply. I gritted my teeth and talked to the bicycle in my thoughts about the purpose of man's existence, the foolishness of trying to cycle uphill and whether I should just give up, fall onto the rocks alongside and die. I was hardly able to admire the scenery, beautiful as it was. The road curved up through the valley. The sides towered up almost sheer and were dotted with houses which appeared to be perched so precariously I expected to see them slip and tumble down like a pack of cards in a heap at the bottom. Many appeared to be deserted and ruined, the former inhabitants no doubt working in Germany or İstanbul or some other foreign place, thinking with a pang every so often of their house on a peak underneath the Zigana Pass. Some of the houses were new. At least some people were returning. Even higher up was the smooth pasture land among the trees and higher still was the snow line where unmelted snow still lay in dirty, white patches. The precipitous rocks and craggy peaks were spitting down small stones and pebbles loosened by the rain the night before. Every so often, I heard a rush and a patter and a clatter and I wondered whether I should be crushed to death before I died from exhaustion. It was taking me hours to cover any distance. Just as my legs gave up, I turned a corner and came across a belt of cafes and restaurants at Hamsiköy. I practically fell off the bicycle, unable to cycle another inch, and pushed her across the road to the first restaurant I got to. I was so cold I could hardly think; I was so exhausted I could hardly walk.

It could have been a lovely spot with the river rushing along in a gorge behind the buildings. But there was a peculiar atmosphere about the place. I had noticed it all the way up from Maçka, a gloomy, brooding kind of a feeling, hostile even. I wasn't sure whether it was because the day was grey and overcast or whether it was because the place had turned in on itself, cut off from the rest of Turkey and the world, going rotten through stagnation and resentment. Or was it because the people were still suspicious of strangers? I felt this so strongly as I leaned the bicycle against the wall and went inside. Although the place was packed, I was totally ignored and even the squinting, restaurant staff was indifferent to my presence, so unusual for rural Turkey. At least the food was bubbling hot and there was tea. I ordered a bowl of moussaka – a dim reminder of the Greek presence – and ate it together with about a loaf of bread, trying to restore the energy which had alarmingly drained away. Looking at the map, I was very close to the pass but I felt so bad that to cover even just a handful more miles felt, at that moment, out of the question.

As I was drinking my tea, a large motorbike pulled up outside and a man encased in motorcycle leathers appeared on the verandah. He too asked for a glass of tea and stood outside drinking it. I couldn't begin to guess his nationality. I went outside to find out. He was French and had come from India where he had met a French woman, also on a motorbike. They had joined forces and ridden together via Pakistan and Iran, heading back to France. The woman was sitting on her motorbike, slightly away from the Turks and the buildings. She was extremely beautiful with her long, blond hair stylishly arranged behind her helmet over the scarves round her neck, cool and poised in that inimitable, enviable French way. Her companion asked her if she wanted any tea but she shook her head. We briefly chatted about her bike, which was British-made. It was splendidly old and painted a magnificent yellow. I asked her what it had been like going through Iran. There were no problems, she said, probably because she had always been covered up by her motorcycle leathers. I gave her a brief outline of my journey. She looked at me. 'The problem if you're travelling on your own is having to stop, even if you don't like the place,' she said. 'I'd be frightened alone.'

I suddenly realised that she too didn't like this place. She didn't want any tea and she didn't even want to get off her bike. There was no doubt her companion was oblivious of how she felt. Before I could ask her if what I was thinking was correct, she announced she was leaving. Without even waiting for the man to get back on his bike, she swept gracefully off, he hurrying to pay for his tea and catch up with her. I too paid my bill and left, fuelled by the food and the tea and somehow reassured by my encounter with the French couple.

Onwards and upwards. That's how the bicycle and I proceeded until we reached 6,590 feet, 2,010 metres. I had arrived at the Zigana Pass. '. . . and when they had all got to the top, the soldiers, with tears in their eyes, embraced each other and their generals and captains.' That's what Xenophon wrote with deep, retrospective emotion. What a moment it had been. Sadly, there were no Greek soldiers or Xenophon to kiss me. What I had to deal with instead was the longest road tunnel at the time in Turkey. A sign at the entrance announced the fact. I had had no idea that there was a tunnel through the pass. I got to the entrance and paused to assess the situation. In other words, I stopped dead, petrified with fear at the sight of the black, gaping jaws of Hades opening in front of me.

The tunnel was pitch dark. I had no lights on my bicycle. They were no longer functioning owing to the disconnection of the wires when the rear mudguard was pulled away from the back wheel on the bus journey to Sinop. I had negotiated previous short stretches of tunnel by cycling through as quickly as possible. This one was different. The Japanese boy had not mentioned this hazard. No doubt he had flown airily through, all lights blazing. Had they been broken, he would have mended them with a flick of a screwdriver. I knew if I tried to cycle without lights through this tunnel, I would be killed by the speeding traffic, which wouldn't be able to see me until it was too late. A pothole or a warp in the tarmac would also be bad news, either throwing me off the bicycle or damaging the front wheel. There was only one thing to be done. I would have to walk through, pushing the bicycle over the 'pavement' running along the side. I hauled her up onto this pavement, which was no more than a rough raised track of large blocks of stones over a drain, and started off into the blackness. At least the tunnel was straight and there was the tiniest speck of light at the other end. So I could aim for something, a glimmer of white hope in the far far distance.

It was a truly awful experience. I couldn't see anything, not even a hand held, like a cliché, in front of my face. I could have closed my eyes and it wouldn't have made any difference. (I tried it, as an experiment.) The pavement was rough and incomplete so the bicycle's front wheel kept disappearing into even blacker holes. I had to keep lifting her over those frequent gaps, the extent of which I couldn't judge. I inched wobbling along, keeping the front wheel almost off the ground so if there was a hole I could control the bicycle more. The noise of the lorries thundering through the tunnel was ear splitting, their lights like the eyes of wild animals shining out of the blackness, to scream past leaving me all alone in a muffled, deathly silence apart from the sound of water dripping from the roof. I hate the dark and I began to feel hysterical. I considered throwing the bicycle on the ground and myself on top of her when I suddenly realised there wouldn't be anybody there to take any notice. I had to keep going. So I did, hanging on to the thought of the speck of light at the end, willing it to get bigger.

And, finally, it did. More than that, the last couple of hundred yards or so were lit by weak, yellow lamps in the roof. The surface of the road didn't look too bad. I waited until it was clear both ways and pedalled furiously but triumphantly out of the tunnel.

I emerged, blinking, into a glorious and transformed world. It was as if I had made a magical journey through space and time. I had left behind the claustrophobic closeness of the damp, grey valley, the heights on either side obscured by low cloud, and entered into a world of dazzling sunshine and beauty. Behind me towered the sweeping, pine-forested amphitheatre of the Zigana Pass, the tunnel like a small, troll-like gateway in. Before me lay a stupendous panorama of the eastern Black Sea mountains, the Pontic Alps, proper mountains, inaccessible, savage, rocky peaks, soaring high and capped with snow. The Turks call this particular range Kalkanlı Dağları, the Shield Mountains. It was a truly uplifting sight. All the previous agonies of the day were worth it for this moment. It was infinitely better to be travelling by bicycle or on foot rather than roaring through in a bus or a car. I had time to look, to drink it all in.

In fact, I could have avoided the tunnel and travelled up the path Xenophon and his Greeks would have rampaged down. Looking up towards the top of the amphitheatre, in the gods as it were, I could see the odd car and van, like toys, balancing right on the edge of a road high up above me. Looking at the map, there were two roads marked over the Zigana Pass, one in red, the main route through the tunnel which I had taken, and one in yellow, which would have been steeper, definitely higher and certainly more beautiful. I had not seen any turning off the main road at all, although according to the map the yellow route began beyond Maçka. It was almost certainly unpaved and would have been ten times more difficult to negotiate. But I still felt sad to have missed it.

I started the descent, speeding down and around the spiralling corners. It was freezing cold and I had to stop and put on my sweatshirt and jacket, my fingers scarcely able to deal with the fastenings. A road sign said it was another ten kilometres to Torul, although I estimated it was at least fifteen. I swooped into the dilapidated rather sad town built at the crossing of several rivers. The heart of Torul was centred around two or three main streets. They were so narrow, I got off the bicycle. As I did so, a lorry came up and stopped beside me. The driver wound down his window and called out something obviously foul to me, careless that he was in the middle of the town and there were people around listening to him. A woman, about my age, rushed up and ordered the lorry driver to clear off, at once.

'Was he saying bad things?' I asked.

'Yes,' she said shortly.

'Men,' I said.

She nodded.

I asked her whether there were any restaurants in town and she pointed round the corner. I got back on my bicycle and cycled off to have a look. I went right to the end of the street, passing a couple of places, to get the feel of Torul, aware of every eye turning in my direction. One of the shopkeepers was hosing down the rubble outside his shop where the road had broken down into unpaved track. His eyes swivelled as he saw me and he launched into a stream of Turkish, none of which I could understand and none of which I wanted to. I turned back and asked a group of men sitting outside a tea house which was the best restaurant in Torul. Eagerly, they indicated the first one I had passed which had, indeed, looked like the best of the selection. I didn't bother to ask whether there was a hotel in Torul. I had already decided that nothing on earth would persuade me to stay there. I would eat and continue on to the bigger town of Gümüşhane which was another fifteen miles or so up the road.

The restaurant was large, airy, clean and civilised inside and so was the nice-looking patron. As I was making a note of where I was and how many miles I had cycled that day, he came and sat at my table. He took my pen and asked for my diary. He wrote his name on a page, Cihangir Aydın, the name of the restaurant, Doğu Kan Kebap Salonu and the name of the town, Torul. Then he wrote in Turkish: 'I will be waiting for your post card. With the greatest respect.' He smiled, handed me back the pen and the diary and went off to talk to his other customers. A great and noble man. I sent him a picture of Norwich Cathedral as soon as I got back home.

My bowl of ezo gelin soup was excellent – and so were the customers, one in particular. He was dark and bearded, clear-eyed and slim, in fact, breathtakingly handsome, a young lion of a man. I fell in love with him at a glance. He was a man in a hurry. He came roaring up outside in his clapped-out chariot of a car, stopped and leaped out. He darted in and out of the restaurant, chatting, laughing and commanding attention. He was an unusually charismatic man and I was sure he was breaking all the hearts for miles around. What is it that makes one human being so superior to all the others. I liked the young lion all the more for the fact that he didn't once glance in my direction. I know because I am sorry to say that I was staring in his all the time. I dreamed over my soup, almost too tired to eat it, of a handsome, noble, clever, sensitive paragon of virtue, you know, like the ones in the stories.

I thought I would use the toilet in Torul and kind Mr Aydın told one of his boys to conduct me to the bus station around the corner in front of an enormous mosque which was being constructed amidst the ruin and decay. I think the boy was pleased when I told him I could find my own way back. I returned to the restaurant and got ready to leave. I went to pay for my soup but Mr Aydin refused to take any money. So Torul had its good points.

I cycled out of the town past the remains of an ancient fortress on a rocky peak – there were to be ruined medieval Armenian and Byzantine castles on virtually every peak from then on – and followed the road to Gümüşhane. It is such a pretty word to say with the soft 'sh' sound in 'gümüş', which means 'silver' in Turkish. Gümüşhane means the 'House of Silver' and was named after the ancient silver mines in the area. Marco Polo mentioned them when he passed through in 1296. Tired as I was, it was a good road for me. I cycled through a serpentine valley between high, craggy, bare, mountain peaks. The river ran green and cool alongside the road, now on one side, now on the other. Some tree planting was going on up there. The Turks were becoming increasingly aware of erosion and environmental damage.

Strangely, considering the terrible state of all the other routes I had travelled on, the largely empty road to Gümüşhane was in the throes of a major re-structure. I lost count of the number of tunnels which were being blasted through. The old road would soon have disappeared completely under a new highway. The Turks were obviously anticipating an increase in traffic from the east. Bulldozers were chewing away at the ground everywhere and workmen were drilling and smashing their way into the rock. I must admit I thought it was rather a shame. The road was the main highway between the Black Sea coast and eastern Anatolia and had once been part of the Silk Route through to China. In its unmodernised form, it was part of the environment rather than a terrible intrusion – although, doubtless, the bus drivers to and from Erzurum would not have agreed with me.

I had a companion for a while in the shape of a teenager, who was also on a bicycle and also apparently heading for Gümüşhane. He buzzed me like a blue bottle and, at one point, took a short cut through one of the as yet unopened tunnels, while I dutifully followed the diversion sign. There he was, his hands in his pockets, pretending he wasn't really waiting for me at all as I sweated round the corner and up a dusty, unsurfaced slope to rejoin the road. It was too much. I wanted to swat him away, splat, against a rock face. As he cycled up behind me, I stopped and hurled myself into his path. 'What do you think you're doing?' I screamed. 'Why are you following me. You've been following me since Torul?'

He was only a lad, fresh-faced with freckles, and, disarmingly, had a set of head phones clamped over his ears. He looked rather sweet and I was almost tempted to ask him what music he was listening to. But the damage was done. 'You think wrongly,' he said, looking frightened, and cycled off ahead of me. This time he kept going. In retrospect, I did think that I had been wrong and, as it happened, I wished I had enlisted his support. Not long afterwards, I cycled into a one-street village through which the road had disappeared under a mountain of rubble. The track rose slightly and wound round a corner, possibly crossing over the river, but I didn't have time to look. As I battled to guide the bicycle up, round and over the heaps of earth and rocks, a group of men, probably in their late teens or early twenties, who were running up a track close by, saw me and with a sort of joint, inarticulate, animal yell hurled themselves in my direction. I had a vague impression of squinting, shambling, heavy-shouldered, goblin-like creatures – definitely not the cream of Turkish youth – running after me. They picked up some small rocks lying around and began to stone me. Fortunately I was on the downward track by then and pulled away, the rocks whistling harmlessly by.

But it wasn't very nice.

I stopped at a shop on the outskirts of the village to buy some chocolate to replace the energy I had lost in all the panic. There was nobody inside so I browsed around selecting something and looked in my purse for the exact amount of money to leave. Just then a man – he looked like a cousin of the stone-throwing group I had just met – scowled in and roughly demanded to know what I was doing. I handed him the money for the sweets and walked out of the shop. Hiding round a corner out of sight, I sat on the ground to eat the chocolate, wondering nervously whether all the locals might not rise up and come and get me. The countryside was very beautiful but I was struck by the same closed-in, insular feeling there had been on the way up to the Zigana Pass, an ancient resentment and apprehension of strangers and what they might want. Xenophon and his band of merry men had a lot to answer for. It was definitely all their fault. They started it when some of the Greek mercenaries completely lost the plot, stoned to death three ambassadors from Giresun and then began to stone the traders in the market. Xenophon described the scene:

'. . . we suddenly heard a great disturbance and shouts of "Strike them down! Throw your stones!" and the next thing we saw was numbers of men running up with stones in their hands and others picking up stones.'

In a de-briefing after the unfortunate episode, Xenophon told his men that their conduct had been 'more like that of wild beasts than of human beings'. But it was too late. The natives had clearly learned the lesson about what to do with strangers.

I regained my composure and cycled on through exquisite countryside with picturesque rock formations and the river winding alongside. It was here – as if to restore my faith in human nature – that I met Yonca, at a point along the Gümüşhane road where the landscape had broadened out and there was room to breathe. Her name appropriately meant 'clover'. Yonca had set up her stall by the side of the road. There were many other wayside stalls but hers was closest to the road. They were all selling pestil, sun-dried fruit pressed into sheets and hung up on string over the stalls, like leathery pieces of yellow cardboard. There were also large jars of golden honey and bottles of a rich, black, fruit concoction. Yonca stood behind her stall. She was wearing several layers of cardigans and various scarves tied round her head. She had a handsome, lively, brown face and she exuded vitality and energy, a Black Sea Mother Earth. In museums all over the Middle East, you can see Hittite figures more than 3,000 years old looking like Yonca. I stopped to stare at the pestil, which I had never seen before, and at Yonca.

'Where do you come from?' she shot at me. I told her. She listened with deep interest. 'How many people are there in England? Is there a queen? Is there a king?' she continued.

It was almost a medieval conversation. I could imagine the locals asking the travellers passing by on the Silk Route similar questions about their far-away countries. Yonca asked for information in staccato, quick-fire questions, pouring out energy and action. She marched off across the road and rummaged in some boxes and came back with handfuls of apricots which she stuffed into my bags. 'Tell them about me in England,' she said. 'My name's Yonca.' She smiled from behind her lovely jars of golden honey and fresh fruit and fruit hanging up to dry like curtains of distilled sunshine along the side of the road, and watched me cycle off.

I finally arrived in the town of Gümüşhane, It was built in a brooding ravine on the banks of a river. The houses climbed up the sides of the ravine in tiers and there was a shut-in feeling about the place. As I cycled in to the main street, I noticed a bicycle shop and stopped outside wondering if they happened to sell hooks of some kind that I could adapt into my missing luggage hook. The loss was not a problem, it was just boring having to tie the bag on every morning. As I gazed thoughtfully into the window, a boy ran up and asked me in English what I wanted. I told him and showed him the other hook still in place. He ran inside and enthusiastically explained to the bicycle repair man what the foreigner wanted. The man came out, sized up the problem for himself and disappeared back inside. After some banging and drilling, he came out with a piece of metal he had fashioned into a hook to fit. The hole wasn't big enough so he went in to widen it. He came back out again and this time it was perfect. It had taken him a matter of minutes to make and he refused to accept any money.

The boy was excited at finding a foreigner in Gümüşhane. He was fifteen, he told me, and lived with his family down the street over a shop. He was learning English at the local high school. I asked him whether he would go on to university. He shook his head sadly. 'There are a lot of us in the family. My father won't be able to afford it.' What would he do when he left school, I wondered. 'I shall work with my father here in Gümüşhane,' he said. I asked him what the hotels were like in town. There was only one hotel I should stay in, he advised, the others were definitely no good, and he escorted me down the street, treating me as if I were a younger sister who needed looking after, which was such pleasant feeling. He left me outside the Otel Gümüş and raced off back home.

The hotel was set in its own rather dusty gardens to the front and rear. It had two stars above its name over the front door. I wheeled the bicycle in to the gloomy lobby and asked the man behind the reception desk if they had a room for one. I was led up several flights of stairs, covered by a loose, dirty carpet, right to the top of the hotel and shown into a shabby room with three beds. The linen looked clean enough but the walls were scarred with crumbling, damp patches. There was a bathroom, with a bath even, but I was sceptical about the possibility of hot water, although I was assured there would be some. The hotel wanted two and a half million Turkish lira, around £10. I simply had no energy to go and look at the other hotels in the town which, in any case, the boy had told me were 'no good'. I knew exactly what he had meant by that. I tried to bargain but failed miserably. After all, the price included breakfast. I would be leaving before breakfast, I told them. Could they make me some sandwiches the night before? They assured me it would not be a problem.

I made several journeys up the stairs, trying not to trip over the carpet, until I was installed in my palatial residence. There was, of course, no hot water so I had to wash the journey away, fifty miles odd, with cold. The price of the room had eaten up more Turkish lira than I had anticipated and I thought I should change some money. The banks or money changers would still be open, so I went to find one.

I quickly discovered there was no exchange bureau in Gümüşhane, although they were a familiar sight in most reasonably large Turkish towns, certainly all the cities. In desperation, I went into every bank up the high street. Although nearly all of them displayed a change money sign, not one of them would accept my sterling notes. It was just like being in Turkey nearly twenty years previously, unbelievable for a country approaching the twenty-first century and which wanted to join the European Union. A helpful customer in one of the banks told me to go and find a jeweller's shop. I dug into my memory and remembered that had indeed been an alternative on my early visits to Turkey. I went into the first gold shop I could find. The miserable goldsmith fixing his gold behind the counter offered me a low rate for my pounds, well below what I had received in Trabzon. I pointed that out to him. 'The pound has dropped,' he said.

It was a bare-faced lie. The pound probably had not dropped against the Turkish lira since Marco Polo rode through on the Silk Road to visit the Kublai Khan. No Western currency ever dropped against the Turkish lira and it wouldn't do so until Turkey got its 80-100 percent annual inflation rate under control. I was furious with the man for thinking me so stupid as to believe him. As I walked down the street, I calculated that if I had changed the small amount of money I had wished to change through the goldsmith, I would have lost about 60p. It wasn't exactly a fortune, but it was the principle of the thing. Had he given me the correct rate, he would have made a profit by the following day. By the end of a couple of months, the money would have more than doubled in value. I was surprised he had failed to take that into account. I couldn't be bothered to go and ask in another gold shop. Gümüşhane would have to lose out on my sterling. I would survive with what Turkish money I had until I reached somewhere with proper facilities.

I made a half-hearted attempt to do some sightseeing around the city and walked up a back street up a hill to get on to a higher level. I could see there were some dilapidated, Ottoman houses dotting the higher terraces. One was a real beauty except that somebody had built a concrete wall right up against it. Every single street in Gumushane seemed to have been ripped up for road mending. The sun blazed down and what with the dust from the roadworks and the noise of the bulldozers and the traffic, I began to feel overwhelmed. I also noticed that some of the town's inhabitants were jeering and sneering at me and I began to feel that some of them might begin hurling rocks in my direction at any moment. There was not a good feeling in the town towards me. I returned to the hotel, buying a surreptitious can of beer along the way, and retreated into the garden where I found a sort of open-air summer house in which to sit and study the map and watch a workman laboriously setting up a sprinkler system to water a patch of grass that was so green and lush it could have fed a herd of cows and when I went to investigate turned out to be already water-logged.

I simply couldn't face exploring the Gümüşhane restaurants that evening and was, in any case on an economy drive. So I finished off the bread and cheese in my bags together with the odd peach or two and, of course, Yonca's apricots. Although they looked wrinkled and small, they were ripely delicious. It meant that I had no food at all left for the following day, but then I was expecting my sandwiches from the hotel, wasn't I.

16
Gümüşhane to Bayburt

Then they descended into the plain and came among villages where the food was good and plentiful.

I suppose I had known all along that those sandwiches would be like the pot of gold at the foot of the rainbow, ever promised but hard to find. A man was awake behind the reception desk as I carried everything down at half past four the following morning, but he was sandwich-less, nor did he have the key to the kitchen. When I told him that I had to eat before starting out, he telephoned somebody and the three-way conversation ran as follows:

Receptionist: 'She's on a bicycle and says she can't go without eating something. Yes, on a bicycle. Her country? What country are you?'

Me: 'I'm English and what difference does that make.'

Receptionist: 'She says she's English. What, you're not coming in for another hour. Can she wait an hour. Can you wait an hour?'

Me: 'No.'

Receptionist: 'She says she can't wait another hour. She's going to Bayburt. What, you can't come in til then. He says he can't . . .'

At that point, furious, I gave up and left, the receptionist still negotiating on the telephone.

It was pitch dark outside and Gümüşhane was still wrapped in sleep. The streets were deserted, but there had to be a bakery somewhere getting ready for the day ahead. I pedalled up the main street but couldn't find anything, so I turned off to cross over the river and on to the road to Bayburt and there, on the left, I found one, the lights inside shining out into the street. The baker inside was busy and his machinery was making such a noise he didn't hear me hammering on the door and screaming outside. Just then, a van drew up and the driver jumped out. He had come to take delivery of a batch of fresh loaves. The baker opened the door, surprised to find me waiting as well. I told him my sad story about the hotel promising to make me some sandwiches but letting me down. I took great delight in telling him exactly what a problem it was, that I was about to cycle off to Bayburt and had to eat something before I set off. I knew the story would go round the town and the hotel would be ashamed. At least that's what I hoped. The baker let me tear off half a loaf of fresh bread and offered me a wooden stool to sit on while I ate it with my last peach. He was curious about the journey and how I was managing on my own. I told him about the behaviour of the lorry drivers.

'It isn't just Turkish men who are bad, is it?' he said. 'It's men everywhere, isn't it?' He looked at me appealingly.

'Yes,' I said. 'There are bad men everywhere, not just in Turkey.'

I told no lies.

I left the warm, comfortable heat of his bakery for the mountain cold of the early morning outside. Cycling on and out of town, I passed at least two more bakeries on the way. It was fifty miles, eighty kilometres, from Gümüşhane to Bayburt and that day was to be one of the best cycling days of the trip. Although my map did not have the route marked as scenic, it was truly spectacular, with high, bare peaks and massive, limestone rock formations rising up on either side. Sparkling, lime-green poplar trees, like guards of honour, lined the way and a belt of rich green grass filled with wild flowers ran along the roadside, watered by the ice-cold river. It was as if I were in a lovely, landscaped garden, and the atmosphere was good too, unlike the bad feeling I had experienced on the way up to Torul and in Gümüşhane.

The road wound and twisted through the valley in relatively gentle climbs and descents. I was looking out for the place called Kale, which means simply 'castle' or 'fortress' and was marked on the map. I wondered if it was going to be another crumbling ruin, eaten away by the eroding weather, as most of them were. In fact the kale itself was a spectacular sight. It was built on a toweringly high, cruel, needle-sharp peak on one side of the road, the walls and battlements clinging on by some magic down the sheer, rock face and continuing into and over the rock formations on the other side of the road. The medieval fortifications had been built from blocks hewn out of the black, basalt rock itself so it all looked like one living shape. The castle must have been a spectacular sight when it was in its heyday, commanding the whole area and no doubt extracting lucrative tolls from the trading parties and travellers, who had to pass, literally, underneath and in its shadow. I shivered as I cycled by the brooding thing shrouded in memories of the past. I could almost hear the clank and jangle of the stirrups and the splash of the horses' hooves through the streams and rivers, and see the local girls running out of their houses to stare at the foreign young men passing by, marvelling at the strange languages they spoke, and then the silence once they had gone, apart from the wind and birds and sound of the water running.

I began to feel extremely hungry and, despite the relatively easy cycling, my legs began to ache. I was losing energy at an alarming rate. I passed by a pretty village; its houses were scattered over a belt of rocks high up and overhanging the road, and continuing over a steep meadow. I could see straight up into one cosy-looking home perched on an inaccessible, rocky ledge. The front door was open and a child was running down the garden path. It looked as if he would run straight over the edge. I could almost hear the water bubbling for tea on the stove inside. I considered the situation, weighing up the energy I would need to go back and walk up to the nearest house in the meadows to try my luck or to continue until I could find a wayside tea house. I decided to go back and hope the people were friendly and had their kettles boiling. I cycled back to the meadows and hauled the bicycle up off the road, bumping her across the grass and laying her on the ground. I headed for the nearest house. A lorry was parked outside and there was a lot of activity going on with people milling around, some of them climbing into the open back of the lorry. A man came to greet me. He spoke in German and I noticed that he was wearing a beautiful and expensive-looking jacket. I asked him to speak Turkish and told him I was looking for tea and something to eat. There was a tea house around the corner just two kilometres further along the road, he said. Everybody was busy because they were going up onto the 'yayla', the high plateau where the animals grazed in the summer. The people were all his relatives, cousins, aunts and uncles. He worked in Dusseldorf but had come home for a holiday.

The man looked busy and excited, pleased to be in Turkey, back home amongst his own people. I glanced at the traditionally-dressed country men and women and wondered what they thought of his smart city clothes and whether they were envious or proud that their relative was doing so well.

'Don't you miss this in Germany?' I asked. 'It's so beautiful here.'

'It's beautiful but there's no work,' he replied. 'What can you do?'

I left them to it, thinking how lovely it would be to spend a day in the pastures soaring up behind the village, and wondering how far I would have to go to get to my tea house. Happily, the man was right. It was about a mile away, along the road in the middle of nowhere. I came upon it, unexpectedly, round a corner, arriving just in time before my legs finally gave out. I leaned the bicycle against the railings around the verandah and hurried inside the gloomy, shed-like shop. I asked the man if he had tea. He did. And what about food. He had eggs so I could have an omelette made with cheese and tomatoes together with a plate of olives. He even had some bread, and I also picked up a melon from a crate on the earthen floor in his shop. I was given a plate and a knife and went outside to sit in the sun and savour the day. When you are really hungry and supplies are severely limited, the simplest food tastes like a banquet. Which, of course, it is.

The man came out to keep me company as I ate. He was going into town later that day and was making a shopping list. I watched him as he wrote down onions, bread, potatoes, eggs . . . I was lucky. Supplies had almost run out. He was also going to take his film in to be developed, but there were still a few photographs left to take. He took a couple of shots of the bicycle snoozing against the railings among the roses he had planted to grow up the side of the verandah, and then he asked me to take a photograph of him sitting on the saddle. He beamed as he struggled to hold her up. To him, the bags were heavy. He was a small, slim man and, like so many Turks, obviously underweight. A daily diet of cheese, olives, rice and beans can never put the muscle on. Meat was expensive and out of reach of the purse of the average Turkish family.

I asked him what the road was like to Bayburt. Just beyond his tea house, he said, there would be a stiff, five-kilometre climb, but after that the road would be manageable. How was his business? I asked. Although the Gümüşhane to Bayburt road was a main road through the mountains, I had seen virtually no traffic that morning. He shook his head sadly. Business was very bad. It was difficult to make a living and he had a wife and four children to support. I looked at him. He was still a young man and I thought of the children yet to come. From Gümüşhane, I said, a car would speed around the corner and past the tea-house before the driver had time to see it tucked away off the road. He should put up some advance warning signs, I suggested. It was obvious that he had never thought of such a thing. Just then a Mercedes car shot past from the Bayburt direction. It screeched to a halt as it saw the tea house. 'See,' I said, 'you need a sign in BOTH directions.'

Three extremely wealthy businessmen got out. You could tell they were rich from their clothes, their absolute self confidence and the gold jewellery, bracelets and rings dripping from their wrists and fingers. They looked slightly shady and I wondered if they were crooks. Half the Turkish economy operated outside the law so that wasn't such a far-fetched assumption to make. They sat down at a table next to mine and ordered tea, casting discreet, curious looks in my direction. They drank their tea, got up to go and an argument broke out about the best way to get to Tokat, one of Turkey's wine-growing areas, which was over the mountains and back towards Ankara. I offered them the use of my map. They spread it out over the table and pored over it, jewellery clanking, as they traced the various possible routes. They argued their way to a decision and, in a flash, were back in the car and roaring off.

'Did you see all the jewellery?' I asked the tea house man as we watched them drive away.

'They were rich men,' he said. 'All those lovely rings.'

'One of them had TWO gold bracelets on.' I said.

'Really, I didn't see that.'

And we both sighed together over the wealth of others.

I was in no hurry to leave, it was such a pleasant place and the day so lovely, but I was thinking about the five-kilometre climb just ahead. I wanted to tackle it before my energy ran out again. I packed up the half of the melon still uneaten, reminded the man about the signs needed in both directions and cycled away towards Bayburt. The climb was almost a pleasure, the way smoothed by the beauty of the place, the lush, rich green along the sides of the road hosting an enormous variety of wild flowers. Giant mauve cornflowers (Andy later told me they were probably *Centaurea dealbata*) mingled in with a rock plant, which was hanging with red berries looking like wild strawberries. There were exquisite, soft, rippling, brush-like grasses, the kind that would have cost a fortune in specialist shops in England. The meadows were dotted with beehives, and honey-yellow hay was being harvested in all directions. It all combined to give a feeling of well being that lifted the spirit and made one glad to be alive. If this was something like England a few centuries previously, no wonder the poets rushed off in all directions, drunk on emotion, to gambol with the violets and daffodils. I too wanted to walk among the trees in the shade and lie among this sensuous wealth of flowers. I limited myself to leaning the bicycle against a rock and walking among the plants, savouring every second of the moment, feasting my eyes on every leaf, petal and flower to try to remember.

It was indeed a pleasure to cycle in such a place, forgetting aching legs, an easy slow turn of the pedals to keep the wheels just about moving, sitting on the saddle leaning back slightly as if it were an armchair, every muscle and bone completely relaxed, head turning from side to side, a silly grin of delight on my face. My sense of exultation was heightened as I passed a Wuthering Heights farm, perched on a plateau and a sign outside that proclaimed we were 1,800 metres above sea level, nearly 6,000 feet up. The road descended in big spirals, swinging and circling down like a lazy glider plane, through glorious, open countryside of rolling, circular lawns and meadows, where cows grazed peacefully watched over by lone shepherds. The air was so clear, I acquired x-ray eyes that could see to the far distant horizon, able to make out every blade of grass, the curving horns on the head of every cow and the budding ones on their calves by their side. And I felt perfectly and unusually safe in the magic of the place. There would be no stones thrown in resentment and anger that day – at least not here.

The road into Bayburt was a switchback, rising and falling like the coils of a serpent. Just as I got tired peddling up one hump, I was at the top and speeding down, heading for another. I passed a turning off to the left to Aydıntepe – the 'luminous' or 'happy hill'. According to the sign, which was only written in Turkish, there was an underground city to be visited. I made a mental note.

Approaching from the direction of Gümüşhane, the medieval fortress at Bayburt was invisible until I was practically into the town, and then, suddenly, there it was, its vast, empty-eyed, battlements and walls crowning the acropolis hill, which dominated the town on the banks of the Çoruh river beneath. Later that day when I managed to get up there, I saw that, although the fortress appeared to be buried in the hills, in fact it commanded a view over the whole area. The main street in Bayburt led directly in a straight line along the river to the foot of the hill and the fortress. The townsfolk went about their business every day in the shadow of one of the largest citadels of its kind in Turkey.

The premier hotel in town was on the left going along the road towards the acropolis. The man sitting in the posh reception area looked mean and unfriendly and quoted me a price of $30 for a room with shower and hot water. Closer into town and past Bayburt's town hall was a string of cheap hotels on the right, backing onto the river. One of them was called Otel Sevil and Mr Sevil junior, who was watching television while manning reception, offered me a high-ceilinged room with a double bed and a shower room with an old-fashioned, marble basin, the kind you find in a Turkish hamam. Looking out of the large window, I could see the river beneath with a walkway running alongside, which was crowded with chairs and tables laid out for lunch under shady parasols. The price of the room was the equivalent of a couple of pounds. I asked Mr Sevil if he would mind while I went to the hotel next door to check the rooms there. Feel free, he said, and continued to watch television. Next door, I was shown a small, cramped room with no bathroom of its own, for the same price. There was no comparison and Mr Sevil didn't look at all surprised to see me return so quickly. He insisted on helping me put the bicycle into the boiler room, manoeuvring it past an enormous satellite dish lying on the floor at the entrance and squeezing it in past an array of iron levers and handles sticking out of the Heath Robinson bits of machinery which made the Sevil Hotel tick.

My room, of course, had not yet been cleaned, so I took the sheets off the bed to dump outside the door until somebody came to change them. The top sheet was of linen but the bottom one was a rough, nylon affair, like a tablecloth. It crackled and sparked unpleasantly as I removed it. While I was waiting, I took a quick shower and discovered that the problem with the hamam basin was that you could run water into it but you couldn't get it all out because there were no holes in the basin. There was always a cold, soapy puddle of water left at the bottom. I scooped away furiously at the water, trying not to think who was last in my bathroom and what he might have done there.

I had just finished when there was a knock at the door. It was the chamber boy, no doubt thrilled to find a foreign woman inside, although his reserved face did not give anything away. I asked him for two linen sheets for the bed, and he hesitated for a moment before going to a chest of drawers just outside my room. He opened the bottom drawer, rummaged around inside and brought out two crisp, thick linen sheets instead of the regulation one. I think they were in actual fact all tablecloths, but at least I wasn't going to get the nylon job. I started to help him make up the bed but he stopped me. This was his work, not mine.

There was still plenty of the day left to explore Bayburt and I hurried out of the hotel, turning up the street, marvelling again at the incredible sight of the massive fortress, its walls honey-coloured in the sun, straight ahead on the hill. There was another even more immediate sight to marvel at: two heavy, mountain bikes propped up on stands outside the hotel next door, groaning under the weight of bags which hung from either side of both wheels, and sprouting mirrors and gadgets of all kinds. They had to belong to Westerners. As I stared – exactly like a gawping local – a woman with short, fair hair stepped out of the hotel.

'These must be yours and I bet you speak English,' I said in excitement.

Of course she did, and so did her partner. They were Dutch people, who unfailingly speak every European language going. They had just arrived and seemed pleased to meet a fellow cyclist. They were as amazed to find me as I was to find them. I admired their steeds, so different from my light, slim one asleep in the boiler room. I could hardly hold one of theirs upright let alone have hoped to move it over a mountain. I wanted to ask a million questions and we arranged to meet early in the evening. They went off to eat and sleep while I went off to explore.

Bayburt was a small town. The busy main streets were laid out in a tight cluster on the west bank of the river underneath the castle. There was an infinite choice of restaurants, which mostly backed on to the river and in which scores of waiters in white jackets were preparing the tables on the walkway for Saturday lunch. Spitted lamb was spitting and turning in all directions. I looked forward to my own lunch later. I walked up to the central clock tower, ducking underneath the sun-canopies pulled low over the shop fronts and manoeuvring past the boxes, crates and trestle tables packed on to the pavements, overflowing with purple aubergines, orange-red tomatoes, cucumbers, spring onions, apricots and luscious peaches. I stopped to stand on the bridge to look back from the castle down the river. It looked like an impressionistic painting, all moving water and shadow and flickering sunlight filtering through the poplar trees overhanging the river. The gaudy parasols balanced drunkenly over the tables provided a splash of spinning, bright colour.

The old wool market was hidden in a quiet back street. Ancient, stone caverns were piled high with sacks crammed to overflowing with fluffy, white and brown sheep's wool and the coarser, creamy-coloured hair of goats. I stroked the wool and marvelled at its softness as the shopkeepers marvelled at my pleasure. The wool was used to stuff traditional, Turkish mattresses, fit for kings and queens but still used by ordinary families. In the spring in Turkey, you can see people everywhere outside their front doors in the country or on the balconies of their town flats taking out the wool from their bedding, plimping it up with a stick and then leaving it to air before stuffing it back into their mattresses. Our duvets and sterile bedding cannot compare with a real Turkish bed with its hand-sewn, shiny, satin quilts, feather pillows, wool-stuffed mattress and luxurious, snuggly blankets. Even in the cheapest hotels I had been staying in on the trip, the beds had been marvellously comfortable – except for the one in the hotel in Trabzon which had had a narrow, modern mattress, stiff as a board.

Bayburt was a traditional, conservative town with the Welfare Party (Refah) ruling in the town hall. Many of the women on the streets were bundled up in what looked like rough, brown-striped blankets. I felt hot just looking at them. Even the youngest teenaged girls were wearing headscarves. Portraits or busts of Atatürk were conspicuous by their absence. Later, I commented to Mr Sevil about the blankets and how hot they must be to wear. They weren't blankets and they weren't hot at all, he said. In fact they kept the women cool. I found this hard to believe until I came across some of the material in a shop where I felt it for myself. Despite its thick and rough appearance, it was in fact extremely light. I considered buying a length to throw over myself when the lorry drivers got too bad.

I browsed around the kitchenware shops opposite Bayburt's big mosque behind the main streets at the foot of the hill. One was selling a vast range of the plastic goods you can find everywhere in Turkey, including jugs, bowls, plates and containers of all shapes and sizes in bright red and sky-blue. I admired a large blue jug which cost less than 50p but which I knew I couldn't easily fit in beside the bedspread. Sadly. The shopkeeper, a large, jolly man, was chatting to a friend but broke off to invite me in to have a look. He was pleased when I complimented him on his artistic display outside. Inside the shop, the shelves were packed with goods like a serendipity, heavy tea sets painted with flowers Chinese-style, vases, ashtrays, tea pots and glass bowls. Out of reach on a high shelf, I noticed a row of blue and gold decorated bottles with enormous, glass stoppers. These were painted with the face of a stiff-looking, moustachioed, Russian military man. You could find them in most bazaars and antique shops in Turkey, sometimes in red and gold. I had once been offered a large one in a tumbledown shop in İstanbul near the Egyptian Spice Bazaar. The man had wanted £20 and to my eternal regret, I turned his offer down. The shop was later demolished.

'How much are you selling these for?' I asked the Bayburt shopkeeper.

He lifted one down from the shelf to show me. I could hardly lift the stopper let alone the bottle. 'They're two hundred dollars,' he said. 'The gold that's used is real gold leaf.'

My mouth dropped open and I was unsure whether to believe him. 'Who on earth pays that sort of price?'

'You'd be surprised. All kinds of people,' he replied.

I gave him the bottle back nervously, clutching the glass stopper in anguish, frightened of dropping it on the floor and smashing it into a thousand pieces.

Close by was a shop selling bowls, pots, jugs and coffee pots in traditional copper as well as in the new and cheaper aluminium. The copper bowls and pots, glowing richly, were stacked up outside. Inside, coffee pots dangled temptingly from hooks and water jugs lined the shelves. The aluminium replicas looked grey and lifeless by comparison. Even more tempting was the young man minding the shop. He was darkly good-looking with the clearest of brown eyes and the sweetest of smiles. Wouldn't those men have been surprised if they could have seen what I was thinking about them. (Horrible thought, maybe they did.) It was his father's shop, he told me, and it was a good business. We chatted about my journey and I mentioned the malevolent way some of the people had regarded me on the streets of Gümüşhane compared with the more relaxed mood in Bayburt. Gümüşhane, he said, was a small, narrow town (he indicated this with his hands) and so were its inhabitants. The countryside around Bayburt was wider, the town bigger and the people's minds corresponded. The two towns, he said, had always been traditional enemies.

I thought of Xenophon's description two and a half millennia earlier of what was then called Gymnias, which is thought to have been Gümüşhane. He described it as a large and prosperous city which was 'at war' with its neighbours. The governor, wrote Xenophon, gave the Greeks a guide, who told them he would lead them to a place from which they would be able to see the sea. But this apparently generous offer had been made out of pure self-interest. When they reached the territory in which the enemies of Gümüşhane lived, the guide urged the mercenaries to burn and lay waste the land.

I lingered in the shop wishing I could buy the young man and take him home with me. He would probably have been a bit more expensive than his copper pots and pans, whose value depended on their weight.

By now, I was extremely hungry. My omelette breakfast at the tea house on the road to Bayburt had been hours before. I walked back through the streets to the river and the restaurants. It was still far too hot to consider walking up the hill to the castle. I chose a restaurant close by the hotel, ordered a kebab from the man with a knife beside the lamb spit and went through the back of the restaurant out to the walkway to sit down. I hid under a parasol and thought about the rest of the trip. I wanted to be in Rize by the following Tuesday to buy my ticket and catch the boat back to İstanbul on the Wednesday. It was only Saturday. I would stay two nights in Bayburt and that would leave me two whole days to get down to Rize. I kept looking at the road on the map from Bayburt, through a village called Akbulut (White Cloud), over Soğanlı Geçidi (which, loosely translated, meant Onion or Flower Bulb Pass) and down to the sea, and wondering for the millionth time what sort of condition it would be in. It was marked as a non-road, yellow with white, empty patches. The Japanese boy had been told that it was a good road. He had not believed it. I decided that if it really was too difficult to cycle on it, there was bound to be a truck or a bus or at the worst a taxi to rescue me. It would be an Adventure. I ate my bubbling-hot kebab and then my delicious pudding made with honey and nuts, and washed it all down with endless glasses of cold water. I tried not to watch as the boys, whose job it was to clear the plates away, scraped the leftovers from all the plates over the side and into the river. I hoped the fish liked lamb kebabs with a smear of yoghurt.

The sun was still hot, but I wanted to get to the castle. I walked back through the town and stopped to ask the way. I felt a bit like Alice through the Looking Glass. She was told by the Rose that to get somewhere she should proceed in the opposite direction to the one in which she wanted to go. This is a brilliant Carrollian observation and an accurate reflection of life generally. The castle towered up, sprawling over the hill, close enough to touch. As I asked a shopkeeper standing in his doorway about how to get there, a crowd gathered to listen to what was going on. The man was grinning broadly and speaking in a language I couldn't understand at all.

'What are you speaking? I can't understand anything of that.' I said in Turkish.

'I'm speaking my language, Laz,' he said proudly and helpfully for me in Turkish.

The crowd roared. The Laz originally came from the Caucasus close by and their language is related to Georgian. They were among the most feared of the Turkish warriors and Atatürk chose them as his personal bodyguards. Like the Kurds and other ethnic minorities in the new Turkish Republic, the Laz people had had to suppress their own culture and had been banned from speaking their own language. They have a reputation for being tough, business people. I looked at the smiling, good-natured faces in front of me. It was hard to believe they were the descendants of some of the fiercest of the region's warriors.

The way was quite simple, they told me, head up the road and keep winding round. I continued on and immediately got lost when I went on a detour down some narrow, rubble-strewn tracks squeezing their way through an older quarter of the town. Some of the houses were collapsing into sad ruins; others were still inhabited and their walls were freshly white-washed. I stopped at a doorway through a wall into a secret courtyard as two girls, both wearing headscarves, emerged. I asked them the way to the castle and they offered to take me there. Their mother was sitting close by chatting to neighbours and, after the girls had presented their find and won everybody's approval, we set off. We passed a man washing his car. He was the girls' uncle. To my amazement, the girls asked him the way. It turned out they rarely, if ever, went to the castle. They certainly were never allowed to go on their own.

We walked up slowly. It was hot, I was tired and the girls obviously were not used to walking in the sun. The views over the town stretched out below beside the river were lovely, and we kept stopping to admire them. The girls pointed out where their school was. I tried to ask them about their lives in Bayburt but I had difficulty understanding their Turkish and they were unused to being asked questions about the things they took for granted. We almost reached the level of the first outer set of walls when they suddenly decided to leave me to continue on by myself. I wondered whether they had got too hot or frightened – or whether there was somebody they wanted or hoped to meet.

The walls towered overhead. I felt no more than an ant next to them. The fortress was much bigger than it had looked from down below. Many parts of the walls had been repaired, too much I felt. The regimented whiteness of the new stone and concrete used contrasted with the worn, mellowed look of the old. It was a stiff climb up, through the arched and vaulted entrance. The fortress with its series of walls and battlements had stood for centuries. It had been built by the rulers of the medieval Armenian kingdom of the Bagratid, but nearly everything inside had been destroyed. The culprits were the Russians, who destroyed the lower walls of Bayburt castle together with much of the town in 1829 during their invasion of eastern Anatolia. The lines of the inner walls could be traced on the ground and parts were still standing but, in the main, the enclosed hill or series of hills had become grassy meadows where people went to have their picnics. I had just about enough energy to struggle up to the top and gaze out at the rolling farmland stretching to the horizon, the ribbon-like roads heading off to Gümüşhane in the north-west and Erzurum south-east over the mountains. From the northern side and looking down almost underneath the castle, I could just about see the road that I planned to take towards Soğanlı Geçidi and back down to the Black Sea. Looking at the countryside, the road ran comfortably over the meadowlands but would then rise steeply to more than 7,500 feet, 2,330 metres above sea level and over the pass.

I stopped and chatted to a family from the Bolu region, west of Ankara, a beautiful area with parts of it richly forested. The man and woman with their children must have been in their early forties. They were enjoying their visit to the fortress but were quick to criticise Bayburt. It was just like Iran, the man said, his wife nodding her head vigorously in agreement. It was bad for Turkey, he went on, all the women having to cover up like this. The couple were also scathing about the treeless landscape. They spoke about Bayburt as if it were an uncivilised, foreign country and they couldn't wait to get back home.

One of the first questions the Turks ask each other on meeting is: 'Which city do you come from?' They don't use the ordinary Turkish word meaning 'city', but always use the word for 'country'. 'Memleket' is an old word and comes from the Arabic. So they literally ask each other what 'country' they come from. To the couple from Bolu, Bayburt was figuratively and literally a foreign country.

I scrambled back down the slope to the outer walls of the fortress and found my way out through the vaulted gatehouse. Half way down the path, I came upon a group of young women. One of them, scarf slipping off her head, was looking earnestly through a pair of binoculars. I wondered what she was focusing on and looked down in the same direction. She had fixed her sights on a couple of soldiers home for the weekend.

'Are you looking at the soldiers?' I asked. 'Are they good-looking?'

She laughed, a little embarrassed, but she was too busy sizing them up to reply. I took a detour down a flight of stone steps, half following the soldiers wondering what they did look like. At that moment, a herd of boys spotted me and pattered down behind, shouting and giggling. They began to throw stones. I turned and yelled furiously. It was a disgrace for Turkey, I roared. A group of women came to help and they too shouted at them to stop. The boys ignored the women. They may as well not have existed.

I thought about my appointment with the Dutch couple and about the promise I had made to drink some beer with them. By then I very much liked the idea of a beer and some like-minded conversation. I went up and down the streets looking for a shop that sold alcohol, a million eyes staring at me wondering what I was doing. I felt more and more embarrassed to be asking those traditional, very Muslim shopkeepers whether they sold alcohol. All of them just shook their heads.

At last, I gave in and went into a tailor's shop to ask for help. The tailor broke off from rolling up his bolts of black cloth to guide me to the town's tiny liquor store tucked away discreetly in a street nearby, disguised by an ice-cream cabinet outside the shop door. He understood exactly how I was feeling. 'The people make you feel uncomfortable, don't they,' he said sympathetically. He asked if I were an archaeologist. I told him I was a journalist. He was pleased I had come to see his town and pleased that I was enjoying my trip to Turkey in spite of the problems, he said. As I walked away, I tried to memorise where the liquor store was for future reference.

On my way back to the hotel, I bought some apricots thinking of Yonca's fruit stall and hoping the apricots in Bayburt would be as good. The shopkeeper asked if I were Azeri. I said I was English but could speak some Turkish except that I couldn't remember the Turkish word for apricot. Could it be like the unforgettable Arabic slang word for apricot, 'mish mish', I asked. The shopkeeper roared. He had never heard anything so funny. As I went down the street and round the corner, I could still see him bent double, clutching his stomach and repeating 'mish mish' with great gulps of laughter. I still can't remember the Turkish for apricot, but I bet he remembers the Arabic.

By then it was five o'clock and time to find the Dutch couple. The man behind the reception desk in their hotel let me go upstairs to knock on their door. Their room was tiny, with two beds crammed inside and no room for much more. Their bicycles were on the balcony. The curtains were drawn over the window against the heat of the sun, but the room was still stiflingly hot. The couple asked me whether I kept my bicycle in my room. They said they always insisted on keeping their bicycles with them. A set of mirrors had been stolen from one of their bikes just a few days before in a hotel. The owner had agreed to pay them $50 after they refused to move until they were paid compensation for the loss.

I got out the beer and we began to swap information. The couple had come to Turkey from Holland via Eastern Europe. They hoped to be able to cross from Turkey into Iran and continue on to Vietnam. The journey, they estimated, would take about two years. They had been travelling together since they first met in their early twenties nearly twenty years before and had begun to make their trips by bicycle relatively recently. To cut costs, they had sold their flat and bought a boat moored on a canal just outside The Hague. They rented it out whenever they travelled abroad which was roughly every two years or so. She cared for handicapped children and always managed to get the same job back again after a trip. He found work fairly easily as a draughtsman. Both admitted they were worried that it might get more difficult in the coming years when they might be considered too old and too expensive. They had no intention of stopping their trips, however.

I asked them how they had coped with cycling in the mountains. They told me that they had arrived in eastern Turkey via central Anatolia and Cappadocia. The Black Sea route had been their first choice, but they had found the journey from İstanbul out to Şile so tough, spending an entire day doing just forty kilometres, that they had dropped back inland. They laughed when I described my sweaty struggles to Şile and onwards. I felt secretly gleeful to learn that other travellers, experienced cyclists too, had found the route so difficult they had abandoned it.

The couple had seen nothing of the town. We went out of the hotel and I led them up the street and through the wool market to the central mosque. I had seen it earlier from the outside but had not gone in. We descended the flights of stone steps, took our shoes off and entered through two magnificent, stone doorways. They looked as if they might have come from the citadel. Inside, there were high, vaulted archways and a spectacular ceiling constructed out of whole tree trunks. I love the atmosphere in a mosque. It is similar to the peace of a cathedral or any large religious building where you feel that, occasionally, mankind can aspire to greater things. Mosques have a particular kind of silence inside, a muffled soft silence. It is because of the carpets that are spread over the floor which absorb much of the noise. I always want to lie down and go to sleep. I must have been a cat in a previous existence.

We browsed around Bayburt and ended up sitting outside a tea house along the river walk in full, spectacular view of the fortress on the hill. It cast a brooding shadow over the town, its empty eyes looking even emptier as the sun set. Although it was the end of the day, the barber in his shop opposite was still busy covering his customers' faces in white foam and then expertly applying his sharp razor to scrape it all off again. There was a whole queue of people waiting. The men looked so comfortable having it done, I almost wished I were a man to be able to experience the luxury of having my face shaved. Next to the barber of Bayburt was, unexpectedly, a fish shop, the word 'Akvarium' proudly written across the window. We could see the gold fish swimming around in their tanks inside through the glass. A disturbed man came along the path, shouting and singing. One of the customers got up and began to dance with him, the man shrieking with delight and clapping his hands. It was lovely for me to be sitting there unremarked and unremarkable in a group rather than on my own, but I wondered at the idea of always having a companion. I told the Dutch couple I could not imagine travelling with somebody all the time. They could not imagine travelling without each other, they said.

We parted and I returned to my hotel, luxuriating in the thought of having yet another lie-in the following day. I was going to cycle out of Bayburt the next morning and visit the underground city nearby. It was peculiar to think that the same time the following week, I would be back at home in Norfolk, watching the ducks on the lake, a world apart. I looked out of my window and watched the waiters dismantling the parasols and putting away the tables and chairs, that melancholy feeling at the end of the day, all light and hope extinguished. My room was a large one; a door shut off the shower room area and another door beyond that shut off the room itself. I felt protected in my inner sanctum. I thought of my bicycle compared to the Dutch couple's, theirs large and heavy, mine so slim and slight, their tyres wide, mine so narrow. But my bicycle had managed to get over the mountains from İstanbul.

Tirra lirra!

17
Aydıntepe – an interlude

Everywhere he found them feasting and merry-making and they would invariably refuse to let him go before they had given him something for breakfast.

The sun was well up over the river gliding and sparkling down towards the castle hill when I got up the following morning. The muezzin calling from a nearby mosque had woken me up at four o'clock and I had almost enjoyed it, revelling in the fact that I didn't have to get up but could go back to sleep. I thought of the Dutch couple, who would be back on their mighty steeds and heading towards Erzurum and the Iranian border. They were unusual people, continuing their adventures when most were settling down to middle age. They had no children and didn't want any, content with each other. I looked at myself in the battered mirror on the wall, skin clear and eyes very blue, the lines underneath faded. Oh joy, life in the old girl yet.

I suppose I should have been flattered by the assiduous attention paid to me by the young waiter who brought me my breakfast bowl of rice and lentil soup in the restaurant. He offered me everything he could think of, bread, water, spoon, fork, knife, glass, pudding. I expected him to offer to drink my soup to save me the bother. Buzz buzz. A man outside in the street was lovingly cleaning his blue van, polishing, wringing out, washing, rubbing, sparkle and all, with a few bottles of water. The Turks are obsessed with washing their vehicles. You see them doing it in the most unlikely places. Earlier on the trip, I had come across a man down a country lane, his car pulled up beside one of the many roadside fountains, doors open, the radio belting out music. He was cleaning his car and blissfully happy in a world of his own. I almost felt as if I had intruded into somebody's front room. Most of the water fountains along the way had warning signs up: 'Strictly no washing cars'. The signs made no difference. The motorists would drive up, spring out, unload their brushes, brooms, buckets and dusters, and get to work.

I went back to the hotel to extract the bicycle from the boiler room and the hub of the satellite dish. I decided she would stay with me in my room for the last night. She looked lonely. Mr Sevil was still asleep and snoring, stretched out on a row of chairs in the hotel lobby, although it was nearly nine o'clock. The day obviously got off to a slow start on Sundays in Bayburt. I wheeled the bicycle past quietly trying not to wake him up and set off back through the town, past the park and up the hill out of Bayburt, and onto the Gümüşhane road. I cast an anxious look at the small road leading off to the right. It wound underneath the castle and would, hopefully, lead me the next day through the meadows, over the Onion/Flower Bulb Pass and back down to the sea.

It was only a few miles over the switchback to the intriguing signpost pointing off into the empty countryside in the direction of Aydıntepe and the underground city. I skimmed along enjoying the space and the illusory feeling of freedom. There was virtually no traffic at that hour. The road was all mine. The open countryside was beautiful, cradled in a bowl of brown hills and behind them, dimly in the distance, a range of mountains, which were still capped with snow. This was nearing the end of July. The inner rim of the brown bowl was dotted with villages, green pockets in the brown, pierced with needle minarets and surrounded by willow trees and meadows, which were kept well-watered by intricate systems of channels and control dams. There were many new, gleaming, white marble fountains along the road, the taps made of copper and fashioned into animal heads in traditional, Ottoman style. The fountains bore plaques inscribed with the names of the people who had paid for them to be put there as an endowment. The villagers were haymaking in the fields, gathering in the fodder for their cattle during the long, winter months. Round cakes of animal manure were piled up outside their houses for winter fuel. There was a peppery smell of dung mixed with hay hanging in the air. This was a timeless scene. People had been doing these things in the short summer months for thousands of years. When Xenophon and his men trudged over this plateau with its isolated valleys in the winter of 401 BCE heading northwards, it lay frozen beneath deep, winter snows. Then, the indigenous people were Armenians, excellent farmers and well organised, with plenty of food despite the seasonal difficulties.

As I cycled through the villages over terrible, potholed roads, I stared at the teenagers, who stared back at me. They were hanging around, sitting together on the bridges, watching the world and the odd, very odd, cyclist go by. No doubt they were reflecting on the meaning of their lives too, dreaming of a different world in a big, bustling city where they could find work, earn money, go to bars, buy a car and get married.

I arrived in Aydıntepe, a tiny town with ancient, stone buildings, and stopped to buy a bar of chocolate in a shop and ask the way to the underground city. I sat on the steps outside the shop and a shopkeeper rushed to give me his chair to sit on and to bring me a glass of tea. A group of boys around ten years old cycled up on their mountain bikes to stare at my bicycle leaning against the wall. Three of them could speak some words of English. They told me they went to a school just outside Bayburt where they were being taught Arabic and English. Their school could have been one of the private, Muslim, religious schools springing up in Turkey. This was very much a Refah-controlled region. There were many signs advertising Koranic classes with classical Arabic lessons offered as well. They were charming kids, sweet, enthusiastic and bright-eyed. I didn't think they would be hurling any rocks in my direction. One of them, a good-looking boy with large brown eyes, told me in great excitement that they were about to go off for the day in the tractor. He pointed to one up the street. They were going to the pastures up in the mountains to see his granny who lived up there. Would I like to go too? I told them I wanted to see the underground city that day but would be heading up Soğanlı Geçidi the following morning. They escorted me round the corner and pointed up the road to a small park. That was where I could find the city, they said.

Cycling towards the park, I noticed how old the houses of stone were along the way, with their heavy, carved, wooden doors studded with rusty nails. A few families were in the park drinking tea while their children played on the swings. The caretaker of the underground city was thrilled to see a foreign visitor. It was his job to switch the lights on for visitors to be able to see. He would take me down personally and show me the sights. It was free. I wouldn't have to pay anything.

We clattered down the steps into a labyrinth of narrow, winding passageways. We had to bend down to creep through them. He pointed out ledges hewn out of the rock, where the inhabitants of the city had kept their lamps. The rocks were still blackened by the smoke. He shone a torch into one hollowed-out chamber, directing the beam at the floor. The chamber was inches deep in the clearest of water welling up from a deep, underground source, filtered clean by the rocks and stones. The water was ice-cold and so clear that at first glance I couldn't see it. I could only see the floor of the room through the water. It was a magical spring. I wondered how on earth the people had managed to hollow out such places in the solid rock.

The caretaker was vague about how old the underground city was. There are even more spectacular cities elsewhere in Turkey, particularly in Cappadocia, in which archaeologists believe people were living anything up to 4,000 years ago, using the complexes of underground chambers as secret retreats whenever they were threatened by invaders. The complex near Bayburt was almost certainly built by Armenians. It is probable that they built these cities to protect themselves and their animals during the long, winter months when the ground was covered in deep snow. The journey of Xenophon and his fellow generals over the Armenian plateau in that winter of 401 BCE, together with thousands of men and animals, was made far more difficult because of the weather. There were many casualties. Xenophon vividly described some of the gruesome scenes:

'The snow was six feet deep and many of the animals and the slaves perished in it, as did about thirty of the soldiers . . . Soldiers who had lost the use of their eyes through snow-blindness or whose toes had dropped off from frostbite were left behind . . . It was a help to the feet if one kept on the move and never stopped still, and took off one's shoes at night. If one slept with one's shoes on, the straps sank into the flesh and the soles of the shoes froze to the feet.'

Xenophon recorded how the Armenians advised the Greeks how to protect their horses from sinking up to their bellies as they made their way over the snow by tying small bags around the feet of the horses and baggage animals. He also described the underground cities and the Armenian hospitality he and his men enjoyed when they travelled through the area:

'The houses here were built underground; the entrances were like wells, but they broadened out lower down. There were tunnels dug in the ground for the animals, while the men went down by ladder. Inside the houses there were goats, sheep, cows and poultry with their young. All the animals were fed on food that was kept inside the houses. There was also wheat, barley, vegetables and barley-wine in great bowls . . . When one was thirsty, one was meant to take a reed and suck in the wine into one's mouth . . . So for that night all the soldiers were quartered in the villages and slept there with all sorts of food around them . . .'

My experience of this very ancient place was also memorable and far far easier than the Greeks' visit had been. The caretaker and I were joined underground by a group of men out on a Sunday visit. They were drunk on high spirits and laughed their way through the passageways and chambers as if they were a bunch of kids. One of them was a teacher at a local primary school. He invited me to join them outside for tea. It was pleasant sitting underneath a shady umbrella sipping glasses of sweet tea. We skipped over my general lack of male companions and children but got stuck on the question of religion. It would probably have been easier if I had said that I was a Christian rather than trying to explain, in Turkish, that I did not subscribe to any particular belief and did not feel it was necessary to do so. It was also difficult to explain that I believed that some of the teachings of Jesus Christ and Mohammed had been re-shaped, let's say, along the way, especially when it came to the status of women. The teacher was a devout Muslim and the answers to the questions about the meaning of life were simple for him, he said. It was all there written in the Koran for everybody to read. In the end, we agreed on the universal nature of mankind, how people throughout the ages wanted the same things out of life, whatever their creed or culture and that 'kardeslik', which means 'brotherhood' in English, was the key. What was so impressive for me was that he and his friends treated and spoke to me like an equal.

I told them I planned to cycle from Bayburt up to Soğanlı Geçidi the following day. It was a good road, they said, and the climb over the pass itself was only about five kilometres. They also told me that mini buses ran along the route, leaving Bayburt in the morning. Meanwhile, I was missing an event that very day on Soğanlı Geçidi, where there was going to be music and entertainment. It was the last day of the Bayburt pastures festival. No doubt the boys going up on the tractor to see granny would be dropping in. I wasn't too upset at missing the fun, shuddering at the idea of how I would probably have become part of the entertainment.

I parted from my new friends and went to sit at a table to write my diary and watch a group of small girls, probably sisters and cousins, packed on to two very comfortable, armchair-like swings in a corner of the park. They were laughing and shouting with pleasure and clinging on to each other as they swung backwards and forwards. The clock was ticking for these girls, some of whom would imminently be wearing headscarves when they reached the age of maturity. Their public shrieking and squealing would have to stop. I was aware so often, not just in Muslim countries, of the male discomfort and unhappiness at females drawing attention to themselves by laughing loudly and immoderately. It is women and their ability to choose how they wish to live which the followers of religions betray so badly.

I cycled back in the heat of the day with the sun overhead like a round, orange fire. It was difficult to imagine the area enveloped in a deep blanket of snow. Giant crows swooped and wheeled overhead. They cast sinister, flapping shadows on the ground and over the clumps of majestic thistles, whose purple flowers, like crowned heads, decorated the sides of the road. The women, bent over in the fields underneath their brown blankets, worked away at the rich earth, despite the fact that it was a Sunday and the weekend.

Back in Bayburt, I drowsed around the town, fruitlessly making my way back to the liquor store for some beer. It was shut. Time was running out. There were just a handful of days left. I went shopping in a supermarket close to the hotel and bought the usual bread, cheese, olives, tomatoes, peaches and biscuits. I also invested in a jar of thick, hazelnut chocolate. I thought it might come in handy on the road the following day. Bottled, instant energy. Whatever the men had said about the wonderful road over the pass, I didn't believe them.

Otel Gümüş was swarming with policemen that evening; maybe it was something to do with the festival. Some of them seemed to be staying in the hotel and all the rooms were taken. I made a joke about how lucky I was. I meant, of course, that I would be well protected that night, but from the look on one policeman's face, I realised you should never ever make a joke in a foreign language.

18
Bayburt to Çaykara

The Greeks ascended the mountain and camped in a number of villages, which were well stocked with food. There was nothing remarkable about them, except that there were great numbers of bee hives in these parts.

I was not as pleased as I had been the morning before to be woken up in the early hours by the very loud call to prayer from the mosques. It deprived me of at least fifteen minutes more sleep wrapped up in my comfortable table-cloths. The bicycle had been spared another night in the boiler house and was balanced against the table, no doubt dreaming of bicycle shops, spare parts and sea views. I forced myself to eat some bread and cheese and then began the task of getting everything downstairs without waking up the sleeping policemen. There was a kink in the staircase, which had taken a while to negotiate coming up with the bicycle and was even more difficult going down. One of the policemen was wide-awake and on guard in the hotel reception. He hovered around as I carried everything outside to load up, almost breathing down my neck as I picked up the bags to attach them onto their hooks. It was the last thing I needed that morning of all mornings with Onion/Flower Bulb Pass looming ahead.

'What do you want?' I enquired ungraciously.

'I want to chat to you,' he said with a sweet hopefulness.

'I'm sorry I'm a bit busy,' I said with suppressed fury, and he drifted back inside, disappointed.

Morning was hovering in the air, the glimmer of dawn approaching. The fortress squat on the hill looked grim, locked into its memories. I cycled away from it, down the street, past the park along the river – somebody had decided to dig the road up overnight – and up out of Bayburt. I crossed over the Gümüşhane road and slipped down the small turning off to the right marked to Çaykara. The first hundred yards or so of the road had a surface of tarmac but after that the road became a stony track. I thought for a while that the tarmac would reappear, but it didn't and obviously wasn't going to. I tried to keep going over the track but the stones were round and loose and thick on the ground. The bicycle wheels couldn't get a grip and kept grinding to a halt in a slither of stones. I wove from side to side, thinking it might be easier to cycle right on the edge, but whoever had laid the stones had done a successful job of it, pouring them in thick layers over every inch of ground. They made a reasonable surface for the lorries, which came lumbering up like lonely pre-historic monsters every so often from the opposite direction. Their heavy tyres could get a good grip but it was hopeless for mine. I had to keep getting off and pushing the bicycle, virtually lifting her over the waves of stones, which crunched and slipped under foot. It was hard work. I felt as if I were walking along a stony beach and the tide was coming in.

I began to panic. I couldn't possibly walk to Çaykara pushing/carrying the bicycle. The town was over the pass and at least fifty miles, eighty kilometres, away. I would have to take a mini bus, the first of which, I estimated, would be passing through in about four hours' time. Until then, I would have to keep walking and do the best I could. I had stopped to panic opposite a picturesque waterfall. The day had arrived, rose pink, chasing away the mist lying in folds over the streams and water channels and the river running alongside. This was clean and clear, the stony bed having filtered out all the lamb kebab and rubbish scraped into it in Bayburt – unless the fish had eaten it. Although it was daylight, the full moon was still there, hanging in the sky, round and enormous like a white balloon. I could have reached out and squeezed it. It was a beautiful world, and apart from the occasional lorry on its way to work (the sight of which was almost reassuring), there was no other traffic. I was off the beaten track at last. Why worry? The whole day stretched ahead.

So I continued on, sometimes cycling, sometimes walking over the track, which was now alternatively made up of the loose stones and deep, muddy ruts, and which frequently turned into a horrible, rigid, corrugated iron-earth that jarred every bone in my body and was almost impossible to walk or cycle over. I could probably have made much better progress had my bicycle been a mountain bike instead of a touring bicycle, but I gained in confidence as we manoeuvred together over the obstacles, realising that her beautiful, hand-made frame and reinforced tyres were strong enough to cope. Thank goodness the bags were light, despite the addition of the Trabzon bedspread

It was a day of water. The river continued to rush along on one side of the track or the other, while the countryside was criss-crossed with streams and brooks, irrigation canals, rivulets and rivers. The enchanting sound of water gurgling, pouring, trickling and swirling was to follow me through the day. The water kept the air cool and made the heavily cultivated countryside rich and fertile. I was aware of people everywhere, working in the fields, hay-making and weeding and hoeing their vegetables including potatoes, onions and dark-green cabbages like footballs. I could hear their voices, but I couldn't see them. They were hidden behind bushes and belts of tall silver birch and poplar trees that lined the tracks, the sunlight filtering through the leaves and branches. I was reassured by the voices. I only had to shout and somebody would come running. I felt safe and protected, safer in some ways for being off the main roads. Not one lorry driver was to harass or even look at me that day.

I arrived at my first village. The road through it looked like a disaster area. As

I plodded through, the front door of one of the tumbledown farmhouses opened and a woman wearing strong boots emerged. I asked her if the track improved further on. She looked at me in a pitying kind of way and tried to encourage me by saying the way should become slightly smoother after a few kilometres. I pushed on, distracted by the cocks crowing and the hens clucking, a sound which always reminded me of my grandmother, who kept hens outside her back door, and I remembered the sacks of pellets piled up in her outhouse and the way the hens pecked at my fingers as I scattered the feed on the ground.

I was not sure if the track did get smoother that day, but I felt as if I began to stay on the saddle for longer as I cycled down shady lanes smelling of hay and with the ever-present streams running alongside. There were several villages along the way and they must have included Akbulut (White Cloud), which I had been looking out for because it was marked on my map. But I didn't see it. There were few road or village signs. If there were any, they were faded and mainly illegible. Who needed them, apart from me.

The views broadened out and the hills became visible on the edge of the horizon, which looked like the rim of a bowl, bare, round and brown. The green cultivations were concentrated on either side of the road where the water tumbled. Tracks ran off in all directions to villages scattered across the countryside. Sometimes I was unsure which track was mine, and either I guessed or somebody came along to put me right. It was an idyllic day. I had rarely felt so happy. This was so much better than slogging along the awful Black Sea coast road, which I now wished I wouldn't be rejoining quite so soon.

Just as I was wondering how close I was getting to Soğanlı Geçidi and how nice it would be to have a glass of tea, I came upon rows of beehives busily spread out on a smooth, grassy, buzzing slope rising steeply opposite the river. Two men were in charge of the bees, and they stared at me as I stared at their hives. Of course I was immediately invited up the bank to join them for breakfast. They could offer me their own sweet, thick honey ('bal'), which was made from the best, mountain flowers, they said proudly, together with some bread and the tea boiling in a Turkish teapot over their fire. It was an irresistible invitation.

The men were thrilled to have an unexpected visitor. They described how they left their families down below in Trabzon every year and stayed up in the fresh air amongst their nine hundred bees, living for two months at a time without any amenities, although there was plenty of water. Their bread was stale, but they didn't mind. They were used to it. They slept in the little shacks they themselves had constructed. They loved it all, the peace, the silence and the nature. Apart from their work with the bees, they said, it was just like being on holiday. They told me that I had covered twenty-five kilometres from Bayburt (around fifteen miles) and that Soğanlı Geçidi was virtually around the corner, although, they warned me, it was going to be a perpendicular climb of about eight kilometres. They made a slanting motion upwards with their hands. I would have to walk up. Well, I could manage that.

We ate in companionable silence, the men so used to each other and their own company that they didn't feel they had to talk all the time. It gave me a chance to reflect on the taste of the honey, something I had avoided eating by itself before. I had only tasted it in Turkish sweets like baklava. I carefully dipped a piece of bread into the golden stuff and popped it into my mouth. It was very sweet but it felt as if I were eating oozing dollops of sunshine. Wasps dive-bombed us while we ate. The men called them 'eşekler' which also means 'donkeys'.

Bee-keeping is one of the oldest traditional activities in the Black Sea mountains. Xenophon described the great numbers of beehives he saw as he passed through with his army. His men found the honey irresistible and gobbled it down, with dire results. They suffered from vomiting and diarrhoea and were unable to stand upright. 'Those who had only eaten a little behaved as though they were drunk, and those who had eaten a lot were like mad people', wrote Xenophon. Some of the men appeared to have died and lay on the ground 'as though after a defeat'. This created 'a general state of despondency', he went on. 'However, they were all alive on the next day, and came to themselves at about the same hour as they had eaten the honey the day before. On the third and fourth days they were able to get up, and felt just as if they had been taking medicine.'

You could not blame the Greeks. I could quite see how it happened. It was very tempting to lie down in the grass and eat the lotus all day too, but I had to press on. I shook the bee men's hands, left them in their bee and wasp-loud glade and headed for the pass.

The countryside narrowed into a river valley and the hills turned into rocks crowding the track. I came to a small village, its houses spaced out among the trees over the slopes. Now the track was too steep for me to be able to stay on the saddle and I got off and began pushing the bicycle up and over the ruts. Rounding a bend, I saw that the trees stopped and there were just bare, rolling hills with the track winding through and over in lazy, serpentine coils. I passed the last farm perched on a hillside commanding a view over the valley. The son was in the yard and I asked him how much further it was to the top. It was eight kilometres and I should wait for a lorry, he said. He laughed when I told him I would walk and wondered how I planned to get back to İstanbul. I told him about the boat from Rize and how it would take two nights. He marvelled at the idea, as if I were planning to sail off on a great journey to lands far away.

The climb was not too bad. I was mentally prepared for it and had decided the five miles should only take me a couple of hours. The countryside up to the pass was completely different from that around Zigana. This was pastureland and the mountain peaks were tipped with snow far away in the distance. I felt as if I were an eagle circling high up in the air, able to look down on this little, large, circular, piece of land. As I climbed higher and higher, slowly ticking off the bends, I could see for miles over the folding green and brown hills and back down to the plateau from where I had come. The flocks of sheep and goats, like children's toys, looked as if their feet had been glued on to the sides of the pastures so they would not slip down the slopes. By a trick of sound, the bells tinkling around their necks and the swish of the water rushing down below in the riverbed were clearly audible. It was very beautiful and I kept stopping to take in the views and give my arms a rest from pushing.

About half way up, there was a village built into the side of the hills, the fine, chalet-style houses spaced well apart and situated so that all of them commanded a view over the spinning hills, the plateau and back down to Bayburt. Mountains now loomed on the rim of the bowl. The track ran along and underneath the village so that the houses were high above me, sheer on the steep, grassy slopes. I could see up and onto the balconies, the lines of washing with underclothes in descending order draped across, but it was difficult to reach them with a loaded bicycle. There had to be a way. I needed to fill my water bottle. I continued on winding around the outside of the village and found another track which branched off and climbed steeply among the houses, too steep and rough to get the bicycle over. I leaned her against a useful post, walked up the track and climbed up to the nearest house, feeling that if I slipped, I would end up back in Bayburt. This was like living on the edge of the world.

A good-looking, strong, young woman was washing clothes in large, flat, plastic bowls outside the front door. The feed of water came from a rubber hose attached to a standpipe. She didn't look at all surprised to see me. I asked if I could fill my water bottle from her pipe. She handed me the hose and I directed it into the bottle. It broke away from the standpipe shooting water all over me. It was icy cold and I gasped from the shock. The woman laughed and said it was like diving head first into the sea. Which it exactly was. She reconnected the pipe and I drank and drank the water. It came straight from the mountains and was cold and sweet. I took the opportunity to fill up my bottle.

I carried on up the slow zigzag, past the village and climbing high behind it, so I could look from my eagle's eyrie down into the vulnerable gardens and back yards and the valley opening up to swallow them from below. Now the people were like small, black pins walking way off in the distance. I stopped to eat peaches and apricots on a smooth outcrop of pastureland. The tough, short grass was so soft and springy I wanted to bounce on it as if it were a trampoline, lie down and sleep in the sun on this natural feather mattress. I resisted the temptation; there were only another few coils to negotiate up this real ziggurat of zigzags to reach the top of the pass.

It took me, as I had estimated, two hours to walk to the top, 2,300 metres high, 7,544 feet. I felt triumphant as I plodded up the track and onto the slightly swelling sweep of the pasture, although my heart sank when I saw the mess left by the festival goers. There were plastic bags and rubbish scattered everywhere, blowing in the wind and collecting in hollows. The bandstand was still in place and I hoped the local council might have enough sense to send people to pick up the plastic, as well as the bandstand, later on in the day. Vague hope or delusion is sometimes better than bleak pessimism. It hurt so much to see that lovely countryside scarred and dirtied by careless human beings. The wind was now blowing strongly. A crowd of men sat outside a shack drinking tea, hangers-on from the party the day before. One of them was a primary school teacher, who spoke English. He offered to drive me down to the town of Of on the coast. I declined his offer. Having got so far on foot and bicycle, I thought it would be a shame to give up at this point. One of the men usefully told me that the way to Çaykara bore right where the track forked into two.

I began the descent. The track cut through the grass, which was thick with wild flowers. I stopped for lunch sitting on the cushion of the grass verge and spread out my princess banquet of bread, cheese, olives, tomatoes and fruit. The views over the pasture land and mountain peaks in the distance were spectacular, but the clouds began to get lower. I hastily packed up my picnic, got back on the saddle and bumped off, ever downwards, glad I had been told about the right fork because there was no sign or indication to show which track led to the coast. By then I was cycling through banks of flowers including wild thyme which smelled so sweet. There were purple, pink, yellow and red flowers. I recognised saxifrages and enormous, mauve geraniums, the true geranium, the cranesbill of old, not the artificial red pelargonium grown in pots in Britain. I was able to identify one of the flowers growing in profusion everywhere as the plant that popped up tentatively underneath my buddleia back home and which, occasionally, grew inch-long flowers of pink and red swirls. The Black Sea variety boasted flower heads like church steeples or mosque minarets. It was *Polygonum bistorta* or snakeweed and it was growing side by side with alchemilla or lady's mantle, which, up there in the Black Sea mountains, was growing twice as big and luxuriantly as it did in England. There were variations of forget-me-nots and exquisite, richly-purple michaelmas daisies. I kept stopping to bend down and smell and look and wonder, but the cloud was billowing across and getting even lower. The weather was closing in and I began to feel cold. I took my jacket out of my bag and prepared for the worst.

Once again, I was running before the storm, but this time there was nowhere to hide. I just had to keep going. The trail of beaten earth, which I had been enjoying through the pastureland, turned into one of stones, while the pastures were transformed into precipitous needle rocks amongst which lay pockets of dirty snow. The cloud was closing over the path behind me, rolling, billowing and swirling like artificial smoke used in theatrical performances. A shepherd, together with his flock of sheep and goats marching behind him in a tight line, was silhouetted high up on a mountain peak against the darkening sky. They looked like cardboard cut-out figures in cribs at Christmas. The figure of the shepherd looked unconcerned about the weather rolling in. Perhaps the sun was still shining where he was and he was observing me, a frantic, spidery figure on two wheels scrambling in front of the icy breath of the clouds.

In the end I used the bicycle as a mountain bike, crashing heedlessly headlong downwards over the rocks, which turned into large, heavy boulders, and skidding round the precipitous bends worn into slippery ski slopes by the passing traffic. Two mini buses from Bayburt lurched and jolted past me at one point, although I was so busy I hardly noticed them. I had no intention of hitching a lift. It was all far too exciting and anyway, given the steepness of the slopes we were travelling down, I preferred to rely on my own driving skills than on somebody else's.

The cloud was still just about behind me so I could see exactly where I was going. Unfolding in front of me was a panorama of awesome rock formations with valleys cutting through, veined and criss-crossed by a zigzag route as if somebody had drawn a series of sharp lines with a pencil. The sun was shining down there in the lowlands. I had to get down the side of the mountain, cross over the river running through the gorge and continue along the twists and turns on the other side, winding down to the floor of the valley.

I rode my beloved bicycle down paths over which I would have normally carried her, hanging on to the brakes to stop her running away out of control, dismounting every so often to negotiate a bend when it was too precipitous and slippery to cycle, digging my feet into the ground to stop myself from slipping over, and getting back on the saddle as soon as I could. There was scarcely time to think. The clouds followed me down the track like a sinister joke. I occasionally stopped to look up and marvel that where I had just been was now impenetrable, hidden in a swirling, damp, white wetness. The bicycle, rattled and jarred, strained to the utmost. The brakes were being worked so hard I could feel them getting tired and loose. I had to pull on them now to get them to work. Bump, crash down that track heading for the river.

By the time I got there, I was surprised that it still had not started to rain – that was to come. It was a beautiful spot there in the gorge with the river thundering down from out of the mountains in waterfalls and foaming pools. I crossed over a ricketty bridge to the other side where a barn-like shack was being turned into a restaurant. A car came up the track towards me. The driver stopped when he saw me and wound the window down. His eyes stared in amazement. I stopped too and before he could speak, I spoke: 'Yes, I've really and truly come from Bayburt and I can't believe it either.' He roared with laughter and drove off, crossing over the bridge to follow the path I had just come down. I didn't envy him the drive up those boulder-strewn slopes in thick cloud. I continued on, wondering how much further I had to go before I would reach the town of Çaykara where I would definitely have to stay the night, however bad the facilities were.

As I wound along through the gorge, I was low enough now to be back among the fir trees, which had reappeared, twig-like, on the edges of the peaks. The clumps turned into pine forests, the trees growing at extraordinary perpendicular angles straight out of the narrow sides of the valley, straining to catch the light and the sun. Water streamed down the sides everywhere, over the rocks, running in streams and rivulets across the path at every bend and bringing with it showers of stones and rocks and the odd boulder. My shoes were soon soaked. I stopped to eat chocolate biscuits dipped in the jar of gooey, hazelnut chocolate, a double burst of energy. A lorry and a car came shuddering down the track behind me. I waited for them to pass me, pressing myself and the bicycle against the rock face. The car stopped and the driver wound the window down. It was the primary school teacher I had met on the pass on his way to Of on the coast. Once again, he offered me a lift, but again I declined. I was hoping that the rain would continue to hold off. I asked how much further it was to Çaykara. I apparently still had another thirty miles or more to go.

Who cared? I didn't. It was a stunning route. As I dropped lower, the villages began. The first looked like something out of the Swiss Alps with large, wooden chalets perched on the edge of the slopes. Around the sides ran balconies from which the people could enjoy tumultuous views up to the peaks and down into the valley. I slithered to a halt outside one house when a dog rushed out enthusiastically to eat the unexpected thing on two wheels. The people came out to see what was going on. They were a whole crowd of brothers and sisters who had come up to the mountains for their summer holiday. They offered me a glass of tea. As I waited, a figure emerged onto one of the higher balconies overhead. He was playing a Turkish pipe. I suddenly realised from his blank, empty eyes that he was blind. He was unable to see the wonderful view at his feet. I was told that he was a brother of the family and had gone blind unexpectedly when he was a child. His music made me shiver. He was smiling even as he produced the incredible, lonely, wailing music of the eastern steppes.

The villages lower down were farming settlements made up of substantial family houses. They were constructed out of timber and were well spaced out away from each other. Many of the verandahs, banisters and stairways were intricately carved and decorated. Every available storage area, including balconies, spaces under the stairs, passageways and lean-tos, were crammed with neatly chopped logs of wood and round cakes of manure ready to burn for heating and cooking in the winter. There were tight bundles of hay entwined with wild flowers, bursting with goodness for the cattle to eat during the long and hard winter months. These people spent the short summers preparing for the siege of winter and the coming snows, which would cut them off from the valleys beneath. The sheer slopes were dotted with people, entire families, scything and raking in the hay. I could not imagine how they were keeping their balance. It looked as if they would slip down on top of me as I passed underneath. I felt dizzy just looking and practically lost my balance as I tried to take in the whirling meadows, the craggy slopes and the valley winding down below. The whole world rocked and rolled and spun around me. Only the bicycle kept her head.

The people were even cutting the precious grass with its wild flowers along the roadside. Not an inch was being wasted. It was hard work to get it back to the villages. It was all done by physical labour. A haystack would stagger towards me up the track on two legs. I marvelled at how the person underneath managed to navigate where he or she were going. The forests were alive too, mainly with women, girls and the youngest boys, collecting up every scrap of stick and branch they could find, to carry it back home, bowed down under the weight. I passed a woman sitting on the ground, almost hidden by an enormous load of wood strapped on to her back. Her small son was trying to help her up. I stopped and offered to help too but she smiled and said her son was strong and capable. I felt like a dilettante, a vicarious observer of all that hard work and energy geared towards survival.

The villages were clean and organised with every house in excellent repair. The land was also loved and cared for: the meadows beautifully terraced with immaculate, dry walls of stone, and man-made water channels pearling through. How different it was from the lowlands. These were mountain people whose ancestors had followed the same seasonal routines for generations. The winters were so hard that if they were not ready for them, they would not be able to survive. They were proud and reserved people and were too busy to pay any attention to me. I surprised one woman loaded up with sticks and twigs when I cycled up behind her. To my horror she began to run, tottering under the weight of her load, muttering and cursing me. I accelerated past her and she shot me a baleful glance and then quickly averted her eyes as if I were the devil incarnate. (Could she have spotted my blue eyes!?) It sounded like she was praying to the gods to preserve her from all evil spirits. I felt discomforted and embarrassed that I, an alien, was intruding on her world.

As I passed through one village, a scream of children turned out in force to tear after me, trying to touch the bicycle. I braced myself for stones but none came, just the little monsters thundering along beside me. A woman shouted at them to stop but pooh, it was only a silly woman telling them what to do, somebody to ignore. In the end, frightened one of them would fall and slip under my wheels, I stopped. They screeched to a halt too, laughing and shouting.

'Am I or am I not your guest while in Turkey?' I asked, hoping that the use of that magic Turkish word 'mısafır' for guest would fix the little buggers.

'Yes,' they said meekly, 'You are our guest.'

And they actually stopped following me and retreated back home, so powerful was their tradition that the guest passing through must be protected and looked after.

By now I was getting tired and my hands and arms ached under the strain of hanging on to the handlebars and the brakes. I continued to ask how far it was to Çaykara but was getting a bewildering variety of answers. The town was not getting any closer and, in fact, if anything, seemed to be moving further and further away. The bicycle was filthy and my shoes and legs were soaked and covered in mud and dust. The clouds continued to roll down and rain was imminent. I was aware of cycling past a covered, wooden bridge which, under normal circumstances, would have required closer examination. But I didn't want to lose any time. (The bridge was indeed worth an inspection. It was without doubt one of the remaining bridges over the river that dated back to the mid-eighteenth century.) I kept going, the valley narrowing, the sides getting even steeper and the forests more dense. The rocks were jagged and high, like castles and battlements, a natural defence system. Such countryside breeds stories and legends. Rocks take on particular shapes and become inhabited by magic creatures.

The light was fading and it began to rain as I crossed over the river again and passed a scatter of houses, all of which seemed to be empty and deserted. It was an eerie, lonely place. Everything was made worse by the sound of the raindrops pattering noisily through the branches. I cycled past a woman and her son trudging miserably along the track and asked them how far it was to Çaykara. They didn't have the energy to reply. A car roared up the track and I stopped to get out of its way. The driver leered out of the window. I was back in the lowlands.

The rain now poured down. The trees and overhanging rocks afforded some shelter but I was getting steadily wetter and wetter. The brakes, always difficult when wet, were becoming worse than useless. The track was turning into a sea of mud and the rocks were even more slippery. What with the failing light, the bad weather and my weariness, the situation was not ideal. Surreally, I met two girls strolling along apparently oblivious of the rain. They were deep in conversation and eating nuts as comfortably as if it were a hot, sunny day. There was a village just round the corner, they said reassuringly. As I cycled off, they shouted to me, asking where I was from. I didn't feel like staying to chat.

I slithered around a few more corners and into the village. I felt frantic and must have looked a sight. The tea house was opposite a mosque. A couple of steps led up to a verandah on which most of the elderly gentlemen of the village seemed to be sitting, sipping their tea and watching the rain as comfortably as if they were at a Sunday cricket match and rain had temporarily stopped play. They started to laugh as I dismounted and prepared to carry my dear, wet and muddy bicycle up the steps and under cover.

'Don't laugh,' I snapped, furious, and they stopped abruptly, struggling to repress their snorts of mirth. I could have murdered them all. After such a ride and such a day. I wheeled the bicycle inside the tea house, leaned her against a table and sat down, trying to coax my gloves off my freezing hands. There was a stunned silence, so I announced to the assembled throng where I had come from and where I was going. Somebody rushed up with a glass of tea. A young man, who fell in love with me at once, moved his chair as close as he could to mine and, as soon as I had finished one glass of tea, brought me another. I found myself sitting in a semi-circle of men, my adoring audience hanging on my every word. They couldn't believe that I had done such a journey that day and that I wasn't married.

The rain continued to pour down. It felt exactly like being in England when you're on holiday and it rains, that pervasive, damp smell, the wet clothes you know will be difficult to get dry, waiting around in a café and wondering what to do next. Fortunately, all the various plastic layers in the bicycle bags came into their own. Everything inside was still dry. My shoes, socks, leggings and jacket were, of course, soaked. I asked how far it was to Çaykara. It was again much further than I had estimated, although they told me the track stopped and became a road with a proper surface further down. I tested my brakes. What with the wet, the mud and the day's excessive usage, they didn't respond at all. I sipped my tea miserably, wondering what to do.

I was saved by a good Samaritan in the shape of a lorry driver, who was delivering bags of flour. He would take me to Çaykara, he said, after he had finished his business in the village. I felt looked after and protected once more, and my main admirer sitting by my damp right elbow, ordered another glass of tea to celebrate. I complimented him on the beauty of his village. From the window, I could see some fine, timbered houses opposite.'

They're dusty to live in and the women have to work hard,' he said, and laughed when I suggested the men should help with the housework.

The lorry driver hurried in to collect me. The bags and the bicycle were dumped unceremoniously among the flour sacks in the back and I sat high up in the front next to my saviour. We set off down the winding track. By then it was dark and the rain was still pelting down, I didn't envy him having to negotiate those hairpin, narrow bends. The road turned out to be properly surfaced further down, but roadworks had closed the way to Çaykara. We had to follow a diversion. This added even more kilometres on to the journey. My driver was a very nice man indeed. He had not been going to Çaykara at all. He was heading with his load further up the mountains to a resort, but was making the detour for me. He thought I was 'brave' and 'courageous', those words again. His wife, he said, would not even get into a dolmuş on her own.

I was so grateful I could hardly speak and didn't feel brave or courageous at all. The windscreen wipers were scarcely able to cope with the force of the driving rain and the lights of the oncoming traffic were dazzling. Some of the bends in the road were so steep and tight, I thought we were going to pile into the trees and rocks along the side. It seemed to take hours to get to the town. The man looked at me in worried alarm. I knew what he was going to say before he said it. There was a hotel in Çaykara, he said, but it was a dump, not suitable for a woman to stay in. I assured him I was well used to places like that having stayed in so many over the years. I could look after myself and it was only for one night, then I would be off to Rize.

The centre of Çaykara was also undergoing roadworks. The street the hotel was in was virtually impassable. There was just enough room for one line of traffic to squeeze past between the mounds of earth thrown up and the deep trench dug down one side. But, of course, bulldozers and cars from both directions were trying to get down it all at the same time. I shut my eyes as my man battled to get as close to the hotel's front door as he could, stopping, reversing, gears crashing, tyres slipping in the mud and the rain.

'This is Turkey,' he said grimly, cursing the drivers who refused to wait their turn, all piling in together and adding to the confusion.

Finally, he made it and stopped the lorry outside. We rushed to get the bags and bicycle out, carrying them across a ricketty gang plank, over a heap of earth and into the hotel's tea house. I had a vague impression of run-down dilapidation as I turned to thank the lorry driver, who disappeared back into the night still looking most unhappy about having to leave me in such a place.

The hotel was ancient. There were even faded photographs of the last Ottoman sultans on the wall as well as the usual ones of Atatürk. The tea house customers ignored me, for which I was grateful. The owner shuffled towards me. He looked like Scrooge. His crafty eyes shifted around in all directions and he appeared to communicate in grunts. However, he went to get a key and led me upstairs. We squeezed through a couple of narrow doorways and up a cramped staircase. It was pitch black and, reluctantly, he put a light on. This lit up a couple of light bulbs dangling from wires hanging down from the ceiling. There were sloping floors and claustrophobic, windowless corridors. Everything was made of wood. It was a potential tinderbox.

The man jiggled the key around in a keyhole and opened the door into a small room in which there was a single bed covered with filthy sheets and a battered bedside table. I asked him how much the hole was. There was no charge for it, he said. This made me instantly suspicious. Were there any clean sheets? I asked. He shuffled off and, with another key, fumbled open a door into a cupboard-like room filled with linen. He extracted a couple of sheets and a pillowcase, which were all reasonably clean, and followed me back inside the room. I couldn't bear the idea of him changing the bed and virtually pushed him outside so I could do it myself, first asking him where the shower room was. It was right down the other end of the building. I followed him through the gloom, ducking underneath the low beams, up and down some steps and manoeuvring past a pile of dusty broken-down chairs and tables crammed into the hallway. The door was padlocked. I made him open it and returned to my room to change the bed. When I emerged to go back downstairs to collect the bicycle, I found he had turned the lights off and it was pitch dark again. But I remembered where the switch was and turned them back on.

I managed to get the bicycle and the bags up into the room and shut and locked the door behind me. Even though the bags were covered with mud and flour from the lorry, I could hardly bear to put them down on the even filthier floor. I peeled off my wet clothes, hanging them up on hooks on the wall. I got out as few things from my bags as possible and went to take a shower. I wore the plastic sandals always left under the bed for guests to use in old-fashioned, Turkish hotels. The bathroom was tolerably clean, its walls and floor tiled, but I was glad of the sandals. I found a man's gold necklace on the floor. I picked it up and put it on a wooden stool to give to old Scrooge downstairs. I hoped whoever owned it wouldn't come hammering on the door while I was in there.

After the shower, I skittered down the corridor back to my room, fumbling with the key in the stiff, old keyhole, hoping nobody would emerge from one of the rooms and catch me. I had already been stared at by a young man, who was occupying a room close to mine and who had spotted me struggling along the corridor with the bicycle in my arms. I didn't want anybody thinking I was a down-market Natasha. I put on all my warm clothes, what there was of them, and put the jacket back on top. It was wet on the outside but not on the inside. My shoes were soaked and smelt disgusting but there was nothing for it but to put them back on too. Hurrying back downstairs, I handed the necklace in to shifty, old Scrooge, meanly wondering if he would really return it to its owner, and went out into town. I wanted food and beer.

It was still pouring. I raced up and down the street desperately trying to find a shop that sold alcohol. Somebody pointed me in the direction of the liquor store. It was a small kiosk, hidden in a back alleyway and heavily padlocked. I went back into the street and tried some more shops. A man sitting behind one of the counters looked like a Shakespearean actor. He had a well-clipped, black beard, large, dark, expressive eyes and a perfectly poised head. He was immaculately dressed and had superb timing. He timed the way he moved his head to look at me and even adjusted his blinking to add force to the scornful superiority in his gaze. 'What do you want beer for?' he asked, looking directly into my eyes. 'Why can't you drink juice or tea?'

There was simply no answer to that. I couldn't bear to get into another religious argument. I had to accept I was in another beer-perish-the-thought kind of town, no doubt ruled by Refah. I decided to lower my profile and find something to eat. Most of the restaurants were packing up for the night but I found one close by, which was able to offer me a bowl of yoghurt with cucumber and garlic and a plate of green beans in oil. The boy manning the place obligingly ran out to a shop to buy some bread. As I was eating, a man came in.

'You were looking for beer, weren't you?' he asked.

'Yes,' I replied, wondering what was going to come next.

'There's a shop behind here which is still open and where you can buy it,' he said. He asked the boy to go and buy me some and, turning on his heel, he disappeared back outside. The boy shifted from foot to foot and looked uncomfortable. I guessed what he was thinking. 'I promise I won't drink it here,' I said. 'Get them to wrap it up and I'll take it away.' He smiled with relief and asked me how many cans I wanted. Only one, I said. He returned a few minutes later carrying a packet done up carefully in newspaper. They only had fanta, he said (it was a joke) and laughed when my face dropped with disappointment.

I scurried back to the hotel clutching my precious packet, whistling in through the door and up the stairs, hoping nobody had seen me, fumbling with the wretched lock and slamming the door behind me. Minutes later, there was a knock at the door. It was Scrooge with a glass of tea. I opened the door, grabbed the glass and shut the door quickly. Furious, I threw the contents including the sugar in the saucer out of the window, hoping nobody was underneath, just remembering to hang on to the glass and the saucer. Minutes later, another knock came at the door. 'Go away,' I screamed. The knocks became persistent. It was impossible to ignore them.

'Now what do you want,' I shouted.

'I've come to get the glass.'

I opened the door a crack. The old bugger was standing outside holding a carrier bag. I just heard him say, 'I've brought some beer. You were looking for some. We can drink it together . . .' before I threw the saucer and glass into his hand and slammed the door shut again, double locking it. I could hear him sniggering outside. I couldn't believe it. How had he got to hear about my hunt to find beer in the town? I decided that if he returned I would go downstairs and disgrace him in front of his customers. Maybe he guessed what I was thinking, because that was the last I heard from him or anybody else that night.

I unwrapped my can of beer from the layers of newspapers folded around it and sipped it slowly, savouring every warm, flat mouthful. I ate some apricots which had turned into a strong-smelling soup in their plastic bag. Opening the window to let some air into the room, I peered out. Çaykara looked a dump in the daylight but night had transformed it into a magical little city, lights winking out from the houses dotted over the hills rising sheer above it. I watched the rain pouring down and wondered what I would do if it were still raining the next day. I would get a bus to Rize, I decided. Despite the view, nothing would induce me to stay a second night in this hotel.

I went to bed early – there was nothing else to do – but I was also shattered from the journey. The hotel was a dump but its beds had traditional, voluptuous, wool mattresses and feather quilts and pillows. I snuggled down thinking of the day's journey. It was my best ever, given the conditions and the length, around fifty miles over non-roads, including the mountain pass.

You can do almost anything if you want to.

19
Çaykara to Rize

Speaking for myself, soldiers, I am already tired out with packing up baggage, and walking and running, and carrying arms, and marching in the ranks, and going on guard, and fighting.

It was still raining when I woke up and peered out of the window. It was like an Irish rain, a gentle patter of warm, slightly oily water. 'Sure and it's a fine day', the Irish would say, and no doubt the Black Sea people say it too, throwing in the word 'grey' as an extra compliment. (It is always a good morning in Turkey, a very good morning, in fact. They say 'gün aydın', which literally means 'luminous day'.) I quickly got dressed, trying not to touch the floor too often, and sat at the window as if I were at the theatre, waiting and wondering if the rain would stop that day, and eating my bread and cheese breakfast.

I could see Çaykara by day now, a small town tucked away in the gorge, hemmed in by densely green hills with the river rushing straight through the centre. The stately houses climbing up the hillsides had been built to accommodate large families. The walls were solidly made of plaster and wood in latticework, like Elizabethan houses in England. A mosque had been built half way up one of the hills. The crown of lights around the tip of the minaret had been among the lights twinkling out the previous evening. There were a handful of houses tucked away at the top of the peaks and among the trees. They perched like toys in the clouds, which billowed and swirled around them. Most of the houses bristled with satellite dishes. I had passed one coming down the mountain the previous day. It lay beside the side of a house, a monster of a dish, practically bigger than the house itself. As I watched from the window, the town began to wake up and the shopkeepers rolled up the shutters of their tumbledown shops in the street below with a noisy rattle. There were some fine, old buildings amongst the dilapidation, their roofs of rich, brown tiles, hand-made and covered in moss. Above, the clouds were almost imperceptibly lifting. It felt as if the rain might stop. I was impatient to get moving.

There were only a couple of customers in the tea house as I manoeuvred the bicycle back down the narrow staircase, returning for my filthy, muddy, flour-covered bags. I was expecting Scrooge to demand payment for the night, despite his claims to the contrary when I arrived. After all, he'd been disappointed in his hopes of getting drunk and doing god knows what with the foreigner. But I wasn't going to make it any easier for him by offering him a payment. I wondered how he would do it. He had no shame. He stuck his hand out and rubbed his fingers together.

'How much,' I said.

He wanted the equivalent of a couple of pounds. I gave him the money, loudly telling him he was a disgrace to Turkey and informing the customers of his antics with the beer. Unfortunately, I became so indignant again that I tripped over the Turkish and I am not entirely sure they understood, although old Scrooge looked slightly red-faced. I had to go and write my details down in a little booth in a corner of the tea house in the hotel book, name, address, passport number etc. The young man there making the tea looked at me sympathetically. He had understood. We looked at each other, then at Scrooge and raised our eyebrows. I love it when people understand each other without having to speak, especially when they come from completely different cultures.

I carried the bicycle and then the bags out of the door over the earth-mound and across the walkway thrown over the trench in the road, and put everything together in the shelter of a doorway opposite. I cycled down the street wondering if I should explore the bus possibilities to Rize. But the rain had at last stopped. Although the weather was still overcast and the air heavy and damp, it felt wonderful to be back on the saddle, that heady feeling of space, freedom and movement. The time for my adventure was running out. I was going to Rize and that would be the end of the cycling, at least for the time being. So I dismissed all thoughts of buses and cycled over the bridge, the river rushing underneath in black torrents, and off down the road in the direction of the coast. The battery in my clock had expired. I stopped and asked a group of men waiting at a bus stop what time it was. They looked at me as if I were a creature from outer space. I was past caring, almost drunk on the warm, wet wind that blew so softly against my face. The tyres of the bicycle hissed as they sped over the soaked road that was going to be downhill all the way back to the coast. The brakes were hardly working at all. If I wanted to stop, I had to start pulling on them well in advance. Fortunately, it was a good, wide road without too much traffic, and I swooped and hissed along feeling as if I were flying.

It was around sixteen miles, twenty-six kilometres, back down to the coast through the narrow valley. There were more fine houses of wood on the heights, but as I got closer to the sea, the valley widened out and 'civilisation' loomed. The concrete buildings began and piles of dirt and rubble scarred the environment, although the hills themselves remained beautifully and fiercely green. The lower slopes were covered with thick tea bushes and, looking up at the higher levels, there were clearings in the forests, which were also planted with tea. The olive-green bushes appeared in the most inaccessible places, tenaciously clinging on to the billows and hummocks of the slopes. Despite the sad mess on either side of the river, the tea plantations were a marvellous sight.

I cycled out of the valley through the urban sprawl of the town of Of. (I looked up the word in my best Turkish dictionary much later on. The English translation was 'Oh! Enough! My God!') I was already missing the clean villages and mountain passes that I was leaving far behind, but it was fine to smell the Black Sea again, such a remote-looking sea compared with the easy accessibility of the Mediterranean. I turned right onto the coast road. I was back in the traffic and the maelstrom. Negotiating along that familiar, narrow and ill-surfaced road was even more unpleasant without proper brakes. I was grateful that it was only a short ride into Rize.

It turned out to be a fairly easy run, through ugly Black Sea towns with extensive tea plantations in the hills above. I passed several tea factories which smelled, of course, like tea. A feature of the factories were the tall chimneys belching out nasty plumes of thick, black smoke. After the explosion at the nuclear power plant at Chernobyl some ten years previously, the Turkish government had tried to minimise worries about the risk of pollution to the Black Sea tea crops, even going on television and sipping glasses of tea to reassure the watching public – who didn't believe a word of it. It must have been terrible for the plantation owners, watching that soft, gentle, Black Sea rain raining like poison onto their beautiful tea bushes.

The mountains came right down to the sea at Rize. The town sprawled in concrete blocks along the sweep of the bay, an ugly interruption in the dense, green vegetation. I passed what looked like the entrance to the harbour from which I assumed the boat would leave for İstanbul the following day. It was about half a mile out of town. A crumbling esplanade ran along the sea but there was no attempt being made to create a park or leisure area. There was just the usual sprawl of bus, taxi and dolmuş stops, piles of broken rocks and debris and cheap market stalls. I would explore the markets later but the first task was to find a hotel.

There were many new hotel blocks clustered on the sea front and around the centre of town, doubtless built after the opening of the borders with the former Soviet Union to take advantage of the trade. I found a hotel which, conveniently, had a long, dark passageway into which I could wheel the bicycle off the street. The young boy behind the reception desk was expressionless and detached. He told me the price of the room in US dollars. The Büyük Rize Oteli was cheap, around £5 for the night. My room was large and shabby with three beds and its own toilet and shower room. Outside in the corridor, an empty gin bottle had been slung on top of a rubbish bin. The chatter of female voices leaked from the rooms next door. A couple of girls hurried down the stairs. They were dressed in tight tops and jeans. They had a profusion of hair and their eyes were startling, beautiful and painted. I admired and envied their air of total indifference as to what people might think. They simply did not care. Why should they?

Downstairs, the men waited around in the sitting room next to reception, staring at me for an indifferent second before going back to the television and their glasses of tea. The hotel was obviously half hotel, half brothel, but it all felt well organised, respectable even. I knew I would not have to worry about anybody hammering on my door in the middle of the night.

I asked Mr Cool at reception where I should go to buy my ticket to İstanbul. He telephoned a couple of numbers and told me to go back to the harbour where there was an office. He also told me how much the ticket would cost and offered to go after he had finished work. I told him that I wanted to go myself. He shrugged and smiled, the smile lighting up his face. He was a poppet of a boy and we were by then the best of friends. I asked him if he were the son of the owner. He laughed. He was only an employee of the hotel, he said. His father and brother were away working in Holland. He was poised and relaxed talking to me. He had obviously become used to dealing with the women coming to stay at the hotel. I was sure he was popular with the Natashas and would treat them as if he were their elder brother, just like he was dealing with me.

I collected the bicycle and we whizzed together into the town centre up the street and round the corner. I found a money change office which gave me a low rate – always check first – and headed off back to the port entrance. The office selling boat tickets was to be found in a collection of pre-fabricated buildings through the gate. The port was less busy compared with those at Samsun and Trabzon. There were fewer buildings and cranes and it was less closed in. From here, the view over Rize along the bay, nestling at the foot of the green mountains, was stunning, the ugly, concrete blocks softened by the distance and their scale minimised in the overall picture.

The man behind the desk was cheerful and pleasant. I had been expecting the boat would be busier, but it appeared to be half empty despite the fact that it was by then peak season. His advice was to take a bed in a double cabin because, he said, it was highly unlikely another single woman would be joining the ship. I would probably be lucky and have the cabin to myself for the two nights. The swimming pool would not be in working order for the trip (I wasn't surprised), but there would be plenty of space to sit in the sun, if it came out. I was still looking forward to a final burst of sunshine before returning to England. There had only been lowering skies and temperamental weather since I had left the coast and headed into the mountains at Trabzon. The ticket cost 6,800.000 TL, the equivalent of £27. This was slightly less than Mr Cool had quoted in the hotel. I was sorry. By going to buy it myself, he had failed to get his commission.

I cycled slowly back into Rize along the double carriageway road, which was shaded by trees running down the middle. I feasted my eyes on those lush green hills and mountains hanging over the town, stretching away as far as the eye could see. I wanted to take it all in, to remember everything. Life suddenly seemed so unreal: that I was in the tea town of Rize on the Black Sea, that I had just cycled 1,500 kilometres, nearly a thousand miles, and that I would be back in England by the weekend. Another Turkish adventure was nearly over.

Back at the hotel, I hauled the bicycle up several flights of stairs into my spacious room and leaned her against the wall where she instantly fell asleep and dreamed of high up and far away pastures. I went to take a shower. There was no hot water and the toilet was filthy and broken. I went back down to reception to complain. This time there was a man behind the desk. The hot water would be on for a couple of hours in the evening, he said, and he would send somebody up to clean and mend the toilet. Two boys arrived, armed with scrubbing equipment and a useful tool to turn a nut in the toilet bowl, which allowed the water to rush through once again. I wondered why it had been closed off in the first place. As they scrubbed and sloshed, cleaning the toilet all over the tiled floor, I retreated into the corridor and happened to observe Mr Cool emerging from one of the rooms. He paused at the doorway and leaned against it while he chatted to a couple of girls inside. He was smoking a cigarette, intimate and relaxed, as if the girls were his big sisters, lovers even. I hoped they were giving him free sex. He deserved it.

I needed to confirm my flight from İstanbul back to London with Turkish Airlines. The office had moved from one end of town to the other, although people were not quite sure where exactly it had gone. I walked backwards and forwards until I located it hiding on the second floor of one of Rize's anonymous look-alike concrete blocks. I could hardly walk up the stairs. I felt awful and, after confirming my ticket, I staggered back to the hotel and 'died' for the usual two hours.

Once I had recovered from the mysterious spell 'underwater', I got up and went out. I had arrived in Rize so early that everything I had already done that day had hardly dented the hours available. Although my way of life could never make me rich in terms of money, I was rich in terms of time. I browsed along towards the sea. The market on the front was largely shut. This was unusual for Turkey where everything was generally open for at least twelve hours a day. It was a poor affair made up of a collection of small cabins selling household goods, tools and clothes. The Russian area was at the back, selling cheap clothes and goods from trestle tables and tents. Some of the stuff for sale was spread out on the ground. Here, the market was functioning in a desultory fashion, run in the main by bored Eastern European and Caucasian women, many of whom looked listless and tired. They wore tight tee shirts whatever age they were, careless that they were exposing quantities of pale flesh, so different from the modest women of Rize, who covered their heads with red, yellow and black striped pieces of Laz cloth. I bought a small compact mirror and a new battery for my clock, both for the equivalent of 20p each. After browsing round the stalls, I went to investigate the 'beach', but I didn't get far. The sea was far away beyond the rocks and the whole area was piled with dumped rubbish and obviously used as a vast, open-air toilet. Poor Rize, off the beaten track, or at least the Western tourist beaten track.

There was hope, at least back in the town centre. I had admired a renovated, Ottoman house there earlier on. It stood in its own landscaped grounds on a hill overlooking the town square, in the middle of which was the biggest statue of Atatürk I had seen so far. The great man stood there powerful and splendid in a long, military-style overcoat and leather boots. Next to the house was a building on tall, stilt-like props made out of whole tree trunks. It was similar to the storehouses in the pension on the way to the Sumela Monastery. The complex was set in gardens behind a wall and I walked around wondering what it was. Just then, a young boy toiled up on his bicycle and tried to cycle up the slope. He skidded sideways and stopped, defeated by its steepness. We looked at each other and laughed. I had a bicycle too, I said, and I couldn't have cycled up such a hill either. He asked if I had seen the town's museum and led me back down the hill, round the foot of the complex and up the other side, stopping in front of an iron gate. This, he announced with bright-eyed pride, was Rize's new museum.

I went in and up the flights of stone steps to find a terrace set out with tables. It was obviously the place to come for Rize's young generation. Youthful couples and groups of students were sitting around drinking tea and coffee. Two men sitting outside the museum entrance apologised that the building itself was not yet open to the public. It was still being finished, they said, but they let me slip inside to have a quick look around the hallway and peer into the rooms leading off it. Everything was made of solid wood, the doors, ceilings, panelled walls, all beautifully renovated or re-done to match the old. The house had belonged to a wealthy merchant, who was able to oversee part of his accumulating riches from his own front door. Opposite, on a lower level, was his huge storehouse which Rize town council had also restored. The intricate lattice-work looked as if it had just been finished by the original craftsmen.

One of the men was pleased with my interest. He told me that the storehouse was at least two hundred and fifty years old. Every part of its construction had been designed to keep the grain and vegetables stored inside fresh and free of vermin. The lattice-work allowed the breeze to flow through but protected everything inside from the harsh sun. There were no stairs in order to stop rats and mice getting in, and the large blocks of wood at the top of the stilts on which the storehouse itself rested made it impossible for vermin to use them as an alternative way in. The buildings, he said, were unique to the Black Sea and the people called them by a special name, 'serander' or 'nayla'. He carefully wrote down the words for me on a slip of paper. The common Turkish name for storehouse, he said, was 'ambar'. I was to see that word over the following two days, written on the less picturesque, modern storage depots at the ports, as my ship stopped by on its way back to İstanbul.

I bumped into the man a few minutes later, now accompanied by his small son. He stopped to talk to me again. I suddenly realised he was a devoutly religious man. I should have guessed from his clear, steady, unafraid eyes, those extraordinary eyes of the truly devout. I had seen similar eyes at a monastery in Bulgaria outside the town of Plovdiv some years before. The monks there had had a similar gaze, a visibly bright integrity of spirit, their eyes like windows into their souls. I had not seen that look very often and when I had, it was more often in the Muslim countries. As the man talked, in clear, slow and precise Turkish, I found I could understand every word. He was well informed and widely read. I asked him where he had gone to school.

'I didn't get much schooling,' he replied. 'My family was very poor.'

'So where did you get your learning and information from?'

'My father was a hoca,' he said simply. (A hoca is a religious teacher and a learned man.) 'I also like information and do my own reading.'

His thoughts poured out. He talked about the Ottoman Empire and what he described as the waste of years under its stultifying rule, the history of modern Turkey and religion, the hegemony of the United States and the lack of a world balance, and the hypocrisy of the West with its unquestioning support of Israel and the Jews at the expense of the Palestinians. I found myself in sympathy with most of what he said. It was almost a relief to both of us to be in such agreement. He asked me why I wasn't married. When I hesitated, telling him it was too complicated to explain, he hastily withdrew the question. But I continued, telling him I wanted to find an equal partner, a man I could respect. I had met such men, I said, but the situation had never been right. We parted and as I walked away, I glanced back for another look at this extraordinary man. At exactly the same moment, he glanced back at me.

I walked slowly back towards the hotel, diverting up a flight of stairs and into an alleyway where I could see something bright and colourful hanging on the wall. It was outside a curio shop which was stuffed with all sorts of things: copper jugs and bowls, beads and silver rings, dusty bits and pieces, flotsam and jetsam. I browsed around, closely followed by the spidery shopkeeper, who insisted on talking all the time, telling me about every foreign tourist that had ever visited his shop and showing me his photographs of the evenings they had gone on to spend together. The piece hanging on the wall outside turned out to be an antique Turkish cradle, woven from multi-coloured wools, like a Turkish carpet. Such cradles were hung in the old days from the ceiling, probably near the stove so the woman could cook and push the baby at the same time. The shopkeeper took it down and spread it out in the shop. It was a fine piece and he wanted just $30.

It was a bargain, but it was large and heavy and I knew I could never carry it on the bicycle. As I admired it with a breaking heart, two blond girls from the East came in to the shop, bargain-hunting. One picked up a cheap print of a landscape in a plastic frame and offered to buy it for $10. The shopkeeper refused. He wanted more, double that, he said. The girl got out a new, temptingly crisp $10 bill, but again he refused, much to my amazement. The picture wasn't even worth $5. The girl was disappointed. I could see her imagining it hanging on the wall of whichever grotty hotel she was staying in. But the shopkeeper was obdurate. After the girls had gone, he hissed in my ear: 'They're here for sex you know.' Maybe he did not want to accept money made in such a way. He told me to think about the cradle and hung it back on a hook in the wall, a beacon of colour in the dark passage to lure people into his web – so long as they were not Natashas.

I ate in an efficient kebab house on a corner close by. It was excellent food but I became suspicious about the time I had to wait before my order arrived. I felt paranoid. Maybe they didn't want single, foreign women in there lowering the tone. When I asked them if anything was wrong, they pointed out that I had asked for a very hot İskender kebab. Finally it arrived, sizzling on the plate in its red tomato sauce with a cold dollop of yoghurt on top like a small mountain tipped with snow. It didn't allay my suspicions but it was a very good kebab, although it turned out to be the most expensive of the trip. Maybe they thought I was busy earning crisp, new dollars in Rize and could afford it. There was a very different atmosphere in Rize from that in Trabzon. It was as if Trabzon had decided it was a big, fast town and could accommodate every kind of visitor. I felt resentment in the much smaller, slower town of Rize, a question mark hanging in the air about what I was doing there, unaccompanied, no husband, no brother. It was a peculiar feeling to keep seeing oneself through other people's eyes and be unable to recognise oneself at all. That isn't me; you've got it wrong. But even as one protested, the impression was further reinforced.

I estimated that by then hot water would be available in the hotel and went back to shower and wash my hair, sluicing the tiled floor down first as I remembered the way the two boys had cleaned the toilet earlier. I wrote my diary and read for the hundred and tenth time a copy of *The Paper Bag Princess*, a Canadian story for children, which my sister gave me many years ago. I always carried it around in my bag. The picture and the words on the front cover were almost worn away and the pages were dog-eared. But inside, the last picture was as clear as ever. It was of a little girl, arms outstretched, feet dancing, bounding off into the sunset and the words of the caption are: 'They didn't get married after all.'

20
Rize to İstanbul

What I want is to have a rest now from all this, and since we have got to the sea, to sail for the rest of the way, and so get back to Greece stretched out at my ease on deck, like Odysseus.

The weather was still overcast the following morning. I had had enough of the unpredictable, moody Black Sea weather. I wanted some sunshine before it was too late. July was about to turn into August and the summer would soon be over. It was early, seven o'clock, but I got up fidgeting, impatient. I had five hours left in Rize before I had to board the ship. Like one of Xenophon's men, the Greek mercenary, Leon of Thurii, who had had enough of packing and unpacking his bag and running up and down mountains, I too was looking forward to stretching out on deck at my ease, doing nothing.

I began to get my things together. Unfortunately, the clothes I had washed the day before were still wet. They included my underclothes, which I had draped over the bicycle's handlebars, and my leggings and a shirt, both of which were hanging precariously out of the window. I leaned out to check how wet they were and to see if anything was happening in the street below but ducked back in quickly. A man was standing on the pavement, and another man, in his underclothes, was on the balcony of a flat opposite, yawning and scratching. He had just got out of his pit and I could almost smell his musty, intimate smell, hot breath and warm flesh. Both were gazing intently at the hotel, no doubt hoping to catch a glimpse of the Natashas to get a free morning thrill.

I left the clothes dangling and wondered what I could do to kill time. I couldn't go and walk along the sea front because there wasn't one. The quick glance outside had told me the town was largely deserted and my heart sank at the idea of going for a walk at such an early hour, a conspicuous actor on an empty stage. But then I thought of the bold, mini-skirted girls in town, noses in the air, indifferent, confident. I could do it too. I hurried downstairs and rushed out into the naughty streets, mentally wrapping myself up in a cloak of invisibility.

A few shops in the main street were already showing signs of life. I browsed along and as I passed a bookshop, my eye was caught by a small paperback in English on display in the window. It was called *Reminiscences of Atatürk*. The shop had just opened and I went in. The shopkeeper guessed what I had been looking at and he found a copy for me. I flicked through it. It was a collection of people's memories of the great things Atatürk had done and said. One of them, written anonymously, went as follows:

'Posters were being prepared for the twelfth anniversary of the Republic. Among them were some like these:

"Atatürk is the greatest."

"It has taken the Turkish nation centuries to produce a Mustafa Kemal."

Atatürk, carefully looking over the wording of the posters, scratched out these words and all those like them, and in their place wrote: "Atatürk is one of us."'

The little book cost the equivalent of 40p. It was a bargain and impossible to resist. Back outside and on the opposite side of the street, the door was open into a junk shop I had noticed the day before, but which had been closed. Clutching my new book, I rushed across the street and squeezed inside. The shop was stuffed from floor to ceiling with things: black and white photographs, ancient tools, jugs, bowls, curved, gleaming swords, nineteenth century guns, Ottoman lamps, beads, leather-bound books, chairs, cushions, rugs and pairs of nutcrackers. It was an incredible shop. A lamp caught my eye. It was one of those magical, hand-made pieces, the sections of which are screwed together with beautifully-fashioned 'keys' and the whole studded with coloured glass marbles. The lamps are made to hang from the ceiling and when they are switched on, they twinkle with multi-coloured lights. I had a smaller one just like it at home. I asked the elderly man, who was sitting silently reading a book behind a desk, how much the lamp was.

'This isn't a shop,' he said, 'it's a museum, my museum.'

And suddenly I noticed that there were indeed little signs up underneath some of the swords, nutcrackers and photographs explaining the history of the item. Some of the swords appeared to have belonged to important people during the Ottoman Empire. The man explained that his business office was next door. Collecting the items had become a sort of hobby, he said, and he had decided to open his own small museum so the people of Rize could enjoy them too. My question about the price of the lamp hung in the air like a bad smell. I felt like a greedy tourist who wanted to buy whatever she saw. I apologised for my mistake. The man shrugged and went back to his book.

I crept out and walked on, heading out of town. The suburban sprawl of Rize seemed endless, but behind the narrow streets I could catch glimpses of the green, tea hills brewing behind the town. I turned back towards the town centre, stopping off to buy bread, cheese, olives and a jar of mussels from a supermarket. I guessed the food on board ship would be expensive so I would take my own provisions. After buying my supplies, I stumbled across Rize's old market tucked away in a series of back streets, selling real food from the pastures above. Trestle tables groaned under the weight of enormous white and yellow cheeses, and sacks spilling over with creamy-white lard. There were bottles and jars of golden honey and mounds of purple plums and orange-yellow apricots. I reflected that it was only a matter of time before the long arm of the European Union reached into

Turkey, which had finalised a customs agreement with Europe although it was not yet a member. They would condemn Turkey's wonderful, fresh food, flies dive-bombing up and down over it, as unhealthy. It would have to be packed and packaged, sanitised, standardised, analysed and labelled and then it would be as tasteless and dull as ours.

The stall holders, many of them elderly men who must have been selling their produce in Rize since they were teenagers, were amused and pleased at my pleasure in their market. I bought a big packet of the hot, red chilli pepper flakes which the Turks scatter liberally over their breakfast soup. In a back alleyway, I came across a whole line of sheds selling coal. The lumps were displayed outside in wooden baskets that rich people in London would have paid a fortune for without the contents. The coal was premier quality from Samsun and looked as if each piece had been selected by hand for its perfect shape and had then been dusted and polished to make it gleam blackly and evenly. There were shops selling piles of pure white cotton and soft wool for those oh-so-comfortable Turkish eiderdowns and mattresses. Tailors worked away close by on their clattering sewing machines in gloomy cabins.

Returning to the town square through a street of glittering gold shops, I found Rize's magnificent central post office. It was situated in a colonial-style building, all wooden balconies and verandahs. It looked as if it should have been in India rather than in north-eastern Turkey. Generally, there were long queues of people waiting to use any public telephone in Turkey, but I didn't have to wait long before a card phone became free. I called İstanbul and left a message for Andy to telephone me back at the hotel. I hurried back to wait. By then, the hotel was up and running and the television was on in the sitting/waiting room. Mr Cool was busy taking up glasses of tea to the girls and administering to their every need. Hopefully. He asked me to help him explain to a couple of tourists from Australia that although noon was officially the checkout time, it didn't really matter what time they vacated their rooms.

I took my call from İstanbul, so strange to hear a familiar voice down the tinny telephone, and went to finish my packing. My clothes were still damp. I carried the bicycle downstairs and said goodbye to Mr Cool. He kissed me on both cheeks. I wished I could have taken him home with me. I cycled sadly and slowly back down to the sea and the markets along the front. Only a few of the shops appeared to be opening up for the day. I found a small pide hut and watched as the man wrapped up a long, thin, boat-shaped piece of freshly-cooked pide, filled with minced meat and tomatoes. I bought a melon, like a small, yellow football, from a fruit stall and then cycled off along the pavement along the sea to the 'feribot' pier.

The boat was late of course so I began to eat my supplies. I had only eaten half my pide before the men in the customs office invited me to share their lunch of döner kebab, rice and yoghurt, which had been brought steaming in large metal containers from the town. After lunch, I sat on a chair outside and once again took in the magnificent, olive-green panorama of peaks behind Rize, the perpendicular slopes terraced and planted out with tea bushes, and the tea chimneys belching their smoke out at intervals along the coast. Behind the main harbour was a port for the fishermen. It was lined with wooden shacks at the water's edge. A few fishermen were sitting outside checking their nets for holes. I listened to the 'put put' sound of the boats juddering and shaking their way over the water. Three large fishing boats, like beached whales on the shore, were being repaired, their ribs sticking out like those of the teenaged boys larking around in the water nearby. One of the boys was snorkelling in the shallows. He could only have been looking at the bottles, jelly fish and filth under the water. It was amazing that he was still alive and hadn't been poisoned.

My fellow passengers began to turn up. One young man roared onto the pier in a snazzy, bright yellow sports car. He was wearing blue, Adidas leisure clothes, baggy trousers and a loose sweat shirt and looked very pleased with himself. His family had come independently to wave him off. We all stared at his car.

At last, the ship chugged into port. It was the Truva. I had seen her so often tied up in İstanbul. The plaque on her side proclaimed the fact that she had been built in Nantes in Normandy in 1966. Although we were very few in number, everybody enjoyed the crush and excitement of boarding. The handful of cars went in first with the sports car taking pride of place. Then I went up the gangway with my bicycle, followed by the foot passengers. Inside, the bicycle was roped up so she was immoveable and I went to find my cabin. It was a neat affair with two bunks, the top one folded up against the wall. I hoped it would stay that way. The tiny bathroom was so tiny, I could only use the toilet with the door half open, but all the various water sources functioned properly. I dumped my bags and rushed up to the deck to watch the ship cast off and swing slowly out of the harbour into open waters, the passengers frantically waving their goodbyes to the people left behind, as if we were going to another country altogether. Which, in a way, we were.

The sea was blue and a shoal of big fish put on a sparkling display alongside the ship, leaping fast and free in and out of the foaming water. The sun was shining. At last. I sped back downstairs to the cabin, put my bikini on underneath a dress and rushed back outside again. The deck to the fore of the ship was empty. I chose a spot where I couldn't be overlooked by the captain or his crew on the bridge and took my dress off. It was very windy but oh how delicious to be sitting in the sun. I felt safe. I was in international waters. I could do what I liked. No more questions about what I was doing and where my husband and children were, no more explanations and amazement about the bicycle. I didn't want to talk to anybody. Two whole days of being able to sit and do absolutely nothing stretched ahead. Time to think, to consider my next move, which had been the whole point of the trip but had been continually postponed until now.

It was all wonderful for about twenty minutes. As the ship sailed further into open waters, the wind increased and despite the sun, I was freezing. There was nothing for it but to go back down to the cabin and put on a lot more clothes. As I emerged once again, a girl passing along the corridor saw me. She stopped, her mouth open with amazement. My heart sank. Just when I thought I was safe . . .

'I was looking for you just now,' she said in halting English. 'I can't believe I've found you. I want to talk to you. Do you mind?'

She looked so pleased and excited at the coincidence. She had been looking for me and had – so unexpectedly – found me. I knew how significant these coincidences were to the sensitive, intense Turks. I couldn't disappoint her. I forced my furious face into a ghastly smile. 'Of course not,' I said. 'It would be a pleasure.'

We went back on deck together and Emine told me her story. A young boy stood smiling by her side as she spoke. She was seventeen, although she looked much younger, and she lived with her family in Trabzon. She had announced to her parents that she wanted to experience a boat trip. They had allowed her to take the boat to Rize that morning and return to Trabzon in the afternoon, with the proviso that she was accompanied by her aunt – Emine gestured vaguely into the distance – and her 15-year-old cousin, Temel, to whom she introduced me. Both of them stared at me so proudly and with such excitement on their faces. They had rarely been out of Trabzon and were having the time of their lives. Emine could hardly stop talking. Her command of English was impressive. Despite her youthful appearance, she was self-confident and in control. I thought it was more a question of her chaperoning her aunt and cousin rather than the other way round. What did I do? Who were my favourite pop groups? Did I like football? She bombarded me with questions, which were at least a little different from the ones I was usually asked, although I was as clueless about how to answer them as I was with the more usual ones. Fortunately, I didn't have to reply. Emine was much too busy telling me about her own life. She wanted to run her own textile company, own a Mercedes car and a motor-bike and get a pocket telephone. She planned to go to England to improve her English and learn French as well, and she thought the fact that I lived on my own was simply great. She shrieked with laughter as she told me these things, half shyly, as if awestruck at her own temerity and yet with absolute determination to make it all happen. I looked at this sparkling, bright girl, who had managed to organise her first desire, a trip on a ship. That was a big enough thing for a girl from a traditional Turkish family to have organised. I wondered how much Emine would manage to achieve. Probably quite a lot if she carried on the way she had started

We stood on the deck while Emine talked and I stared at the coastline. The countryside looked bigger and cleaner from a distance, the mess, created by man within it, softened and absorbed. Distance always lends a different perspective from the one you get when you are in the thick of things. From the sea, I was unable to see the crowded, sweating traffic negotiating along the narrow roads or the concrete suburban sprawl along the front. What I could see were the layers and layers of misty mountain peaks rising up gloriously inland, the Pontic Alps. Next time, I thought, I would spend more time in those magnificent, high places.

It took about two and a half hours to sail from Rize to Trabzon. The town was recognisable from far away by the large storage towers in the port and the high, green hill of Boztepe, busy with antennae on top. I looked for the road I had cycled up towards the Sumela Monastery just six days ago – it felt like six years – but it was hidden by a factory. Emine and her cousin excitedly pointed out the suburb on the hill where they lived and said I could visit them any time. She gave me her address and asked if I would write to her. I gave her mine and told her she would have to write to me first. Emine, you haven't written to me yet. I'm still waiting for your letter.

As the ship swung in towards the harbour, a pilot ship, painted a bright red and bottle-green, sped over the water to guide us in, buzzing around like a gadfly round a rhino. There was no other sea traffic and only a couple of other ships tied up in the port, but manoeuvring the ship alongside the quay was a serious occasion. There was a crackle of walkie-talkie radios, a scurry of sailors and a frantic uncoiling of the ropes. The captain was magnificent at the wheel while his mate, eyes concealed behind dark glasses and wearing exceedingly tight jeans, decorated the stern of the boat from where he barked orders at the men. The Turks take themselves very seriously and yet generally manage to inject it all with an element of good-humour. They are, by nature, a theatrical people. We all stood on deck and admired the performance.

Emine, Temel and the aunt, who finally materialised, disembarked, and a whole crowd of people, many of them backpackers, got on. I hoped very much there were no single women among them to invade my cabin. There was much to observe before we set off again. Shiny, black lumps of coal were being unloaded from a boat tied up alongside and deposited straight into the back of a lorry waiting on the quay, practically underneath our ship. As one lorry filled up, another would take its place. The operation was not a scientific one and a substantial amount of the coal slipped down the sides and crunched onto the ground. I wondered whether that was counted as a kind of free overspill for the dock workers. Much of the quay was occupied by thousands of new cars lined up in neat rows.

The ship pulled out of the harbour and swung away westwards. I wanted to pick out St. Sophie perched on her hill but I became confused where to look amid the huddle of houses and buildings on the hills. There was no view of Trabzon's fortifications, nor the plunging chasm behind. I could see how built up it was outside the heart of the town and how eroded and less green the hills were along this part of the coast. We were heading for Giresun and would arrive around midnight. It was going to take almost as long to get there as it had taken me to cycle. The weather was getting cold and it felt as if it was going to rain. The driver of the yellow sports car sat slumped on deck looking traumatised, a different man from the one who had so joyfully driven up on the quay at Rize. Pale and loitering, he stared sightlessly out to sea. Was he missing his family or a lover? A group of tourists, who had embarked at Trabzon, sat nearby. One of their number, an American, was describing to them loudly and in minute detail about where he had been, what he had seen and how much it had cost him – a bit like me really. I went to get a beer from the bar. Two Germans were getting stuck in to the brandy and the rakı; the barman could hardly tear himself away from them to serve anybody else. He was enjoying himself too and I reckoned by the end of the evening, he was going to be under the bar along with his customers rather than standing behind it. The self-service cafeteria opened for business but I only saw a Japanese couple using it. I guessed that all the Turks and most of the backpackers, as I was, were living off their own much cheaper provisions.

The sea had turned an inky, silvery-black, and spectacular, red flashes and white forks of lightning lit up the sky in the north. It was the crazy man backstage switching the lights on and off again. In the west, the clouds were tinged with the red of the setting sun. In the south, the lights twinkled out from the coastline, and the mountains loomed high behind. It was spectacular but too windy and cold to stay outside any longer. I scuttled down to my cosy cabin. To my relief, I was still the sole occupant. I read some more Reminiscences of Atatürk:

'Atatürk was asking questions in a history examination at Ankara Lycee.

"Who is a friend of Turkey?"

"England."

"No."

"France."

"No."

"America."

"No, my son. A friend of Turkey is a Turk himself."

There was a terrible storm later in the night and the ship creaked and groaned and I lay in my bunk trying not to think about all the various, great maritime disasters nor what I was going to do with my future if I did survive the journey.

The next day was a sparkling one, the sun streaming down a path of light onto the sea, the moon still half awake opposite. The ship was swinging in towards Samsun. I could see how the town stopped suddenly half way up the bare hill as if somebody had drawn a line beyond which the town could go no further. The sea was filthy. It was a browny colour with enormous jellyfish pulsating in the mirk, the horrible kind that can be seen in the Bosphorus, the sort that proliferate in highly polluted waters. The pilot boat roared up alongside and everyone took up position to press the levers and undo the ropes, the mate clutching his walkie-talkie radio and still wearing his blue shirt, tight jeans and dark sunglasses. By now, he had a designer stubble.

I breakfasted on melon and went back on deck to sunbathe until it got too hot and then, along with everybody else, actors in a play, guests at an endless cocktail party, I perambulated around the ship, sitting, staring, changing the view, reading, writing, thinking and drinking beer. It was almost an art form to fill the time. The German, who had been carousing the night before in the bar, appeared looking terrible; his face was white and puffy and his hair dirty and uncombed. He could hardly walk and was shuffling along smoking a cigarette. I noticed a large, fresh cut on his arm. The sports car driver, still wearing the Adidas outfit, looked as if he had slept propped up in a corner all night and was by now seriously considering suicide. One of the tourists was writing furiously in his diary. He looked so earnest, he had to be an American. I wondered if I looked as earnest when I wrote in my diary. Just think, I thought, he's now in my diary. Was I in his?

Quite a few of the tourists were sunbathing and the swimming pool in front of the bar had been unexpectedly filled up overnight and was open for business after all. Despite my dreams of swimming on board, however, I kept well away. The pool was more of a deep hole and so small that the handful of boys using it filled it up. What was more, after they had jumped in and out a couple of times, there seemed to be more water on deck than in the pool itself.

It was pleasant not having to do very much except make lots of good resolutions for the future. I realised that all the issues and situations I wanted to resolve were melting away even as I thought about them. One can't force these things. I was only able to open the drawer, turn it upside down on the floor and start sifting through the pile in front of me. I was merely re-organising things rather than throwing them away and starting anew. Life changes cannot be summoned up with a click of the fingers, even after a few weeks along the Black Sea with the very focused Xenophon and the Ten Thousand – who I was beginning to miss and who were sailing far far in front of me. I sat slumped in a chair looking in the direction of the coastline, which had disappeared. The ship had sailed right out to sea and we were alone in the middle of the Euxine.

The next bit of excitement came when we swung in towards Sinop, sticking out on its peninsula and visible for miles, as it had been when I cycled away from it all those days ago. The ship did not sail in to the harbour but waited, bobbing around in the sea just outside, in full view of the splendid fortifications. If one ignored the rest of the peninsula with its horrible, dense and hideously painted apartment blocks, Sinop was exquisitely situated. I was able to see my pension and the balcony overlooking the port. I wondered if the Turk and his eternally kissable Azeri wife were still there, looking out at the ship and getting ready for their next party.

We waited for passengers from Sinop to be brought by boat out to us but nobody came. They were probably too busy carousing in the bars to remember the ship returning to İstanbul, another world away. My fellow passengers came on deck to take photographs of Sinop and shake their heads over the apparently needless delay. To the east, the sea looked like spilt mercury, silvery and un-catchable. Closer to the shore, it was a deep, enigmatic, shiny, blue-black colour. Mythical monsters lurked in the depths as they had done for thousands of years.

And still we waited, almost falling asleep as the afternoon wore on. I didn't recognise the captain's mate, who emerged shaven and resplendent in gleaming white uniform. Men should obviously wear uniform all the time. They look cleaner and less smelly. He got into position at the front of the ship ready with his walkie-talkie, but nobody came to give him a reason to use it.

The sun was low in the sky by the time we abandoned the people of Sinop to their fate and sailed away around the tip of the peninsula busy with concrete blocks and bare of trees, the hills bristling with listening devices and tumbling straight down with a splash into the sea. On the other side of the peninsula, the cliffs were soft and green, like cushions. Now I could see the bus station by the castle tower and all the stretches of wall which one was unable to see inside the town because they were hidden by buildings. Much of it was still substantial. From a ship, one could appreciate why Sinop was so difficult to capture, protected as it was by the sea and the mighty city walls. The ship sailed on past İnceburun on the tip of the bulge before Ayancık, the northernmost point on the coast of Asia Minor. The cliffs, splashed red with the sinking sun, stretched westwards. Far away in the distance, way beyond the plains, the mountains loomed, almost 4,500 feet above sea level, 1,370 metres, according to my map. It was impossible to think that I would be in İstanbul the next day and in London the day after that.

I had such bad dreams in the night that I fell out of my bunk. This was quite an achievement because the bunk was almost on the floor. I hurt my wrist. This made writing my diary over the following day painful. It had again rained overnight and it was another liquid day, the early sun shining on the puddles on the deck. The sea was the colour it had been when I had glimpsed it at the start of the trip from the cliffs near Şile, a deep, enigmatic blue. I felt as if time were running out. and went to sunbathe in the sun lounge area where high perspex walls kept out the wind. I was joined by the captain, who announced that he always kept his feet higher than his head when he was lying down. It was good for the blood and the circulation, he said. He lay heavily on the wooden deck, propping his surprisingly fine, white feet up on a chair, and proceeded to interrogate me about my sex life. There was no escape. There never was. He could not seem to understand that cycling through the Turkish countryside on a bicycle was not the best way to form relationships. To divert his curiosity, I asked him about his own family. He had just one child, he said, a seventeen-year-old son who was studying in Rome. His son could already speak English and French and wanted to learn all the other European languages. He treated me to a resume of his philosophy about life. You should do or try to do whatever you want to do, and do it as well as you can, he said. And then he gave me some advice. 'It's the first day of the rest of your life. You've got to make the most of it.' It was a cliché but it was perfectly in tune with my thoughts, which I had not told him. Again, I was surprised by the Turkish ability to get straight to the heart of the matter, to somehow fathom what was beneath the surface, to understand how one felt.

The captain was called away on business. I continued to cook in the sun until I feared for my skin. I got dressed and began the perambulations around the deck. There was no sign of the sports car driver and I wondered whether he had finally thrown himself overboard. There was an air of subdued excitement among the passengers. Some had already taken up their positions in chairs and were staring intently out to sea. One group studied the shoreline through binoculars. Everybody was waiting for that gap in the coastline, waiting, just like the sailors in times gone by, to spot the only exit by sea into the rest of the world from the pond of the Black Sea.

And, like everything you wait for, when it arrived, it came all of a sudden. We sailed, magnificently, out of the Euxeinus Pontos and into the Bosphorus, Europe to our right and Asia to our left. All the passengers were crammed onto the front deck, jostling for a clear view. This was the highlight of the boat trip. Smoothly and steadily, the Truva negotiated her way through the narrow straits between Europe and Asia, past Byzantine and Ottoman fortresses, castles and palaces, past summer houses, villas and suburbs and underneath the two massive, suspension bridges, blowing her horn to warn the container ships, fishermen's boats and passenger steamers of our approach.

Everybody stared and beat their breasts and gnashed their teeth over the concrete development spreading over the Bosphorus hills, but the views were still wonderful. And I gazed and gazed and tried not to blink in case I missed something, looking to get that first view of the skyline that stretches back from Topkapı Palace jutting out into the sea from Sultanahmet like an ocean liner straining at its anchor to be off and away. Painters had been inspired for centuries by the silhouettes of the palace, the mosques, the domes and the minarets, so clearly defined against the sky. The Turks had so far preserved the famous view; there was not a whisper of a high-rise in sight. For the time being.

On we sailed, past the splendidly restored Çirağan Palace and the Dolmabahçe, like a wedding cake, where Atatürk died on 10 November 1938 and all the clocks were stopped in it for ever, and then the docks, Galata Tower and Beyoğlu spread over the hills, a glimpse of the spire of the Crimean Church, and past the nineteenth century apartment blocks and tumbling-down warehouses like a row of old teeth stained tobacco-brown. The evil-smelling, murky waters of the Golden Horn branched off to our right under Galata Bridge, to our left in the distance was Leander's Tower and beyond that was the Sea of Marmara and the Mediterranean. Fingers pointed, cameras clicked, and suddenly we were there, tying up at Sirkeci in the shadow of Topkapi Palace. 'The whole army crossed to Byzantium', wrote Xenophon triumphantly in his *Anabasis*. I rushed down below to untie the bicycle. Together, in the footsteps of Xenophon and his men, we went down the ramp and into the noise and sunshine of that great city.